DESPERATE MEN

MEN

REVELATIONS FROM THE

SEALED PINKERTON FILES

BY

JAMES D. HORAN

BONANZA BOOKS • NEW YORK

To Gertrude and Howard who deserve the credit for the virtues of this book and are in no way to blame for its faults

PREFACE

SINCE the Pinkerton National Detective Agency was founded a century ago by my great-grandfather, Allan Pinkerton, the files were regularly weeded of photographs and records of criminals who had died, or who to the satisfaction of the agency had abandoned their activities. These carefully combed records were then placed in the "Dead and Removal File" and marked for "indefinite preservation."

However, as the years passed, this file assumed gigantic proportions. Finally, in 1939, Ralph Dudley, our vice president, himself a student of the early West, undertook to sift the records and to prepare the Pinkerton historical archives. It was an arduous task to catalogue the many crimes and criminals and still retain the more important original documents.

The records were then wrapped in heavy manila paper, stoutly bound, and stored in special files for protection against moisture and dirt, at the agency's executive offices at 154 Nassau Street, New York City. Access is possible only by permission of one of the executive officials of the agency.

We have received over the years many requests from authors and editors to examine these records. Although we aided them in specific details of their research as much as possible, we have refrained from allowing anyone outside of the agency to examine the complete files.

In the last few years, however, numerous motion pictures, books, and magazine articles on the life of the Jameses and Youngers and other Western outlaws have appeared. Many of them glorified the bandits as misjudged Robin Hoods. To offset this erroneous conception, we decided to open our complete, century-old files dealing with Western outlaws for the first time to Mr. Horan. Although we have cooperated with him to the fullest extent, Mr. Horan's conclusions are his own.

ROBERT A. PINKERTON, II

CONTENTS

BOOK ONE

v

ILLUSTRATIONS

INTRODUCTION

I BELIEVE the desperate men of whom I have written would have flourished and survived had it not been for the powerfully built man with cool, appraising eyes who hurriedly left Scotland one day in 1840. He was fleeing from arrest as a social revolutionist and an active agitator in the Chartists' proletarian movement.

His name was Allan Pinkerton, and he was coming to America in the best democratic tradition.

Pinkerton settled in Dundee, Illinois, where he operated a cooperage shop. On the side he maintained Dundee's station on the underground railroad for runaway slaves. In the 1840's he became agent for the Chicago Abolitionists and took over that larger and more important junction on the underground.

He was appointed to the Chicago police as its first and at the time only detective. Soon he had five detectives working under him and achieved widespread reputation in the Middle West. In 1850 he left the police force to open his own agency—Pinkerton's North Western Police Agency—a few years later to be named Pinkerton's National Detective Agency. In the late fall of 1856 his reputation became nationwide when he arrested and convicted a famous international French swindler about whom the New York City police could do nothing.

His new reputation brought him more and wealthier clients. His agency was soon working for the railroads and the express companies arresting freight-car thieves, express-car robbers, and highwaymen. He rose rapidly in his law-enforcement business, but still studiously maintained the Chicago junction of the underground railroad. Legend has the Pinkerton household so crowded with runaway slaves that Mrs. Pinkerton many times was forced to call in the neighbors to help her feed them. Pinkerton became a firm friend of John Brown, and when that wild-eyed, bearded man stopped by the Pinkerton home on the night of March 11, 1859, the Chicago detective gave him five hundred dollars in cash and tickets on the Michigan Central Railroad to get Brown and his band to Detroit, the next stop on their violent eastward journey.

It was under Pinkerton's protection that Lincoln went safely from Philadelphia to Washington in 1861. The plot at Baltimore is well known; there is no need to retell it here.

The next we see of Pinkerton is in October, 1862. The photographer, Matthew B. Brady, was at headquarters, Army of the Potomac, near Antietam the day Lincoln and his friends from Illinois, Ward Hill Lamon and General John A. McClernand, visited General George B. McClellan, the Army commander. Brady, as always, took a number of pictures. In one of them, with Lincoln and McClernand, was a man with a short dark beard, wearing a sort of bowler hat, long black coat, and checkered dickey. Just before the shutter snapped, he struck a nonchalant, Napoleonic pose, tucking his right hand into his coat between the first and second buttons. This man, Brady was told, was Major Allen, chief of the Secret Service of the Army of the Potomac.

It was of course, Allan Pinkerton. But so carefully was the secret kept that General Fitz-John Porter, one of McClellan's corps commanders, did not know Pinkerton's identity until the war had ended.

After Appomattox the business of Pinkerton's agency increased. His operatives protected railroads, banks, corporations, and express companies. But with the booming industries came the outlaw bands. The Reno Brothers were the first; Pinkerton broke up that blood brotherhood. In 1866, Jesse James and his ex-guerrillas made their first strike, and the war between Pinkerton and the famous Missourian began. It was to last for sixteen incredible years.

One question of which I am aware is the one usually raised about the Pinkertons raiding the Samuel farmhouse and tossing in a "bomb," which exploded, tearing off the right arm of Jesse's mother and fatally wounding his small stepbrother.

The raid made by the agency was the reasonable act of a law-enforcement body hunting desperate robbers and killers. Pinkerton's National Detective Agency maintains that it was not a "bomb" that was flung into the dark farmhouse, but a flare known in those days as "Grecian fire." To this writer it is logical. A bomb blast certainly would have blown out the walls or at least the windows. None of the newspaper reports I have examined—some written by reporters who accompanied the raiders—make any mention of such damage to the farmhouse.

It must also be remembered that the family of Jesse and Frank James had sheltered them knowing they were wanted by the law for not only robbery but ruthless and cold-blooded murder. Can it not then be said that those who side with the forces of evil must accept the consequences for their act?

In the final analysis, however, the reader must make up his own mind as to who was right and who was wrong on that violent, bloody night.

In 1884 Allan Pinkerton died, and his now world-famous agency passed on to his two sons, William and Robert. Between them they broke up the Wild Bunch, also known as the Hole in the Wall Gang, a colorful band of outlaws, and forced their leader, Butch Cassidy, and his lieutenants (one a beautiful woman) to flee to South America. There, for almost a decade, they successfully demonstrated the American technique of outlawry.

Chasing bandits and Western badmen was only part of the agency's work. Forgers, confidence men, swindlers, and murderers were also included. The criminals trailed by the Pinkerton operatives in every part of the globe were the elite of the international underworld; the thrilling stories of how they were arrested are endless.

Through the cooperation of Robert Pinkerton II, present head of the world-famous agency, I was permitted access to the Pinkerton historical files. Almost nightly for more than a year I examined the huge volumes—a Klondike of American history—at times using a powerful magnifying glass to decipher faded and brittle clippings from forgotten frontier newspapers or the report of some operative written, perhaps, by the dim lamplight in a shabby Western hotel room after a weary day on horseback.

There was one disappointment. Having done extensive research both in the United States and Canada on the American Revolution, I found the lack of warm and personal documents in these outlaw papers a constant source of irritation. But upon reflection I see that that was to be expected. Men who robbed trains, banks, and stage coaches obviously didn't have the time, inclination, or literacy to discuss their philosophy of life, hopes, dreams, or ambitions, in letters or private journals. So regretfully, at least to this writer, our desperate men must remain shadows on horseback who thunder across the stage in America's great melodrama of the Middle Border and the Wild West.

I approached the writing of this book with a great deal of hesitancy. I believe that I can speak with some authority on the position of the Iroquois Confederacy in the War of Independence, Butler's Tory army of Niagara, or George Rogers Clark's military control of the Northwest during that period. But of outlaws I knew nothing. Like most Americans, all I knew of Jesse James was a vague remembrance of something I had read which insisted the Missourian was a sweet-faced boy who only robbed the rich to give to the poor.

My interest, however, mounted after a few months of examining the files of Pinkerton's National Detective Agency. These were no distorted Hollywood outlaws wooing a lady fair with a guitar; the men who pounded through the old records were flesh and blood. They were desperate men, evil men, but for all of that, they were fascinating men.

Before examining the files I consulted many books and newspapers of the time to gain some knowledge of American outlawry. To begin with, I would classify the majority of so-called outlaw biographies as trash. It would be a waste of space to list them. Robertus Love's *The Rise and Fall of Jesse James*—prejudiced in favor of the James brothers—is still the soundest work yet written about the outlaw leader. Charles Kelly's privately printed *Outlaw Trail*, a biography of Butch Cassidy and his Wild Bunch riders, is an excellent study of this fabulous Western figure.

I found *Charles W. Quantrill; A True History of His Guerilla Warfare* by J. B. Burgh, as told by Capt. Harrison Trow, the best source of Jesse's service under Quantrill, Todd, and Anderson.

To the reader who is interested in the savage border war, I would recommend William Elsey Connelley's *Quantrill and the Border Wars*. In my opinion—and I am not a Civil War expert—Connelley's work is one of the most comprehensive and accurate volumes on that swashbuckling outfit. Bassett's *A True Life of Chas. Quantrill* fails to measure up to it. There is also a great deal of information to be found on Quantrill and his deeds in the many-volumed *Official Records*.

One of the better outlaw books is Burton Rascoe's study of the life of that fabulous lady, Belle Starr. Rascoe, however, is in error, when he declares Frank James served twenty years in jail. James was acquitted of murder and robbery and never spent a day behind bars.

Some authorities on the Middle Border outlaws may scoff when I say that *The Younger Brothers,* by Augustus C. Appler, is an excellent source book. Appler was the editor of the Osceola (Missouri) *Democrat,* and a friend of the Younger family. His material came from the Younger brothers themselves. Appler strikes this writer as a conscientious newspaper man of the old school.

I found the best source book on the Northfield, Minnesota, bank robbery to be *Robber and Hero; The Story of the Raid on the First National Bank of Northfield, Minnesota, by The James-Younger Band of Robbers,* compiled by George Huntington and published in 1876. It is an important piece of Americana. Additional material is included in *The Northfield Bank Raid,* published by the Northfield *News* in 1933.

Many valuable newspaper clippings found in an old scrapbook kept by Governor Thomas Crittenden of Missouri when he was fighting the James-Younger gang, are reprinted in *The Crittenden Memoirs* compiled by H. H. Crittenden. It is unfortunate that no professional writer ever sat down with the chief executive and dug out the complete and inside story of the Jameses and their position in Missouri's political picture. It would have been fascinating.

Jim Cummins' Book by Himself, published in 1903, is an interesting account of the outlaw's life but many times inaccurate.

I liked Homer Croy's *Jesse James Was My Neighbor,* even though Mr. Croy allows Jesse to retain his somewhat tarnished halo.

The Pinkerton files on Butch Cassidy and his Wild Bunch, also known as The-Hole-in-the-Wall gang, are voluminous. It took weeks to make a preliminary survey of what material was at hand. As I did with the Jesse James section, I first consulted as many secondary sources as I could find before examining the files.

To the reader who is interested in the growth of the West I would heartily recommend Professor W. P. Webb's *The Great Plains.* It is excellent. Theodore Roosevelt, who was a cowboy before he was a President, paints a stirring picture of a puncher's life in his *Biography,* which is always a top favorite on any Americana shelf. One disappointment was Charles Siringo's *Riata and Spurs.* The autobiography of this colorful man is vague and disjointed. A professional writer could have produced a minor Western classic—or at least could have put in dates and locations.

J. Monaghan's *The Last of the Bad Men* is a well-written and painstaking biography of Tom Horn, that strange enigma of the old West. There is also Horn's own story and a batch of magazine articles written about Horn and published at the turn of the century. Most of them are rewrite jobs with little regard for truth.

One volume that belongs on any outlaw shelf is Matt Warner's story *The Last of the Bandit Riders* as told to Murray E. King and published just before the bandit died in 1938. On the other hand, *When the Daltons Rode* by Emmett Dalton has little to offer.

The story of Black Jack Ketchum beating himself every time he made a mistake is told by Colonel Jack Potter in the May, 1941, issue of *Sheriff and Police*. The author has made an extensive study of the well-known train and bank robber.

For years Arthur Chapman's *Butch Cassidy*, published in the *Elks Magazine* in 1930, has been the accepted source of how Cassidy and the Sundance Kid died in South America.

Charles Kelly, author of *Outlaw Trail*, uses Chapman's version. He writes me: "After talking to many of the old timers out here I am convinced that the story of Cassidy's end at San Vincente is true."

I'm inclined to go along with Frank Dimaio's less dramatic but more logical story of how the strange trio met their death. I believe, however, that the new material I have found in the Pinkerton files now rounds out the picture of Cassidy's strange odyssey to South America.

My source for the hunting of Harry Tracy was the dispatches published in the *New York Morning World* from its anonymous correspondent. But it was impossible to pass up without reading *The Hunting of Harry Tracy*, written by that old master of the Western story, William MacLeod Raine, and published in *Wide World* magazine about the turn of the century.

During my research I have consulted numerous newspaper clippings, many of them from long-forgotten frontier newspapers. Rather than slow up the narrative with footnotes, I have indicated in the text when I have used them.

And now for my personal notes of appreciation. I had not supposed it true that it would be impossible for an author to

acknowledge all the help he has received in his work, but I find
now, as I try to do so, that such is indeed the case.

One of my big debts is to Miss Rita Burnside, who not only
labored copying obscure messages, digging for missing links, and
obtaining countless photostats, but who worked alone on the research that had to do with the stockman's invasion of Wyoming.
It was Miss Burnside who discovered among other things, Nathan
Champion's strange last will and testament, in that rare old volume,
The Powder River Invasion; War on the Rustlers, by A. S. Mercer.

It is almost impossible to speak adequately of the help and encouragement my friend, Howard Swiggett, novelist and historian,
has given me. In addition to a fellow writer's sympathy, he offered
clues to sources, information, unflagging interest, and a storehouse
of notes from his own works on the Civil War.

High on the list to be thanked are Robert Pinkerton II, present
head of Pinkerton's National Detective Agency, for allowing me to
be the first to examine the outlaw files and Ralph Dudley, vice
president and general manager of the agency, for his guidance and
encouragement. Mr. William H. Smyth, of the Pinkerton's New
York City staff; Mr. William F. Wagner, assistant general manager;
Barnard F. Boyce, assistant general accountant; Howard W. Nugent, manager of the agency's Department of Criminal Identification; assistant superintendent Charles D. Hey and his assistants in
the criminal gallery and files, and the personnel of the agency's
photographic department, who accepted the numerous requests for
photostats of important documents or copies of pictures, with pa-
tience and good humor.

The historical societies of Missouri, Wyoming, and Illinois have
been considerate and helpful. At the New York Public Library's
American History Room—and what would the historical novelists
and Americana writers do without them—I have received the ut-
most help and consideration from Mr. Sylvester Vigilante and Mr.
Ivor Avellino.

I am greatly indebted to those two fine old gentlemen, Francis
Paul Dimaio and Lowell Spence, both retired Pinkerton operatives.
Mr. Spence, who hunted Harvey Logan, the Kid Curry of the Wild
Bunch and the only man to identify his body, supplied me with
important sidelights of Logan's character and details of the man-
hunts. It was Mr. Dimaio who disclosed how Cassidy, the Sundance
Kid, and Etta Place died in South America—the version on record

and not the romantic one at which he is inclined to scoff—along with other details of how the agency hunted the outlaw trio after they had left the United States.

And last but certainly not least, I must humbly express my appreciation to my wife, who somehow, with great adroitness, amidst the day-to-day pressures, prepared the time to allow this book to be finished.

JAMES D. HORAN

BOOK ONE

PROCLAMATION

OF THE

GOVERNOR OF MISSOURI!

REWARDS

FOR THE ARREST OF

Express and Train Robbers.

STATE OF MISSOURI,
EXECUTIVE DEPARTMENT.

WHEREAS, It has been made known to me, as the Governor of the State of Missouri, that certain parties, whose names are to me unknown, have confederated and banded themselves together for the purpose of committing robberies and other depredations within this State; and

WHEREAS, Said parties did, on or about the Eighth day of October, 1879, stop a train near Glendale, in the county of Jackson, in said State, and, with force and violence, take, steal and carry away the money and other express matter being carried thereon; and

WHEREAS, On the fifteenth day of July 1881, said parties and their confederates did stop a train upon the line of the Chicago, Rock Island and Pacific Railroad, near Winston, in the County of Daviess, in said State, and, with force and violence, take, steal, and carry away the money and other express matter being carried thereon; and, in perpetration of the robbery last aforesaid, the parties engaged therein did kill and murder one WILLIAM WESTFALL, the conductor of the train, together with one JOHN McCULLOCH, who was at the time in the employ of said company, then on said train; and

WHEREAS, FRANK JAMES and JESSE W. JAMES stand indicted in the Circuit Court of said Daviess County, for the murder of JOHN W SHEETS, and the parties engaged in the robberies and murders aforesaid have fled from justice and have absconded and secreted themselves:

NOW, THEREFORE, in consideration of the premises, and in lieu of all other rewards heretofore offered for the arrest or conviction of the parties aforesaid, or either of them, by any person or corporation, I, THOMAS T. CRITTENDEN, Governor of the State of Missouri, do hereby offer a reward of five thousand dollars, ($5,000.00) for the arrest and conviction of each person participating in either of the robberies or murders aforesaid, excepting the said FRANK JAMES and JESSE W. JAMES; and for the arrest and delivery of said

FRANK JAMES and JESSE W. JAMES,

and each or either of them, to the sheriff of said Daviess County, I hereby offer a reward of five thousand dollars, ($5,000.00,) and for the conviction of either of the parties last aforesaid of participation in either of the murders or robberies above mentioned. I hereby offer a further reward of five thousand dollars, ($5,000.00.)

IN TESTIMONY WHEREOF, I have hereunto set my hand and caused to be affixed the Great Seal of the State of Missouri. Done

[SEAL.]   at the City of Jefferson on this 26th day of July. A. D. 1881.

THOS. T. CRITTENDEN.

By the Governor:
MICH'L K. McGRATH, Sec'y of State.

REGAN & CARTER, STATE PRINTERS, JEFFERSON CITY, MO.

FOLKLORE AND HISTORY

HEROES, as George Meredith once said, do not die—at least not before the tale is over. Heroes—and villains—of folk tradition live forever in the stories of those who knew them and on into the pages of history. They are like a great fertile family with collateral branches in many lands running into "the dark backward and abyss of time" to their ancestors who slew dragons, saved maidens, and plundered the rich.

The dragons of America were slain by Daniel Boone, Paul Bunyan and his blue ox Babe, by Rio Grande Robert, John Henry and his powerful hammer.

But there is only one outlaw. Even in this explosive atomic age Jesse James still rides. Nothing, it seems, can destroy the legend of our most famous bank and train robber.

In both juvenile and adult imagination he still thunders across the West, mounted on a big bay, calico mask across his face, the bag of gold stolen from the hated railroad slung across his saddle horn, while coming up far behind is the posse hopelessly outclassed by this Gay Desperado.

He robs because the railroad has stolen his family's land and driven them from the old homestead. He steals from the rich and gives freely to the poor. He is Robin Hood in a faded blue Army coat, armed with sixshooters instead of a yew bow. Such is Jesse James as most of us know him. A decade ago Hollywood upheld this tradition. It is no wonder that Joe Francis, granddaughter of the Missouri outlaw, told the Associated Press after the picture's gaudy premier, "The only resemblance is they both ride horses."

As recently as 1948 an old gentleman proclaimed to the world that he was "the real Jesse James." The pages of the nation's big newspapers were crowded at the time with a tense international situation; seasoned metropolitan editors, their fingers on the pulse of America's news interest, promptly gave the story a page one spot.

Stories about the discovery of a still living Jesse James are not unusual. Every few years someone pops up with a cry, "Jesse James is not dead. I'm the real Jesse James." One cropped up in 1902 when the remains of the outlaw were disinterred from the front yard of the "Samuel Place" and buried beside his wife in the Kearney, Missouri, family plot. That morning, the sheriff's office in Kearney received a grimy postcard sent from a Kansas town and signed "the Real Jesse James."

The card went on to say, "I will not be buried in Carny next Sunday. I am not dead. I was not shot by Bobie Ford. Tom Howard was shot by Bobie Ford. I wasn't there so you can't bury me."

At Jesse's second burial an examination of the skull by his son, Jesse James, Jr., showed the bullet hole beyond the left ear and several easily identifiable gold-filled teeth. The skeleton was beyond a doubt that of the famous outlaw.

Quite recently two young hoodlums held up a railroad train. The name of Jesse James again leaped into the headlines throughout the country. The Associated Press recalled the exploits of the bandit in a feature story. A national weekly, a few months later, in speaking of a prominent statesman of Franco's Spain, described him as a "Spanish Horatio Alger with the overtones of Jesse James." To sum up: Jesse James is one of our cherished folklore legends and nothing seems to diminish our perennial interest in him.

The most persistent legends created about Jesse cast him in the role of a Robin Hood. The legend is not a Sunday-supplement fantasy. Carl Sandburg recognized it, saying, "There is only one American bandit [Jesse James] who is classical, who is to this country what Robin Hood and Dick Turpin are to England, whose exploits are so close to the mythical and apocryphal."

Theodore Roosevelt wrote, "There is something very curious in the reproduction here in this new continent of essentially the condition of ballad growth which was obtained in medieval England; including, by the way, sympathy for the outlaw, Jesse James, taking the place of Robin Hood."

Such tales, however, are woven about every outlaw and freebooter who catches the public's fancy, and are passed along from

generation to generation. An example appears on the first page of
Volume I of the Historical Archives of the National Pinkerton
Detective Agency. It is a brown and brittle clipping from the
Denver Post, May 18, 1890, giving an account of an interview
with "Uncle Dick" Henderton, who claimed to have known
"Jesse James well."

"In one robbery at a place called Blue Cut," Uncle Dick said,
"an old lady in black gave Jesse James $70 in greenbacks and
then cried, 'That is all I have in the world. My husband's corpse
is in the baggage car.' Jesse wept, handing her back her money
and adding two crisp $100 bills. Jesse would never rob a cripple
or a gray-haired old lady. Once in Liberty, Missouri, he gave his
coat to a shivering old man."

And so on.

Of course there was no corpse in the baggage car of the train
the James-Younger gang held up at Blue Cut.

During some of his earlier crimes, Jesse may have had some
chivalry toward his female victims and former Confederate officers.
But not at Blue Cut when the Missouri outlaw leader had begun
to suspect that the sands were running out; the Pinkertons were
snapping at his heels and civilian posses lured by the reward
money were scouring the countryside. He had no time to waste
in gestures.

As for Jesse giving an old man his coat in Liberty, Missouri,
the bandit may have been sorry for some of his friends and neighbors who had their savings in the Clay County Savings Bank
which he undoubtedly helped to loot in the 1866 raid. But the
title of this portion of the first volume of the Pinkerton five-
volume file on the James-Younger gang is, appropriately, "Bunk."

Jesse James is not the only American outlaw to whom our
folklore has given an occasional halo. Further west there is
"Butch" Cassidy and his fantastic Wild Bunch of Wyoming who
ruled the northern section of Wyoming, Utah, and Colorado from
1882 to 1889, from a medieval-like fortress in what is still today
the most desolate section of the West. From this community of
evil they robbed, looted, and murdered. At one time they had an
army estimated at from one hundred to five hundred of the nation's
most desperate outlaws, rustlers, badmen, gamblers, horse thieves,
dancehall girls, and renegade cowboys. From their hole in the hills
they defied the United States government, smashed an invasion by

a counter army hired by cattlemen, and stood off four troops of United States cavalry. At the turn of the century the leaders transferred their activities to South America, where they successfully introduced the technique of American outlawry. Like Jesse James, Butch Cassidy, the leader of this incredible gang, is described as a Robin Hood. The same tale is told about him as about Jesse. It is amusing to match their similarities.

In his privately printed *Outlaw Trail*, Charles W. Kelly, who did a painstaking research job on the outlaws of that period, writes:

> "Frank," Butch Cassidy told Weber, the oldest resident of Hankville, "I'm not as bad as I have been pictured. I've done a poor feller and his wife a good turn this trip. As I was cutting across the hills, I came upon a run down looking outfit but I stopped to see if I could get something to eat. There was an old man and an old woman there. They had tried to make a home but old age had hit 'em quicker'n they imagined, and the fact is they were about to be run off the place by a feller who had a note against 'em.
>
> "I asked them who the gent was and they said they looked to see him about any minute.
>
> "'Which way will he come in?' I asked and the old woman pointed to an old trail. I made the old lady take $500, the amount due, and I told her to give it to this feller. I said goodby and left. I hid out along the trail and along comes a fellow on a horse. He had black clothes and I had a hunch that this was the collector. I watched him and he went to the old log cabin and the old lady let him in. Maybe five minutes later he came out. When he came up the trail I stopped him, took the $500—and here I am!"

Robertus Love, in his study of Jesse James—greatly prejudiced in favor of the James and Youngers, but as near to an authentic biography of the bandit as has yet been printed—tells an identical tale, but Jesse James is the Robin Hood.

Love quotes a Missourian who in turn received the story from Frank James. He tells how the gang was traveling "somewhere in northern Missouri" when they came upon a small farmhouse with a lone woman in charge. After they had produced some money, the woman agreed to cook them a meal.

It was while she was making the coffee Jesse discovered "tears rolling down her cheeks and sobs heaving her bosom."

Questioning the woman, Jesse learned "she was a widow with several children and a $1,400 mortgage on the old homestead."

"Aha!" said Jesse. "And so that's really what's making you cry—you're afraid you are going to lose your home. I see."

That was it, the widow admitted, and then went on to tell the outlaw that the man who held the mortgage—"a hardhearted old miser"—was coming that very morning to foreclose!

The yarn goes on to tell how Jesse, his eyes blinking furiously, cried: "Is that so? Well, now ma'am, I don't know about that; I—well now, I don't think you're going to lose your farm after all."

And then this warmhearted desperado took his sack and "counted out on the table $1,400."

After a hearty meal, Jesse obtained the description of the gent coming to collect his mortgage money, and advising the widow to get a receipt "signed in ink" left the woman "weeping but weeping for joy."

Like Cassidy, of course, Jesse and his gang held up the "mortgage man" and recovered the $1,400.

The naïve stories are endless and probably originated in Richard F. Fox's *Police Gazette*. Hundreds of them were printed in that vivid pink sheet, read by America's male population before the run of the century, in brothels, saloons, and barbershops. There is no doubt that a large percentage of our folklore legends were culled from the pages of that illustrated weekly. There isn't an old-timer from Missouri to the Texas Panhandle who today doesn't tell the same tales as unquestionable truth, only substituting his favorite or regional outlaw in the featured role. But there were long precedent and ancient lineage for these tales.

One of the most fascinating questions about the career of Jesse James is what did he do with the money he stole? Although his share on many occasions was small after the total had been split several ways and the expenses deducted, some of his robberies were successful and profitable. On one or two occasions, minor members of the James-Younger gang were arrested while in the process of "shooting up the town," and it can be assumed that they were spending their share of the loot in the traditional wine, women, and song fashion of the thief after a successful job. But not Jesse James, his brother Frank, or the Youngers.

On the other hand, Butch Cassidy and his Wild Bunch spent their loot in wild sprees, taking over whole towns and ordering at pistol point, if necessary, every male inhabitant to "belly up to the bar."

After a wild and boisterous two or three days, they would ride back to their fortress in the hills nursing hangovers and leaving behind the townspeople, nerve wracked but happily counting the gold in their tills.

There is none of this, at least documented, to be found in the background of the James-Younger outfit. On the whole they appear to be a vicious and moody bunch.

From the evidence at hand, perhaps the best that can be said of Jesse James is that he appeared to be faithful to his wife and to be fond of his children. This is a very small credit against the vast debits of his life. There is one more thing. His personal courage never seems to have been questioned. Jesse could kill unarmed and helpless men without hesitation, but he never flinched in the face of heavy odds.

The superb horsemanship of the Missouri outlaws and Butch Cassidy's Wild Bunch must always be kept in mind. They could outride any sheriff's posse, skimming the rail fences like fox hunters. And of course if they wanted to go on living they had to be expert judges of horseflesh. As one of Jesse's followers put it succinctly:

"Dingus was the best horse thief in the west."

Romance and legend aside, it is best now that our desperate men of the Middle Border be introduced. For sixteen years they will thunder across the West in America's greatest crime wave; they will rob trains, stagecoaches, and banks; they will murder and plunder; they will be merciless and ruthless; they will halt a civilization, wreck businesses, and drive innocent men to ruin; they will defy their own government; they will kill and be killed; in their own lifetime they will become legends.

The leader of the band was Jesse Woodson James, called *Dingus* by his friends. In his maturity he was a man about five feet eleven inches in height, with a solid, compact build. He was fair complexioned with black hair, blinking blue eyes (he suffered from granulated eyelids), and a carefully trimmed sun-browned beard. Thus the wanted posters read. He was a strange man with a dark streak of violence running through his makeup. He was a born leader but psychically lonely. As the old ballad goes: "He was born one day in the county of Clay and came from a solitary race." He was a poised man—even when relieving his victims of their wallets and watches—and at times had a wry sense of humor. He was recklessly courageous and defiant at all times. He justified his murders and his robberies with a snarled "They drove us to it" or by glibly declaring that his victims were "northerners" and as such were not entitled to any consideration. Despite the romanticists, the countless folklore tales of his goodheartedness, and the misplaced sympathy of his defenders, this man, who became a symbol of highway robbery for all times and a distorted figure of eternal youth riding through a purple haze of romantic melodrama, was a completely pitiless killer.

Frank James was the second member of the band. Although he was four years older, he had less dash and personal magnetism than his brother. He was soft spoken, sanctimonious but ruthless. He was a Bible- and Shakespeare-spouting thief who wrote long letters to the newspapers to protest that he was being persecuted, yet a short time after their publication he would apologetically relieve a train or stagecoach passenger of his gold "super." When he surrendered much was made of him, but in this writer's opinion, he was a smug, solemn-faced hypocrite who finally wound up in the job he was best fitted for—doorman for a burlesque house.

The most likable member of the gang—at least to this writer— was Thomas Coleman ("Cole") Younger. Many historians have looked down their noses at him, but it is impossible to suppress the personality of this complete extrovert. He was a handsome man of two hundred pounds and an inch under six feet, with light brown wavy hair and thick sideburns. He was a wearer of conservative clothes, which gave him the air of a prosperous cattleman, and in his more solemn moments, a clergyman meditating on next Sunday's sermon. He loved the flamboyant and dramatic. In one of the stagecoach robberies a "big man" was said to have returned a victim's watch and tie pin upon learning he served in the Confederate army. If the story is true, it was undoubtedly Cole playing to the hilt the role of a champion of the South who was driven into banditry by the war and at the same time building up one of those pretty legends by which so many brigands of history so often manage to win the charity and sympathy they never deserve.

Above all, Cole was a charmer of females from six to sixty. One of the best pictures we have of him is in Scyene, Texas, wooing a farmer's young daughter with his talk of wild raids and boasting how "one of our men, Jesse James, can pick off his man at five hundred yards." This young girl, as Belle Starr, was later to become as notorious as her lover. A child, fathered by the big outlaw, was named Pearl and ended up as the madam of a well-known Western bawdyhouse. Another picture is of Cole—with eleven bullets in his big body—charming the ladies of Madelia, Minnesota, where he and his bullet-shattered brothers had been taken after the debacle at Northfield, one of the most thrilling stories in our western history. His personality so dazzled one lady that she followed him to the gates of the state penitentiary to wave good-by. Cole was undoubtedly born three centuries too late. Elizabeth, the Queen, would have loved him.

Another rider was Jim Younger. Like Cole, he was big and soft spoken. Jim drifted into rather than adopted the business of outlawry. He was apparently easily swayed by his brothers or by Jesse James, but he stuck it at Northfield until the bitter end. Tragedy side-stepped him during his outlaw career but visited him with vengeance during his later years.

The baby of the band was Bob Younger. He was twelve years old in 1863 when Quantrill's riders of the Black Flag Brigade thundered into Lawrence. He was twenty-three when he knelt wounded behind the wooden staircase in Northfield, to trade shots with a courageous hardware merchant. When the going was the roughest, Bob was cool and fearless. But when the reckoning came, unlike Frank James, that repentant thief, he took his punishment.

"We are rough men and are used to rough ways," was all he said to the editor of the St. Paul, Minnesota, *Pioneer Press* as he lay with a bullet in his breast and a shattered elbow in the hotel room in Madelia.

The last member of the Middle Border outlaw trust was John Younger. He was a hard-drinking and gun-slinging young hoodlum who killed his first man for hitting him over the head with a dead mackerel when he was only fifteen. As the story goes, he was taking Cole's Colt to a gunsmith to be repaired when he met a farmer on the road who began teasing him. The boy went back at him and the farmer swung the dead fish. Cole's gun was still in working order and John killed the man. He was arrested but acquitted the next day on the grounds of "self defense."

John's favorite boast was "no damn detective will ever catch me grinnin' through a grating," and to carry it out he and one of his brothers trailed and engaged two Pinkerton operatives and a local peace officer in a gun duel on a small stony hill outside Roscoe, Missouri, on the afternoon of March 16, 1874. In the furious exchange of bullets he was killed along with the local deputy and one of the Pinkerton men.

There were other riders, but Jesse and Frank James and the Youngers were the principals. This can be said about all of them: They arose from the dark complexes of the border warfare, neighbor against neighbor; were schooled by Quantrill and cemented by their strange clannish hatred of outsiders, like that of the Doones. By what personal appeals they were bound together we do not know, but they pursued their Godless, goalless circle of robbery and violence until at last, gradually seeing the bonds which tied them to each other originally in trust—perhaps even in rough affection—burst asunder by the inexpiable crimes they perpetrated, they turned, betrayed, and killed each other. They were not only outlaws but symbols of an era in our history.

2.

THE DARK AND BLOODY GROUND

L IKE better men, Jesse James was the son of the Middle Border. The pressure, the dreams, and the tides of land hunger which brought the Lincolns, the Grants, and all the homesteaders west, brought the James family to break the plains. They were apparently better off intellectually, morally, and even financially than the great masses rolling across the Mississippi. There never seemed to be any question of real poverty or want. Medicine and theology are strangely mixed in the bloodlines.

The parents of Jesse and Frank James were Robert James, of Logan County, and Miss Zerelda Cole, of Lexington, both in Kentucky. Their families were of pioneer stock whose forebears had traveled the old Wilderness Road.

Robert James was twenty-three and a third-term student preparing for the Baptist ministry at Georgetown Academy, Georgetown, Kentucky, when he first met Zerelda Cole, then seventeen. They were married a short time after. Miss Cole, who was educated in a Roman Catholic convent, became a Baptist after her marriage.

The young couple were still honeymooning when they visited Robert's widowed mother in Clay County, Missouri. Attracted by the grand sweep of the land, they decided to settle there. Shortly after Robert James was ordained and became the Reverend Robert James, acreage was acquired and a small house built near the village of Centerville, now Kearney. A few years later a second house was built.

On January 10, 1843, their first son was born. He was named Alexander Franklin James.

Meanwhile, the Reverend Robert James expounded the gospel to two neighborhood congregations known as Good Hope and Providence. As did every frontier preacher-farmer, the young clergyman worked his land during the week and preached his sermons on Sundays.

On September 5, 1847, a second son was born. He was named Jesse Woodson James.

Avarice and restlessness must have been strangely present in the young country minister. After about ten years of married life he left his small family for the California gold fields. He never swung a pick, for three weeks after his arrival he died and is said to have been buried in Maryville, California.

Some writers have hinted that perhaps the strong-willed Mrs. James was too much for her husband. In his *Life and Adventures of Frank and Jesse James,* published in 1898, J. A. Bacus wrote: "It is said by those who knew the couple in early years, they were ill-mated, he gentle and amiable, while she strong in passion with

1. [LEFT] The Russellville, Kentucky, bank, an early James robbery victim. Jesse took $14,000 from this bank March 20, 1868. 2. [RIGHT] John Reno and Frank Sparks. John Reno invented the technique of train robbery. Jesse probably learned the trick when a member of his gang returned from the Missouri State prison where he was imprisoned with Reno. Frank Sparks was one of Reno's lieutenants. *(Courtesy Pinkerton's National Detective Agency, Inc.).* 3. [BELOW] Type of train James-Younger gang used to rob. *(Courtesy Library of Congress)*

THE ADAMS EXPRESS Co

THIS COMPANY HAS FACILITIES UNSURPASSED BY THOSE OF ANY OTHER EXPRESS LINE IN THE WORLD, FOR THE SAFE & EXPEDITIOUS FORWARDING & PROMPT DELIVERY OF

BANK-NOTES, GOLD & SILVER COIN, PARCELS, PACKAGES, FREIGHT, &c

ALSO, FOR THE COLLECTION OF NOTES, DRAFTS & ACCOUNTS IN ALL THE CITIES, TOWNS & VILLAGES IN THE EASTERN, WESTERN, SOUTHERN & SOUTH-WESTERN STA

4. The Adams Express Company was the first train company to be robbed by the James-Younger gang. They engaged Pinkerton to track down the bandits. *(Courtesy of the New York Historical Society, New York City)*

5. The seated figure at the right is Allan Pinkerton, founder of Pinkerton's National Detective Agency, which proved to be the only concrete threat to outlawry in the West. This picture was taken of Pinkerton and his agents during the Civil War. *(Courtesy James D. Horan Western Americana Collection)*

6. *A Harper's Weekly* artist's step-by-step representation of the James-Younger train robbery at Muncie, Kansas, on December 12, 1874. Appeared in the January 2, 1875, issue of *Harper's Weekly*. (*Courtesy James D. Horan Western Americana Collection*)

7. View of the square in Northfield, Minnesota. Picture taken about the time of the raid. (*Courtesy Pinkerton's National Detective Agency, Inc.*)

8. Zerelda James Simms Samuels, thrice-wed mother of Frank and Jesse James. Note empty sleeve. Her arm was accidentally blown off when detectives surrounded Dr. Samuels' house on January 5, 1875, in a fruitless attempt to catch the James' boys. (*Courtesy Pinkerton's National Detective Agency, Inc.*)

9. Dr. Henry M. Wheeler, who at the age of nineteen first noticed the outlaws' presence in Northfield and gave the alarm to the town. (*Courtesy Pinkerton's National Detective Agency, Inc.*)

10. Joseph Lee Heywood, Northfield's bank cashier, who was shot to death by the robbers. (*Courtesy Pinkerton's National Detective Agency, Inc.*)

a bitter and unrelenting disposition, traits of character which she handed down to her two sons, Frank and Jesse."

In 1851 when she was twenty-six Mrs. James married for the second time. The bridegroom was a fifty-year-old local farmer by the name of Simms, a "widower with children." The union was an unhappy one and resulted in a separation a short time later.

There are two versions of why the marriage broke up. One has the mother of the future outlaws insisting that Simms was "unkind" to "the boys"; the other has the farmer declaring he "could not stand" his young stepsons.

In 1857 the mother of Jesse and Frank was married the third time to a farmer-physician, Dr. Reuben Samuel. The union was successful. In spite of the scarcity of marriageable womenfolk along the border, it is a curious sidelight to consider the widow James, burdened with two small children, apparently having no difficulty in making not only a second but a third marriage.

The second stepfather of Jesse and Frank James belonged to a Kentucky family and had been educated in a Cincinnati medical school. He first practiced in Greenville, Clay County, Missouri. Throughout the sixteen years the two outlaws were rampaging across the West, Dr. Samuel apparently never made his sentiments known. He is a vague and shadowy figure who never comes to life. But it is a strange triangle—the physician stepfather sheltering his two notorious stepsons.

The "Samuel place," described as "an ordinary farmhouse," was only a few miles distance from Lee's Summit, the home of the Youngers. Less than a half day's horseback ride away were the Dalton's. This interlocking family network, the first impregnable defense of the outlaws, produced in classic border fashion countless cousins, kissing kin, and henchmen.

The forebears of the Younger brothers, like the James family, were of pioneer stock. Charles Younger, grandfather of the bandits, originally lived in Virginia but moved to Missouri with his family in 1825. He had three sons and a daughter, Adeline, who by that extraordinary aptness of romance was to become the mother of the Dalton boys, Grat, Bill, Bob, and Emmett, all train and bank robbers. By a weird coincidence the Daltons met their end in a crackle of gunfire strangely paralleling the Northfield, Minnesota debacle where the James-Younger gang crumbled.

The reign of both brotherhoods was ended by an outraged citizenry.

Blood will tell, and in the Youngers it tells strange things. Adeline's brothers were Colonel Henry Washington Younger, father of the outlaws; Thomas Jefferson Younger, who served in the Missouri State Legislature; and Benjamin Franklin Younger, who served as peace officer of St. Clair County, Missouri. Outlaws and public servants.

In 1830 Colonel Younger married Miss Busheba Fristo. The union produced fourteen children, eight boys and six girls. Of the boys, those who became outlaws and killers were Thomas Coleman, John, James H., and Robert Ewing. In a family of strange coincidences it is not bewildering to discover that Cole and Jim were both born on January 15, Cole in 1844 and Jim in 1848.

In 1861 Colonel Younger opened a livery stable in Harrisonville, Cass County, with the finest horseflesh in the Middle Border, and bought two large farms, one in Jackson County, ten miles from Independence, and the other in adjoining Harrisonville.

Living must have been primitive during the years the James boys and Younger brothers grew to manhood. Burton Rascoe in his *Life of Belle Starr* describes the dining room of a fairly decent Missouri tavern of that time "as swarming with flies, midges, and mosquitoes with the meager food fried in deep grease often used many times over." The evening meal—"supper"—consisted of what was left over from the noonday meal. Food would be salt meat or game in season and occasionally fish.

Roads were impassable during the heavy snows and the spring rains; food and clothing were often difficult to secure. The chores were back breaking: splitting wood, planting, hand cultivating and reaping, and fence building. But this rugged outdoor life made them all tough and gave Jesse the whipcord body that stood up under his ghastly wartime wound and the rough, hard riding life of a western outlaw.

There is no record to show that Jesse and Frank James, or Cole, Jim, John, and Bob Younger ever received anything but grade schooling at the nearby Pleasant Grove School.

The childish games of the future outlaws and of all the children along the border states were grim and imitative of their time: the brave-hearted Missourian against the thievin' murderin' Kansan. For seven years before the Civil War was fought, a conflict raged between Kansas and Missouri, equaled for savagery in American history only by the Mohawk and Westchester's Neutral Ground in the Revolution.

Since 1818, Missouri, peopled mostly by southerners from Kentucky, Virginia, Tennessee, and other slave states, had been the bone of contention between free soilers and slavery advocates. Slave states were equal in number with the free states, and each faction was unwilling to allow the balance to be tilted. This was broken finally by the Missouri Compromise, which provided for Maine to be admitted as a free state and Missouri as a slave state.

In 1856 the Dred Scott Decision fanned the fire; after John Brown's raid on May 24, 1856, it exploded. Settlers from Kansas raided Missouri and carried off slaves; Missourians retaliated with swift, deadly raids, burning and looting. The Kansans contemptuously called the raiders "Bushwackers" while their neighbors sneered "Red-Legs" or "Jayhawkers."

Many a thrilling and exciting story must have been told on the porch of the Samuel place or the Younger farm by men who had taken part in these border raids. One can see the boys squatting in the dust, drinking in the bloody tales.

After Sumter, Frank James, who was about sixteen, enlisted in the Missouri State Guards commanded by Sterling Price. Three weeks after the first battle of Bull Run, on August 10, 1861, he fought at Wilson Creek near Springfield in southwest Missouri, one of the most important and bloodiest battles in the first year of the war. Dingus, his more famous brother, was then only twelve.

After Wilson Creek, Frank returned home on a furlough trumpeting the glories of the Confederacy. He was promptly thrown into the lockup at Liberty, twelve miles from Kansas City, the seat of Clay County, Missouri, by the Federal militia. A few days later he was released after signing an "oath" to uphold the Union. The "oath" was quickly forgotten. The future outlaw went back to war, this time a member of a guerrilla outfit headed by a man named Quantrill—"Charley Quantrell."

Cole Younger, then seventeen, joined Quantrill either in the fall of '61 or in April of '62. Jim Cummins, who rode with James and the Youngers both under the Black Flag of Quantrill and on the outlaw trail, called Cole "the cool and desperate Cole who headed the advance into Lawrence. He was grand, noble looking, and a handsome man, and was respected and well liked by all who came into contact with him. He was far superior to the others."

Cole, unlike the rest of the Missouri bravos, joined the regular Confederate army. In the Pinkerton Historical Archives there is a copy of a notarized affidavit made in March, 1898, by a Colonel G. W. Thompson, a recruiting officer in Missouri, who states he swore Cole into the regular army on August 8, 1862. When General Sterling Price was retreating southward in the fall of 1864 during the last raid of that Confederate army, Cole joined the tattered gray riders. He was stationed in Louisiana until the spring of 1865.

Cole claimed in later years he had been forced "to take to the brush" because he was subjected to a series of outrages at the hands of the State Militia headed by a Captain Irvin Walley. There is no reason to doubt his statement; the red tide ebbed and flowed across the bloody ground of the Middle Border during those dark years.

Although Cole was "grand, noble looking and handsome and would remind one of a clergyman" he was a cold-blooded killer. One of the best accounts of the Youngers, and an important source book, is by August C. Appler, editor of the *Osceola Missouri Democrat,* and a friend of the Younger family. Appler obtained most of his material from relatives and intimate friends of the Younger family and also had "several interviews with the Younger brothers in regard to the charges against them." He also declared that "much of the matter stated here was sketched by Coleman Younger himself and merely written out in more detail."

Appler tells how Quantrill's band captured fifteen Jayhawkers after a fierce battle. In camp that night Cole debated with some members of the gang about the merits of an Enfield rifle. One of the guerrillas claimed that if the ball could kill a man at a mile, at a short range it would go through ten men. Cole decided to use the prisoners in a test. He placed them in a line, one behind the other, then measured off fifteen paces and fired. Three men dropped. The guerrilla continued to fire at his human targets "until all had been killed." True? False? Legend? It is difficult to say. The times were hard and brutal. Life is cheap in any merci-

less partisan war. In his last years Cole vigorously denied the story
as "false and untrue in every line."

Captain Trow in his *A True Story of Chas. W. Quantrell*, tells
a story of how Cole spent a great deal of time after his enlistment
as a guerrilla going off into the woods to polish his marksmanship.

"Soon he was perfect and then he laughed often and spoke a
great deal," Trow related.

A few months after he had enlisted with Quantrill, Cole was
joined by his brother Jim.

Then, in 1863, the star of the play emerged from the wings
and came on the stage. Trow described him as "a slim boy with an
oval, peach-colored face, blinking icy blue eyes, and small white
hands with tapering fingers." He was dressed in rough jeans and a
long cavalryman's coat. Two businesslike Navy Colts sagged about
his middle from the bullet-lined gun belt. A well-oiled carbine was
slung across his back. He was mounted on a sleek, spirited horse
which he handled gracefully. He rode beside a giant of a man
with a black beard and bristling with guns. The boy calls him
George; the giant calls the boy Dingus. Once the big man threw
back his head and roared with laughter but the young rider only
let a smile crook his lips; it was cold as sleet. The boy was Jesse
Woodson James; the big man, George Shepherd.

The story is that Jesse had been flogged by the Federals while
plowing a field. Earlier the same militiamen had hanged Dr.
Samuel from a blackjack tree in front of the farmhouse "for his
disloyal remarks and friendship with Quantrill." Mrs. Samuel is
said to have saved her husband's life by following the lynching
party and cutting the physician down as he was slowly strangling
to death. After the flogging Jesse ran away to join Quantrill but
was sent home by Frank. He persisted, however, and a short time
later, with his friend "Jim Cummins from up the road," joined
a newly organized guerrilla outfit headed by "Bloody Bill" Anderson.

The story of Jesse's flogging is also related by Captain Harrison
Trow who rode with the outlaw in the guerrillas. Although the
incident may be true, there is nothing to support it but the repeated telling. It may have been told to lay the foundation for a
"revenge" motivation to account for Jesse's outlawry.

A study of our Western outlaws will reveal in almost every case
a "revenge" motivation to account for their later crimes: Butch

Cassidy turned outlaw because he was "falsely" accused and sent to jail for stealing a saddle; the Daltons commenced their life of crime after being "cheated" at cards in a western gambling den; Quantrill, the criminal lunatic of the Middle Border, used as an excuse for his unspeakable outrages the "murder" of a non-existing "brother" by Kansas Jayhawkers.

Although the motivation for Jesse James becoming a partisan—patriotism, adventure, plunder, a natural blood lust, or revenge—will never be known, we do have these facts. Jesse James joined the guerrilla outfit of "Bloody Bill" Anderson some time in 1863 and served, at different times, under Quantrill, Anderson, and George Todd—three of the bloodiest men in the annals of American history. For two years they tutored the sixteen-year-old boy in every technique of cold-blooded murder, violence, thievery, and arson. Because the violent war years and the three ruthless guerrilla leaders undoubtedly had a powerful influence in shaping the character of the famous outlaw, we must examine them. By no means is the examination an attempt to ameliorate the future evil of Jesse James; rather it is an attempt to explain it. Perhaps in probing the meager records we have of the part played by this hard-eyed Missouri boy in this horrible border war, we can come to some conclusion how—but more importantly why—Jesse James turned outlaw.

The most important of Missouri's three guerrilla leaders is Quantrill. Some historians still spell his name as "Quantrell" and call him "Charley Quantrell." His real name was William Clarke Quantrill and he was an ex-schoolteacher, born in Hagerstown, Maryland, on July 21, 1837. He came from a family of peculiarly criminal tendencies. It is said that his father was an embezzler; his mother possessed an uncontrollable temper; his uncle was a forger and a confidence man; a brother was a thief. Before the outbreak of hostilities along the Kansas-Missouri border, he worked as a horsethief in Kansas under the alias of Charley Hart.

From his pictures he was extraordinarily handsome, the face well shaped and intelligent, the expression grave and severe. He had thick dark hair, well brushed, and unlike his bearded partisans, wore a thin and carefully trimmed mustache.

There is no other like him in our history. Eighty-four years before his time Simon Girty, the ex-wagoneer and woodsrunner, led his red hordes through the Ohio valley with torch and scalping knife, once watching a former friend slowly burn to a charred hulk at the torture stake. But for all his brutality Girty was faithfully serving a cause. Quantrill had none. He was false to himself and to his followers and completely devoid of any moral code. Unknown to his men he played a double game.

A typical aspect of his character is described by William Elsey Connelly, secretary of the Kansas Historical Society and Quantrill's only authentic biographer. He writes:

> . . . late in the fall of 1860 he [Quantrill] made up a party at Lawrence, Kansas, for the purpose of riding into Missouri to steal horses, mules and cattle. This raid was made into Cass County. Quantrill had carefully gone over the roads there and he had marked the farms from which the stock was to be taken. The party secured a large amount of livestock and started to return to Kansas. Quantrill slipped away from his companions and alarmed the people from the place where the stock had been stolen, gathered a number of them together and led them against his own band of thieves who were overtaken before they had reached the state line.
>
> A battle was fought and the robbers resisted fiercely and succeeded in escaping with most of their spoil which they sold along the route home. Quantrill then contracted with the Missourians to find and identify the livestock at so much per head. He secured much of it from those who had purchased it from the robbers. When he returned to Lawrence he claimed that he had become bewildered in the dark and had lost his way to the camp, had been set upon by the enraged owners of the cattle and nearly lost his life but finally escaped by making a long detour to the south. He claimed his portion of the money the livestock had been sold for and it was paid over to him. . . .

Quantrill claimed that he visited Jefferson Davis in Richmond in 1861 and received permission to operate along the border. This may or may not be true. Certainly Jones, the Confederate diarist, exulted, as we shall see, in Quantrill's later exploits and seemed to have known much about him.

In the fall of 1861 Quantrill gathered eight men about him

and started, as Captain Harrison Trow puts it, "to settle some old scores with the Jayhawkers."

Within a few months the band had grown to fifty. Among the first to enlist under the Black Flag was George Todd. Trow described him as "an incarnate devil of battle. He thought of fighting when awake, dreamed of it at night, mingled talk of it with relaxation, and went hungry many a day and shelterless many a night that he might find his enemy and have his fill of fighting." Two years later Jesse rode at Todd's side at Centralia.

With the band rapidly growing, "an organization was effected: Quantrill was elected Captain; William Haller, first lieutenant; William Gregg, second; George Todd, third; and John Jarrette, orderly sergeant."

During these early days Quantrill invented a tale about himself to explain his bitter hate of the North and more likely to explain his activities in Kansas. For years after Quantrill's death, his men, many of whom returned home, unlike the James and Youngers, to become respected members and leaders of their communities, still recited the story and refused to be convinced that it was only pure fiction. In the Confederate Home at Higginsville, Missouri, there may be a gallant nonagenarian who still accepts the story as genuine.

This is the way "Charley" Quantrill told it around the leaping campfires under the frosty stars in that bloody fall of 1861.

He and an older brother who lived in Kansas set out for the gold fields of California. One night, while camped on the Cottonwood River they were attacked by a band of Jayhawkers. His brother was killed, the Negro cook was kidnaped, and he himself was left for dead, shot in the leg and the breast. For days he fought off the buzzards which tried to tear at his brother's decomposing body. Then, out of nowhere, a Shawnee Indian came upon the scene, buried his brother, and nursed him back to health.

Quantrill swore revenge. As his tale had it, he joined the same gang which had murdered his brother. For years he rode with the band. One by one they disappeared. Only two escaped. He, Quantrill, had killed all the others to avenge his poor brother's death!

The rough and embittered settlers of the ravaged border, themselves victims of that bloody tide which flowed back and forth for years before the actual Civil War broke out, were ready to believe anything. They took up Quantrill's tale and gave it a few more flourishes. Before long the ex-schoolteacher was a knight-errant fighting his way through his enemies to rescue the Holy Grail. When they burned and plundered and murdered, his followers did so with a high feeling of justification—look what those Jayhawking bastards did to "Charley's" kin....

While writers and historians, particularly Kansans, paint Quantrill as a bloodthirsty monster, many Missourians indignantly declare that the guerrilla raider is a misunderstood hero. They point out that although the James and Youngers were among his riders, there were also some of Missouri's finest citizens, many of whom became state leaders and respected merchants after the war. One of Quantrill's lieutenants, William Gregg, returned home to Jackson County, Missouri, to become deputy sheriff and hunt the men who, during the war, had ridden with him.

Missourians also pointed out that Union guerrilla forces under Jennison, Lane, and Montgomery burned as many houses and towns and killed as many innocent persons as did the raiders under Quantrill, Anderson, and Todd.

Of the partisan leaders on both sides Quantrill was the bloodiest. By the spring of 1862 he and his followers were outlawed by Union Army Special Order No. 47 signed by Brigadier General James Totten, commanding the District of Central Missouri, with headquarters at Jefferson City, Missouri. Many of the Southern army officers agreed with the Union order. Stand Watie, who led a band of Confederate Cherokees, and who was made a brigadier general in the regular Confederate army for outstanding leadership and bravery by Jefferson Davis on May 10, 1864, replied, when he was compared with Quantrill:

"I am not a murderer."

Murderer or partisan leader, Quantrill undoubtedly had the approval, if unofficial, of headquarters at Richmond. In his *A Rebel War Clerk's Diary*, J. B. Jones noted:

> Aug. 27, 1863:
> Major Quantril (sic) a Missouri guerrilla chief, has dashed into Lawrence, Kansas and burnt the city—killing and wounding 180. He had General Jim Lane but he escaped.

Oct. 20, 1863:

Letters have been received justifying the belief (notwith-standing the forebodings of Lt. Gen E. K. Lurth) that we have taken Little Rock, Arkansas again. This is Price's work: also that Quantrell [sic] and other boldraiders in Missouri have collected some thousands of desperate men and *killed* [Jones' italics] several regiments of the enemy. They have burned a number of towns (Union) and taken the large town of Boon-ville. These are the men against whom Kansas abolitionists have sworn vengeance—no quarter is to be granted there. I suspect they are granting no quarter.

Nov. 19, 1862:

We hear of sanguinary acts in Missouri—ten men (civilians) being shot in retaliation for one killed by our rangers. These acts exasperate our people and will stimulate them to a heroic defense.

From 1861 to 1863 Quantrill's raiders burned, killed, and looted. In retaliation, Jennison's Jayhawkers and Kansan Red-legs swooped down on the Missouri countryside, driving off herds of livestock and horses, killing their owners, and putting the towns and villages to the torch. It was a bloody business on both sides.

In July, 1862, a band of Jayhawkers invaded Harrisonville, the seat of Cass County, and left it a smoldering shambles. The Younger livery went up in flames and the blooded horses were stolen. The same month Colonel Younger—the title is not military but believed to be one of those handed out to all the dignified land-owning gentry—was murdered on a lonely road five miles from Independence, Missouri. Historians insist the murderers were Jayhawkers but do not say *how* they know. However, it may be true. A large sum of money was stolen and the pockets of the corpse turned inside out. From this circumstantial evidence it can be assumed, too, that the murderers of the stable and farm owner were thieves lured by the roll of bills rather than motivated by patriotism. It was common knowledge in the community that Younger carried large sums on his person when he traveled to Independence on business.

That winter the Jayhawkers returned and drove out Mrs. Younger and her children and burned their home, forcing the widow to hide out in their second farm in Jackson County.

The action embittered Cole, and when he was invited by George Todd and four other guerrillas to visit Kansas City "for a little fun" he accepted readily. Captain Trow, who saw them off, explains the "fun" was killing a few of the Jayhawkers who had reportedly murdered Colonel Younger and burned the Younger farm.

Disguised as Federal cavalrymen "carrying four instead of two revolvers" they entered the city. The streets were filled with a wartime holiday revelry. One can see the six bearded guerrillas led by big Cole pushing their way along the crowded wooden sidewalks, back slapping, roaring out answers to the drunken greetings, visiting saloon after saloon, downing the three fingers of whisky, Old Crow or local corn, but all the time keeping an eye on Todd who claimed he knew the men they were seeking. Then at midnight they entered a place and Todd stiffened as he saw six men sitting at two tables pushed together, playing cards. At a jerk of his hand they joined the game. Liquor flowed. Then at a signal from Todd they produced their revolvers and killed the Jayhawkers, one of them shattering the lamp and plunging the bar into darkness.

Outside "an alarm was beating at every corner" but they managed to reach their horses. At the last picket post they were challenged for their countersign, Todd cried "Charge" and they rode head on into a blue patrol killing four troopers and scattering the rest. They were chased but in the brush managed to escape. And so the war continued.

By the close of the year 1863 a new guerrilla leader was making his reputation. As Trow puts it:

"A name new to the strife was passing from band to band and about the campfires to have a respectful hearing."

" 'Anderson? Who is this Anderson?' the guerrillas asked each other. 'He kills them all. Quantrell [sic] spares now and then, and Poole and Blunt, and Yager and Haller and Jarrette and Younger, and Gregg and Todd and Shepherd and all the balance; but Anderson never. Is he a devil in uniform?' "

The man who "kills them all" was "Bloody Bill" Anderson, a brute who earned his title the hard way. Like Quantrill, "Bloody Bill" invented a pretty tale to excuse his murderous actions. Captain Trow tells the story in his memoirs.

In late 1862 Federal soldiers arrested a number of demonstrative southern girls whose only sin had been extravagant talk and pro-Confederacy cheering. They were imprisoned in a dilapidated tenement close upon a steep place. Food was flung to them at intervals and brutal guards sang ribald songs and used indecent language in their presence. With these women, tenderly nurtured and reared, were two of Will Anderson's sisters.

Trow then goes on to relate how the guards started to pull down the building

but it did not fall down fast enough for the brutes who bellowed about it. In the darkness it was undermined and in the morning when the little wind blew upon it, it was shaken and fell with a crash. One of the girls was killed and the other, badly injured in the spine with one leg broken and her face bruised and cut painfully, lived to tell the story of it all to the gentle patient brother kneeling before her at her bedside and looking up above to see if God were there.

It's a very pretty picture in the best hearts-and-flowers tradition of the time, but it is not true. Anderson was a cattle thief in Kansas before the border war and he organized his guerrillas simply to engage in outlawry under the guise of "serving the South."

Jim Cummins, discussing in his memoirs the brutality of Anderson, relates that "every time Bill Anderson killed a man he cut off his ears and hung them on his horse's bridle. He killed more than a dozen men one day in Lawrence, Kansas, and more than a dozen at Centralia, Mo. massacre."

This story is probably true because other guerrillas boasted of it in their memoirs. It wasn't unusual for prisoners to be hanged, quartered, or scalped. Trow describes how they once scalped some Federal prisoners after a small skirmish. When one of the guerrillas asked "Bloody Bill" why he didn't lop off the ears of the dead men he replied that "he had no use for them."

Riding with Anderson was a slim and grim-faced boy with long black hair blowing about his face. His comrades called him "Dingus"; in the family Bible his name appeared as Jesse Woodson James.

It has been claimed and denied that Jesse James was present when Quantrill sacked Lawrence, Kansas, on August 13, 1863, killing one hundred and forty men, women, and children, burning one hundred and eighty-five buildings and five stores, and plundering and looting at will. Frank James and Cole and Jim Younger were on hand, but there is a reasonable doubt that young Jesse rode under the Black Flag that day. Trow, who lists the more prominent names of those who took part in that bloody afternoon's work, significantly leaves out Jesse, although he takes pains to mention him riding on other raids.

While serving under Anderson, the Clay County farm boy had other assignments besides fighting. Because of his "slim boyish body" on several occasions he was dressed in female attire and sent to visit backwoods brothels and prepare the scene for night ambush. It is a little-known role the future bandit leader played in the bloody border war. In his excellent biography of John Hunt Morgan, *The Rebel Raider,* Howard Swiggett writes:

> The massacre of Union officers and soldiers frequenting the brothels strung long the Missouri River was a sinister commonplace. Jesse James with his girlish looks and disguised as a country girl desiring to escape the tedium of her home and meet soldiers, gained admittance to one brothel and prepared the scene for a night ambush.

The ambush took place in the fall of 1863. Jesse, dressed in a gingham dress topped off with "a garish bonnet with pink ribbons," was sent by Anderson to what Captain Trow describes as "a house occupied by Women of Light Love, four miles from Independence and a little back from the road leading from Kansas City."

After Jesse had mounted "woman fashion" upon his fiery horse with the "wind lifting his calico dress to reveal instead of laced boots or gaiters the muddy boots of a born cavalryman," he set out for the brothel followed at a distance by twelve rough-looking guerrillas led by Gregg. It was agreed that if Jesse did not appear within a certain time the band would surround the house, "forcing the inmates to give such information as they possessed of his whereabouts."

Trow writes:

He finally reached the destination without meeting a citizen or meeting an enemy. He would not dismount but sat upon his horse and asked that the mistress of the establishment might come out to him. Little by little with many gawky protests and many a bashful simper, he told a plausible story of parental espionage and family discipline. She could not have a beau, could not go out with soldiers, could not sit with them late, could not ride with them nor romp with them. She was tired of this and wanted a little fun. Would the mistress of the house let her come to her house occasionally and bring some of the neighbor girls who were in the same predicament? The mistress laughed and was glad. New faces to her were like new coins. As the she-wolf and the venturesome lamb departed, the assignation was assured.

The "assignation" was set for that night. Jesse, no longer in calico and bonnet, led the guerrillas to the brothel where they discovered twelve Federal soldiers from the Independence garrison, "who had been made to believe that barefoot maidens ran wild in the woods and buxom lasses hid for the hunting."

Gregg wanted to demand a surrender but Jesse urged a quick raid. At a signal the guerrillas, screeching their blood-curdling cry which was to echo so many times in later years in towns and hamlets and lonely railroad depots of the West, poured through the doors and windows. In a few minutes the twelve unfortunate customers were riddled with bullets or had their throats cut.

The partisans vanished like smoke in the wind leaving the "poor painted things weeping over the corpses."

After the sacking of Lawrence, Quantrill followed his usual custom, after each large-scale operation, of disbanding his guerrillas. "More men; more trails for the blue bellies to follow," he would shout as he waved his men off. A rendezvous and a time was always agreed upon before disbanding. Where Jesse and Frank James hid out is not known, but it was probably at the Samuel place, just outside of Kearney, Missouri.

The North was horrified when news of the massacre hummed over the telegraph. Six hundred Federal troops took the field to search for the guerrillas. A squad surrounded the Younger farm in Jackson County where Cole was visiting his mother, but tradition has him escaping with the aid of an aged Negro woman.

In August, 1863, Ewing's famous General Order No. 11 was issued. It required every citizen of Jackson, Cass, Bates, and a portion of Vernon counties to abandon their homes and either come into the designated lines or the fortified sections. Any citizen who refused to obey was to be treated as an outlaw.

It was merciless but it was war. Rights of property vanished; bandits preyed at will; nothing could be sold; everything had to be abandoned. There were straggling lines of dull-faced men, women, and children, their rickety wagons loaded down with personal possessions, passing the skeleton chimneys rising out of charred boards and stones. Federal troops plundered at will. Officers and men were bedecked with jewelry and carried silverware, pots, or bolts of goods, the loot of men frenzied with hate.

For three weeks the countryside was in the state of panic. Then word went out; lonely horsemen pounded down the darkened roads, many times engaging Federal patrols with a flurry of shots; bars slid away and doors opened an inch or two to catch the whispered password and instructions; small groups of riders galloped across the deserted fields; the grapevine sang with the news: "Charley Quantrell's ridin' again."

With blue patrols everywhere, Quantrill decided that it would be better strategy to split his command into small groups of riders who could strike swiftly and suddenly, then vanish into the shadows.

Jesse James opened the counterattack in the fall of 1863. Leading three other guerrillas he swooped down on a picket post outside of Wellington, Missouri, and killed the eight men who held it. Two days later Frank James and two other partisans ambushed a Federal company of eighty men near Salem Church on the Lexington Road and killed seven and wounded thirteen in their murderous crossfire.

Riding with George Todd at the head of thirty guerrillas a few weeks later, Jesse James saw action at Shawnee Town Road, when the Missourians cut off a train of twenty wagons bringing infantry into Kansas City. More than sixty men were butchered, some being held while their throats were cut.

The killings continued through the year. It was a war without quarter, as Jones, the rebel diarist, suspected.

Jesse James reached the full stature of a guerrilla fighter in September, 1864, at Centralia. In this bloody affair, which started off with George Todd ordering Jesse "to kill every male thing that wears a blue uniform," Jesse James had one of the leading roles. When it was over he is said to have killed nine more men. By this time he had an impressive record in killings for a boy of seventeen.

At Centralia Jesse rode stirrup to stirrup with his brother Frank, Jim Younger, and Captain Trow. On this occasion the guerrillas were two hundred and sixty-two strong, with the independent bands of George Todd, "Bloody Bill" Anderson, and Captain Johnny Thrailkill uniting under the central command of Todd who, as his men boasted about the night fires, "was a man of iron who would have a go at a circular saw."

The events of that day began in Centralia when sixty-one guerrillas, including Jesse James and several of his future outlaw followers, captured the railroad train with seventy-five Federal soldiers aboard. W. F. Bassett, of the United States Military Telegraph, described the "massacre" to the editor of the St. Joseph, Missouri, *Argus* a few days later. Bassett arrived at the scene a short time after the events of that bloody day had transpired and was told the story by survivors and eye witnesses.

"About 11 o'clock the rumbling of the railroad train could be heard," Bassett said, "as it thundered down the grade and slowed at the depot, its occupants being entirely oblivious that they were on the threshold of a monstrous tragedy. Scarcely had the train ground to a halt, however, before the soldiers aboard—75 in number—glanced out of the window and at once comprehended the situation."

With their horrifying scream, the guerrillas tore down upon the train. Most of the soldiers, all going home on furlough, were "poorly" armed and the revolver fighters had little trouble in subduing them. The prisoners were executed, with Jesse James and Frank James and Jim Cummins "from up the road" following "Bloody Bill" down the line of kneeling soldiers as the heavy Colts barked.

With the dead men in blue lining the tracks, "a full head of steam was turned on and the engine sent flying tenantless away to the north."

The Missourians rode off to join Todd at "Singleton's barn"

and the horrified citizens of Centralia broke out spades and shovels and, "digging a long ditch near where the soldiers were killed, buried them in one common grave."

Ten miles away at Paris, the seat of Monroe County, there was a battalion of raw State Militiamen, commanded by a Major Johnson, whom Bassett describes "as brave as a lion but inexperienced in the art of war, especially in coping with those terrible revolver fighters under Anderson and Todd."

In the early part of the afternoon the telegraph broke the news to Johnson of the tragedy. Johnson, "beside himself," ordered his men "to horse and be ready to march in twenty minutes." The long blue column rode out of Paris with Johnson at its head boasting that he would soon return "with the head of Anderson on a pole."

Just before the troopers reached Centralia, Bassett declared, a small girl ran out into the road and seized the bridle of Major Johnson's horse, "begging him to beware of Anderson and his men, saying she had a presentiment that if they looked for the guerrillas they would find them and all the militiamen would be killed. But he (Johnson) pushed her aside roughly and rode on."

Meanwhile, scouts had reported to Todd the approach of the Federal troops. He ordered his men to mount and led them over a ridge about a mile from the barn and onto a small prairie beyond. From this point he ordered Jesse James, Ole Shepherd, brother of George, and Peyton Long, out as bait. Todd's orders were to lure the Federals to within one hundred and fifty yards of the ridge. The future bandit chieftain led his men over the ridge "in skirmishing order." Shots were fired 'which were ineffective at long range, and the Federals urged their horses from a walk to a trot. The Missourians, mounted on the best horseflesh in the state, wheeled and the three guerrillas went over the crest of the slope. And then suddenly it was lined with riders. What a scene it must have been that bright September afternoon with the long line of Missouri raiders silhouetted against the sky, "their eyes flashing and the breeze ruffling their long hair and beards."

Both commands glared at each other. Bassett said that the lowing of the cattle and the bark of a farm dog could be heard in the still air. Major Johnson, apparently from his inexperience, ordered his men to dismount and "drew them in line of battle." While his officers bustled along the line, the more experienced ones undoubtedly cursing the stupidity of their commander, Johnson shouted to the watching guerrillas on the ridge above: "Come on you dastardly cutthroats—we are ready for the fight."

It was Jesse who answered him. Cupping his hands he shouted, "Keep your shirts on, we will get there soon enough for you."

When Todd saw the Federals dismount he gave the same order. "They intend to fight on foot?" he asked Jesse unbelievingly. "Well, it will be a bad day for the home guards." The order went swiftly along the line: "Dismount, secure bridle reins and place fresh caps on revolvers." Then at a signal they swung back in their saddles.

All eyes were on Todd. Next to him was the blue-eyed boy from Clay County. The partisan leader raised his broad-brimmed black hat topped with the flowing white plume and silver star. One can see Jesse James, reins in teeth, mounted on his mettled horse, then, as the late afternoon breeze flattens the leader's white plume, digging his knees into the sides of his mount and gripping the two heavy revolver butts with sweaty hands, his heart, like the hearts of all men going into battle, thumping wildly and the blood roaring in his ears.

"Steady men."

Then the plumed hat fell and Todd's guttural voice cried: "Charge!" The well-trained thoroughbreds "shot forward like catapults and the whole living mass charging down the hill had the appearance of a living whirlpool."

It was cavalry warfare in all its terrifying splendor: the cyclonic rush; the bloodcurdling guerrilla yell rising in the still afternoon air; the first crashing volley; the bodies like straw-filled dummies sliding from the horses; frenzied horses dragging dead men from the stirrups; men pounded into unrecognizable pulps; the desperate clubbing with revolver butts and slashing with bloodied sabers; the cries, the moaning of the wounded and dying. It was all there that bright September afternoon at the base of the small grass-covered slope "in back of Singleton's barn."

The raw militia broke under the first wave. According to Capt. Trow, Frank James shot and killed Major Johnson. Less than sixty troopers managed to mount their horses and ride out of the dust. Waving his revolvers Jesse cried "after them" and gave chase. Todd and several other guerrillas wheeled about and followed him. But after a time even Todd grew weary of the slaughter and drew up his command "to watch." Bassett wrote:

> Rapidly a puff of smoke would be seen, and then another horse would be riderless and dash off into the gathering twilight. But five of the whole command escaped slaughter. Jesse James was accredited with nine victims on the case; Ole Shepherd eight; George Todd eight; Peyton Long seven; Babe Hedspeth six and the others from three to five each. The guerrillas lost but one, a young beardless boy who had joined them the day before in Howard County.

The North was horrified at the news of Centralia. In 1862 they had indignantly called John Hunt Morgan, the Rebel Rider, a murderer when his men had picked off a few Federal vedettes. But an entire trainload of troops butchered; a regiment wiped out...

Blue patrols covered every section of the countryside. But the "guerrillas had vanished like the mists of the morning."

It is fitting to point out that "Charley" Quantrill, at the time his men were gathering at Centralia, was basking in the charms of Katie Clarke, a young and plump brunette doubtless in Trow's phrase "a woman of light love." Their assignation was somewhere in Howard County, Missouri.

The skirmishing continued. The name of Jesse James was respectfully spoken of about the night fires. Tales were told of his daring and his ruthlessness.

"For a beardless boy of sixteen he is the most fearless fighter in the command," Todd said one night. The rough and bearded men who sat about the campfire under the frosty autumn stars nodded. They had seen Jesse James in action.

The next large-scale action in which the young partisan fighter took part was in the fall of '64. It was the last raid of General Sterling Price. By October the Confederates had pushed the Union forces back from Lexington to Independence. The Federals, under General S. R. Curtis, held the west bank of the Little Blue and were firmly entrenched behind stone walls, in houses and barns. Troops under Marmaduke and Jo Shelby in a series of saber-swinging charges broke their hold and the Federal retreat flowed into the streets of Independence. The Second Colorado covered the retreat.

Shelby, a colorful cavalry leader, who was operating a rope business at Waverly near Lexington, Missouri, when the Civil War began, led charge after charge against the Coloradans. In his front lines were the guerrillas led by Todd. Riding next to Shelby and Todd was Jesse James.

Late that afternoon the Federal columns had been pushed back to a crest of a hill. Both sides clashed, and the blues, covering the retreat, broke and fled into Independence. The battle raged in the streets. Shrieking their wild cry the partisans charged one of the strong Federal positions; Todd, Jesse, and Dick Maddox were in the front lines, revolvers blazing. A volley crashed. Todd threw up his hands and slipped off his horse, the black hat with the gorgeous plume rolling in the dust.

The dying guerrilla leader was brought to the nearby house of "a Mrs. Burns" and died within an hour. A Spencer ball had severed his spinal cord. That night, under the hissing torches in the town's graveyard, Jesse, Frank, big George Shepherd, and Dick Maddox swore a "blood oath" to avenge the death of their leader.

After Todd's death the guerrillas continued under Price's command until his southward retreat. At Boonville, Missouri, they were joined by "Bloody Bill" Anderson and the meeting was a colorful one.

Anderson came riding into camp with the roughest command the border war had ever seen. Each man was a walking arsenal, and their bridles were adorned with human scalps. It is recorded that John Pringle, a red-headed giant, had several revolvers hanging in holsters all over his body and, like the Mountain Men of the West, wore tufts of human hair. It is not an exaggerated picture. The border war is unparalleled in our history for brutality and savagery, and in the closing years the so-called niceties of war were scarce among the guerrillas on both sides.

General Price was horrified at the sight and ordered the grisly trophies discarded. But despite his repugnance as a regular army man, for the undisciplined and shiftless guerrilla forces, he realized their importance and that night held a long and serious conference with Anderson, Jesse, Frank James, and several others. It must have been a strange scene in that lantern-lighted tent with the rough, bearded partisan fighters recounting past glories and nonchalantly advising the Confederate General "of the temper of the people, of the forces of the people, of the nature of guerrilla warfare." Price probably remembered that scene many times years later when he read of the exploits and murders of Jesse James and recalled the blue-eyed boy in the cavalryman's coat and muddy boots shifting the two Colts aside as he leaned forward to make a point or move a grimy finger across the map.

Price sent Anderson into northern Missouri. After cutting a bloody path through the state, Anderson was killed leading a charge near Missouri City. John Pringle, the big redhead who had horrified General Price with his scalps, was riddled while trying to bring in the body. The Federal troops were jubilant. That night they cut the head from Anderson's body and stuck it on a telegraph pole as a warning.

A short time later Quantrill, who, it seemed, had tired of the charms of his Katie, returned to his command. But the old magic was gone. At White River, Arkansas, Jesse James refused to follow him into Kentucky—a wise decision as later events proved —and the band broke up. Twenty-five of Todd's old outfit agreed with Jesse and swung away to follow him to Texas. Captain Polk and Jesse shared command. One of the riders was Dick Maddox's wife.

On November 22, 1864, at Cane Hill, in the Cherokee Nation, the hard-riding Missourians clashed with a column of "blue bellies" led by a Captain Emmet Gross of Jennison's Fifteenth Cavalry, whom Trow calls "an old acquaintance." It was twenty-six against thirty-two. Jesse James starred in the battle. He chased Gross and killed him, then cold-bloodedly finished off the Reverend U. P. Gradner, who pleaded that he was "chaplain of the Thirteenth Kansas" as the grim-faced boy blew out his brains.

The following day, the twenty-third, the guerrillas were chased by seventy-five Federal Cherokees. The exhausted raiders wheeled to meet the charge of the redskins. Reins about their necks, they rode like the wind, scattering the riders of the plains, killing fifty-two. One can almost sense Captain Trow's prideful chuckle as he wrote his memoirs more than a half-century later:

"Dick Maddox's wife could not be kept under cover and had a lock of her hair shot off just below her ears."

After a few months in the Lone Star State, the raiders began their long swing home. It was a weary ragamuffin lot that left Sherman, Texas, on a blustery March day in 1865. Their first

stop was Mount Pleasant, Titus County, Arkansas. They crossed
the Missouri border and in Johnson County were ambushed by
a Federal patrol. It was a brief battle in which Jesse skimmed a
rail fence to kill a "gray-haired militiaman." He took four shots
to do the job.

During the rest of the month they played a hound-and-hare
game with the blue patrols snapping at their heels. Mrs. Maddox,
who had the lock of her hair shot away from beneath her ear,
was probably riding in that dusty column. Two years after her
return to Missouri she was widowed when her husband died with
his boots on in a gun battle.

On April 1, the harassed raiders met in a council of war and
agreed to surrender. On the afternoon of the fifteenth, Jesse James
led six guerrillas into Lexington, Missouri, to surrender to the
Union provost marshal, Major J. B. Rogers, who was known to
some of them as a "liberal officer of the old regime." It is significant that Jesse was elected to head the parleying party. There
can be no doubt that by this time the beardless youth had ably
demonstrated that he could lead men and was a cool and shrewd
hand.

With a grimy handkerchief tied to a branch, Jesse rode into
Lexington mounted on what Trow calls a "splendid black horse."
One can see the slim boy in the cavalryman's coat, the carbine
across his shoulders, the two big Colts sagging on each side, slowly
turning from left to right as the big black horse splashed down
the muddy street. He was well known by this time, and undoubtedly southern sympathizers on the wooden sidewalks winked
encouragement or gave him furtive nods.

The details of what happened following the truce parley are
not known. Whether the guerrillas were attacked before or after
their visit to Lexington is lost in a morass of conflicting stories
and legend. Trow claims it was "shortly after the surrender,"
which may be true. It has been authenticated, however, that
Jesse and his men were attacked that afternoon by an eight-man
point of a large body of advancing cavalry, one troop of Johnson
County militia and one of the second Wisconsin. There was
a sharp battle with the vedettes. In a few minutes the main body
appeared and charged. Two riders engaged Jesse. The young
guerrilla killed one trooper and wounded the second trooper's
horse. The dismounted soldier fired a ball which tore through

the boy's right lung, inflicting a ghastly wound. A volley downed his black horse and he was trapped under the body. As he lay there the charge swept past in the wake of the fleeing guerrillas.

Bleeding badly Jesse extricated himself and took to the woods. For two days he lay delirious on the bank of a small creek. On the afternoon of the second day he crawled to a nearby field where a farmer, a Southern sympathizer, found him. That night the farmer delivered Jesse, more dead than alive, to a "Mrs. Bowman" at whose house some of the guerrillas were hiding. Four days later the guerrillas returned to Lexington with Jesse tossing in fever on the bottom of a wagon filled with hay, each breath rasping like the turn of a rusty file as he struggled to fill his lungs.

One look and Major Rogers told the guerrillas that Jesse was so far gone that it wasn't necessary to issue him a parole. He did, however, "order him a wagon, a few dollars and a pass to visit his mother and stepfather in Nebraska."

With some of the guerrillas taking turns driving the team and caring for their apparently dying comrade, the journey to Rulo, Nebraska, began. The trip was completed sometime in the spring and Jesse was placed under the care of his stepfather. In August of 1865 the family returned home by way of the Missouri River. The wounded guerrilla was taken off the river boat on a stretcher and removed to the home of John Mimms, located in what is now north Kansas City. Mimms, according to Robertus Love, the "outlaw editor," was married to a sister of Jesse's father, the Reverend Robert James, who had died and been buried near the far-off gold field of California.

It was at the Mimms house that Jesse fell in love with Zerelda Mimms, who was named after Jesse's mother. It was to be a long and precarious courtship. Nine years later, when his name was known in every American household and in parts of Europe, the young outlaw popped the question to his cousin and was accepted. It was to be a strange and tragic union, tested by gunfire, violence, hate, and madness.

Sometime in the fall of 1865 the emaciated boy with the blinking blue eyes, who had supped long with murder and hate, was tenderly placed on hay in the bottom of a wagon and taken the last several miles to the Samuel place near Kearney, Clay County, Missouri.

3

GUERRILLAS! TO HORSE!

THE Civil War had ended but without the paroles of Appomattox and Nashville for the guerrillas who rode under Quantrill, Todd, and Anderson. Throughout Missouri reprisal followed reprisal. Stiffened bodies swung slowly in the breeze from branches or were found on lonely dirt roads chewed by the wild hogs. Homes and barns were put to the torch with the flames licking at the night. Livestock was stolen. Crude penciled warnings to "git out of the county" were nailed to doors. Night riders of the Vigilantes pounded along the dark roads or stood in grim masked silence in the lantern light as the death sentence was read to a white-faced or a defiant man with a noose dangling over his head.

The times were hard and dangerous. Those who had suffered at the hands of the guerrillas now struck back. Private grudges and family feuds broke out to be continued with murder and bushwacking.

State and local offices were filled with appointees of northern sympathizers. Many had served with the Missouri State Militia under General Nugent and had little love for Quantrill's riders. Conditions soon made it impossible for the citizenry to carry on their ordinary pursuits. Society in most of the desolate and depopulated Missouri counties reverted to the time of the Indian Wars, as described by Edward C. Smith in his *The Borderland in the Civil War*—"when men again tilled their fields with muskets by their sides and slept in expectation of combat."

Law was the Colt strapped around a man's waist.

The ex-guerrillas added to the chaotic condition by continuing to live in their former wild and dangerous fashion. Gun duels were frequent; innocent men were fired upon and killed or wounded in drunken frays; towns were terrorized by the hard-riding bravos who refused to believe that the war was over. What was hoeing a furrow and shucking corn to tearing open a town with blazing guns and shattering glass music in your ears; to see the "charcoals," as the radicals of the day were called, dive for cover, or to put a whole town or miles of prairie to the torch. And what was milking a cow to the blood-tingling minutes when your horse leaped forward and you were one of the two hundred or more screaming demons of destruction at Centralia... when you had lived from hour to hour and day to day in a primitive and savage world where it was kill or be killed...

There was scarcely a Saturday night the guerrillas didn't shoot up Liberty, the county seat of Clay. Cavalry fashion they would gallop into town on their fine mounts shrieking their wild cries and blazing away with revolvers. Then over to Fred Meffert's saloon for a few drinks. There weren't many citizens who protested. It wasn't healthy.

In the fall of 1866 a minor miracle occurred. In solid Democratic Clay County, a Republican was elected to the office of sheriff. His name was Joe Rickards, a solid, stumpy man with gray, flintlike eyes who refused to be intimidated by the "greatest revolver fighters in the country" and said so.

One afternoon Sam Holmes, a hanger-on of the guerrillas, rode up to the courthouse and shouted for the sheriff. Told the peace officer wasn't available, he said:

"Dingus and the boys are over the Platte County Fair and said to tell Rickards that they're coming into Liberty tomorrow and no goddamned Republican is going to arrest them."

Late that afternoon Rickards returned to the courthouse and was immediately notified of Jesse's ultimatum.

"Better leave for a trip tonight, Joe," his friends warned him. "Those young 'uns are bad."

"I think I'll stay around," Rickards replied quietly.

That night the sheriff visited Judge Philander Lucas of the Fifth Circuit Court of Missouri in his chambers. Judge Lucas, who administered a stern but righteous justice in the Jesse James country until the late '80's, told the story to a reporter for the Cincinnati *Inquirer,* on July 26, 1902.

Joe came to me and told me of the message the James boy had sent to him. When he had finished I asked him what he

was going to do. He did not say a word, but turning, gave
me a very comical and significant wink.

Joe Rickards' wink meant more than words and on the following day I remained on the *qui vive* to see what would
happen. I did not want to see Rickards get hurt, but at the
same time I relied on his good judgment to do the right
thing in the right place and time. Besides it was high time
that someone had taken the conceit out of those game roosters
who were dropping in every day or two from a four year
course in bushwacking and who were trying to turn the country upside down with their crazy exploits.

The gang led by Jesse and including Frank, Clell Miller, Jim
Poole, who had led the band on their way to Texas, George
White, and some other ex-guerrillas roared into town that morning. "They did so," Judge Lucas recalled, "in a very disorderly
fashion, yelling and firing off their revolvers."

After driving the citizens off the streets and shattering a few
signs and windows the Clay County bravos dismounted in front
of Fred Meffert's saloon and went in. The jurist continued:

> I looked about for Rickards and sure enough there he was
> right opposite the saloon, with his hat pulled down over his
> eyes and wearing an old overcoat in which he had never be-
> fore appeared. The gang had ridden past without even no-
> ticing him. The minute they entered the saloon he followed
> them and drew forth from beneath his coat two six-shooters
> which he leveled at the gang and said:
> "Throw up your hands."
> They turned, and seeing what confronted them obeyed very
> quickly. Then as they did so, Joe said: "Now then, you—
> scoundrels, you said that no goddamned Republican could ar-
> rest or take you; I'll show you a trick or two about that."

Under the peace officer's gun a deputy relieved the bad men
of their artillery. The sheriff marched the sheepish gang with
empty holsters past the grinning townspeople and into the courthouse where they were arraigned before Judge Lucas. The jurist
recalled:

> As a matter of fact there wasn't any charge against them, for
> what killing and robbing they had done had been committed

in the war and as an act of reprisal on the enemy. After some palaver and efforts on the part of Joe to find some charge against them, we were obliged to turn them loose after a warning from Joe in the future to mind their P's and Q's.

This was to be the first and only time Jesse James was arrested in his sixteen years as America's number one outlaw.

This incident is important. It not only gives a glimpse of the restless wartime partisans but it also squelches the legend that Jesse was seriously ill and could not have taken part in the robbery of a Liberty bank and murder of a young boy a short time later.

In his interview Judge Lucas declared: "Some time after this incident he [Jesse James] organized his band and robbed the bank at Independence." There was no bank robbery at Independence and the jurist undoubtedly meant Liberty, for he added: "This was the start of the career of Jesse James as a professional bandit."

There is no record of what Jesse did between that fall day he was taken into custody by Sheriff Rickards and the second week of February the following year. He was evidently organizing his gang, sending word out to his guerrilla comrades as Quantrill had done when the blue patrols were everywhere. And as before, a solitary horseman, or horsemen in groups of twos and threes, crunched their way up the snowy path to the "ordinary farmhouse" as the bars slid back and the door swung open revealing Mrs. Samuel and her farmer-physician husband shielding the flickering flame in the glass chimney of the lamp as they peered out into the frosty night.

On the morning of February 13, 1866, the pent-up storm broke over Missouri with a band of howling riders pounding their way through the streets of Liberty to commit what is the first bank robbery in the United States. The crime was accompanied by the brutal and senseless murder of a schoolboy only a few feet from his front yard. There was only one witness to the robbery and murder. He was Jimmy Sandusky, a young college student, later the Honorable James Sandusky of Liberty, one of Missouri's prominent lawyers.

The robbery took place at eight o'clock. A few minutes before,

George "Jolly" Wynmore, a chubby, round-faced boy of nineteen with an infectious grin and hearty laugh, walked out on the porch of his modest frame house. As he looked across Liberty's deserted public square, he grinned to himself as he fingered the comic valentine in his pocket.

A lone wagon crossed the square and the boy raised his hand. The hello from the bundled-up man on the driver's seat sounded thin and far off in the frigid air. The wagon squeaked its way out of sight. "Jolly" Wynmore shivered. It was about time to start if he wanted to catch his first class in William Jewell College on the hill just above the town square. He shifted his books higher under his arm and stepped off the porch.

He walked briskly toward the square. The town seemed deserted even by the usual dogs. Along the sidewalks the modest houses, their steps edging shyly forward in the road, looked deserted. There was no sign of life in their front parlors, now cold as marble tombs, concealed behind the heavy drapes or curtains.

Another youngster, bundled to the ears, suddenly turned a corner and seeing him, waved. Young Wynmore waved and helloed. It would be fun to walk to school with Jimmy Sandusky. He quickened his pace. Then the still morning was shattered by bloodcurdling screams and yells.

Both boys paused. Ten riders tore around a corner and crossed the public square. Four pulled up short before the Clay County Savings and Loan Association, dismounted and entered. The others danced their fine-looking horses about in a wide circle. They were rough-looking men wearing blue overcoats and mufflers with holsters strapped to their waists. Their mounts snorted and jerked their heads nervously as they pranced about.

Inside the bank the four men walked briskly toward the counter where cashier Greenup Bird and his son William, acting this day as an assistant, were preparing for the day's business. The elder Bird smiled.

"Well, gentlemen..."

The smile froze on his face. He slowly raised his hands and stared down at the unwavering revolvers. His son quickly followed his father's example. The guns prodded them into the vault. One of the bandits produced a dusty Missouri wheat sack; the other three went along the shelves sweeping in gold, silver, bills, and bonds. After the vault had been bone-picked the leader of the four men eyed the older Bird.

"Stay in here," he chuckled. "Don't you know all Birds should be caged?"

The big iron door clanged shut and the robbers walked leisurely out of the bank. The heavy sack was hoisted across the saddlehorn of one of the riders. For a moment the gang wheeled about like cavalry preparing for a charge, then, shrilling their devilish cries and firing their revolvers, they pounded across the square into Franklin Street.

As the riders swept past him, young Wynmore, apparently confused, started to run toward his house. One of the riders pulled up short. He took aim and fired. The boy stumbled and fell to one knee. The revolver barked three more times. The young college student threw up his hands and crumbled, his books tumbling about and the papers blowing in the wind. With a triumphant yelp the rider raced after the rest of the gang, his sleek-looking bay soaring down the frozen, rutted road with long and graceful strides.

With the whoops of the bandits now faint echoes, townspeople ran to the side of the boy. A nearby doctor was summoned. There wasn't anything he could do; four slugs had ripped through the boy's head and stomach.

The people of Liberty were stunned. The bank held up in broad daylight? It was unbelievable! But it was the sight of the dead boy in the frozen road that brought them to their senses. A posse gathered. Peace officers, farmers, and townspeople took up the trail. They discovered the bandits had ridden east on Franklin Street for three blocks then turned and left the town on the road leading from Liberty to Excelsior Springs. The gang crossed the river late that day somewhere in Ray County and vanished into nowhere. All that day the posse dashed up and down the back roads knocking on farmhouse doors, questioning passing travelers, but they could find no trace of the hard-riding outlaws. As Bassett said of Todd's guerrillas after Centralia, they had "vanished like the mists of the morning."

That night a howling blizzard swept over the countryside. The storm-battered posse returned to Liberty and told the townspeople who still gathered in the sheriff's office:

"Not a sign of them. We searched all day."

A few days after the robbery of the Clay County Savings and Loan Bank the first clue turned up. It was pitifully meager. Just a Missouri wheat sack found at Mount Gilhead Church. Cashier Greenup Bird promptly identified it as the one into which the bank's money had vanished. But the sheriff threw up his hands. The sack was a common type, used by farmers all over Missouri. It could have come from a thousand different farms.

The town was kept in a state of high excitement for days. Some charged—in whispers—that the bandits were the ex-guerrillas Jesse and Frank James, Bud Pearce, Arch Clements, and George Shepherd. But there never was a positive identification.

When the law officers from Liberty visited the Samuel place, Mrs. Samuel was indignant as always when some one implied that her two "boys" were anything but upright, honest citizens. Jesse and Frank robbing a bank...!

In the Crittenden Memoirs there is an account from an un-named Missouri newspaper which reported in 1882—sixteen years later—that "the job was done by four former guerrillas and two Indian boys." One of the riders is said to have been "Andy Maguire who used his part of the swag in dressing himself up in broadcloth and ran away with the daughter of old man Deering from near Independence." Maguire was captured later and hanged by indignant citizens. There was no mention of the Jameses or the Youngers. The dead boy was buried and the crime lapsed into local folklore.

In the Pinkerton archives there is the statement of an R. I. Stepp. The witness, a farm hand, had this to say:

> On the thirteenth of February, 1866, I was working on a farm owned by a Mr. Howard near Lee's Summit, Jackson County, Missouri, when I learned of the Liberty bank holdup. On that day nine or ten men on horses had crossed the Missouri River at Blue Mills Ferry on their way to Liberty. Two of the men stopped at Captain Minter's house. Captain Minter later told his neighbors that among these men were the James boys and Bud Pearce. He said afterwards that these men bought two sacks of meal. When he learned that the Liberty bank had been robbed he said that these were the sacks into which the money had been put. Later he became frightened and said he did not recognize the men who bought the sacks.

Such is the evidence. There is little doubt that restless ex-guerrillas who, as Judge Lucas said, "are trying to turn the country upside down with their crazy exploits," were the men who committed the holdup and murder. But just who they were has remained a secret to this day.

Significantly, in the wake of the robbery was the first appearance of the gang's methods in terrorizing witnesses and suppressing evidence by threats. The bandits were not masked or the newspaper account would have mentioned that. But the Birds apparently never made an identification. Why? Again, why did Captain Minter become "frightened"? In a future chapter we will see how Jesse and his gang treated loose-tongued neighbors. It would be interesting to know what became of Mr. Stepp who, it seemed, was the only citizen with enough personal courage to name names. If he was an itinerant farm hand, he undoubtedly was soon looking for work in another and safer county.

The bandits' loot was reported to have been $15,000 in gold and $45,000 in nonnegotiable bonds. The bonds were only worthless papers to the gang. The gold wasn't much better. Few people used it in daily transactions and it could easily create suspicion. But like the modern stick-up man, the bandits of the early West had their "fence." He was a mysterious Mexican by the name of Gonzales who would accept all the gold that one could steal, at 40-per-cent discount. After riding 300 miles to cash in their plunder, the holdup men received less than a thousand dollars apiece for their morning's work of robbery and murder.

The second of America's bank robberies followed the technique of the first.

It was October of the same year when several men, mounted on horses described by a witness as "fine Kentucky blue bloods," rode down the main street of battle-scarred Lexington, on the southern bank of the Missouri and a day's easy horseback ride east of Liberty, Missouri, and southeast of the Samuel place. It was about noon and the streets were deserted. The men dismounted in front of the banking house of Alexander and Company and three entered.

One man, with a muffler tied about the lower half of his face, asked the cashier to cash a fifty-dollar United States bond. Cashier J. L. Thomas nodded and pulled out the cash drawer to oblige the stranger, when he heard a revolver cock. He looked up. The mumbled command was almost inaudible through the muffler.

"Empty that drawer."

Thomas did as he was ordered and the contents of the drawer clinked into a wheat sack. The men began backing out of the bank, one warning, "Don't shout or we'll blow out your brains."

In a few minutes the gang was fleeing out of town. Suspicion centered again on Jesse and Frank James and Clay County's ex-guerrillas. As before, Mrs. Samuel indignantly informed the law officers that they were "persecuting" her sons. Jesse, she insisted, was so weak from the wounds in his right lung that he could scarcely move from his bed. Frank, she added, was on "some sort of business" in Kentucky. She did not explain the nature of the "business."

As with the Liberty crime there were no arrests, no trials, no convictions. The bandits had vanished into thin air.

In bank robbery number three the bandits met more resistance. They rode away with nothing but experience.

It took place the following year on March 2, 1867, at 8 A.M. Five men rode slowly down the main street of Savannah, seat of Andrew County, Missouri, a quiet little community about two days' ride from Liberty. The five dismounted and walked into Judge William McLain's private banking house. The jurist and his son were behind the teller's cage preparing for the day's business. Each of the holdup men quickly drew a Colt. In a glance Judge McLain took in the picture. Without any hesitation he grabbed a revolver from the cash drawer and fired at the holdup men. He only splintered the doorjamb. Five guns answered.

When the smoke had cleared the illusion that the Middle Border badmen were crack marksmen had been sent galleywest. Only one of the bandits had scored. His ball lodged in Judge McLain's chest. It was not a fatal wound and the brave jurist staggered out of his teller's cage to engage the gang in a one-sided gun duel. The bandits wavered, then turned and fled. The banker followed them to the street, still firing, while his son roused the town. A few minutes later the elder McLain collapsed. He later recovered to become a local celebrity.

Two men named Samuel Pope and William "Bud" McDaniels were arrested a short time later for the holdup but presented

11. Alonzo E. Bunker, bank teller in the Northfield bank. Wounded by the robbers. *(Courtesy Pinkerton's National Detective Agency, Inc.)*

12. Frank J. Wilcox, bank bookkeeper, who was covered by the robbers' guns. *(Courtesy Pinkerton's National Detective Agency, Inc.)*

13. Anselm R. Manning, Northfield hardware merchant. Manning is but one of the citizens of Northfield who finally became enraged enough to fight off the James-Younger gang. *(Courtesy Pinkerton's National Detective Agency, Inc.)*

14. The seven captors from the Madelia posse. Captain Murphy asked for six volunteers from the posse to accompany him in surrounding the bandits. These seven men literally tore apart the bandits. From left to right, top row, Captain W. W. Murphy, Ben M. Rice, C. A. Pomeroy. Bottom row, Sheriff James Glispin, G. A. Bradford, Colonel T. L. Vought, S. J. Severson. *(Courtesy Pinkerton's National Detective Agency, Inc.)*

15. Cole Younger, the only extrovert in the James-Younger gang. Picture taken in 1876 after injuries inflicted upon him during his, Bob Younger's, Jim Younger's and Charlie Pitt's capture. (*Courtesy Pinkerton's National Detective Agency, Inc.*)

16. Bob Younger, who impressed the reporters questioning him after his capture with his dignity. He told them, when asked how he and his brothers felt about capture, "We are rough men and used to rough ways." (*Courtesy Pinkerton's National Detective Agency, Inc.*)

17. Jim Younger also captured by the Madelia posse. Picture taken in later years. *(Courtesy Pinkerton's National Detective Agency, Inc.)*

18. John Younger, who did not share in the attempted robbery of the Northfield bank. He was killed in 1874 in a Missouri gun fight by Pinkerton man, Louis J. Lull. *(Courtesy Pinkerton's National Detective Agency, Inc.)*

unquestionable alibis and were set free. Other ex-guerrillas were named as the robbers, but none was apprehended.

After Savannah came the fourth stickup at Richmond, seat of Ray County, Missouri, which was to become a stronghold of the James-Younger gang. It is only a few miles northwest of Lexington and directly east of Clay County. The robbery was one of the most ruthless in America's crime history.

The attack was more of a wholesale jail delivery than a bank robbery. When the powder smoke had cleared there were three dead, one a young boy. At least six other violent deaths can be attributed to the raid in the chain of events that followed.

It began on the morning of May 23, 1867. Early shoppers, merchants, and farmers gave the quiet little community a bustling, businesslike air. Just before noon fourteen men galloped down the main street of the town, shrieking like banshees and firing revolvers and carbines. The street emptied quickly as windows and street lamps shattered. The gang milled in front of the Hughes and Mason Bank, the largest county bank in the state.

Six of the bandits dismounted and tried the locked door of the bank. It was quickly battered down after one of the bandits fired and smashed the lock. Inside the terrified tellers were waved to one side as $4,000 in gold was swept into the reliable wheat sack.

Meanwhile, despite the terrorizing tactics of the gang, several armed citizens had taken positions behind trees, hedges, and in the upper stories of buildings. One, Mayor Shaw, calmly took a position in the middle of the street and began, courageously but foolishly, exchanging shots with the bandits. In a few minutes he went down under a volley. Seven bullets were later found in his body.

The outlaws came out of the bank dragging the sack. It was quickly strapped across the nearest saddlehorn.

"Let's get the jail," one shouted.

Next to the courthouse was the county jail which, local tradition insists, held several ex-guerrillas. The bandits, hooting and firing, rode down on the jail. For fifteen minutes they desperately tried to break down the front door, but it was too sturdy. B. G. Griffin, the jail's warden, and his fifteen-year-old son took up a position behind an elm tree and began to harass the raiders with a steady fire. Three of the outlaws rode down on the brave pair. The boy fell, and in a few minutes the father, riddled with seven bullets, was sprawled across his son's body. After giving up the jail delivery as a hopeless job, the gang took over the town, dashing up and down the main street and blazing away at windows, men, signs, or anything else that took their fancy. Tiring of this they wheeled about and with a final yip-yip-yaw, raced out of the terrified community.

The outrage set Missouri on edge. Public demonstrations were held. At night saloons ran full blast filled with grim-faced men swearing that a hemp necktie party awaited the first member of the gang arrested. Jesse and Frank James were accused, but curiously enough when the warrants were subsequently issued they were not named.

The eight named were James White, John White, Payne Jones, Richard Burns, Isaac Flannery, who rode with "Dingus" at Centralia, Andrew Maguire, Thomas Little, and Allen H. Parmer, who later married Jesse's step-sister, Susan. When he was accused, Parmer promptly proved that he was working in Kansas City when the robbery took place. The ex-guerrilla later moved to northern Texas where he became a prosperous and respected citizen.

On the day of the funeral of the Richmond victims a posse from Kansas City raided a house near Independence, Missouri, after they had received information that Jones was hiding there.

The bandit refused to surrender and ran from the house, both guns blazing. He escaped, killing a peace officer and wounding a young neighborhood girl who had acted as a guide for the posse. She died within a few hours. Jones was killed in a gun duel two years later.

The night following the Independence raid, a second posse surrounded a farmhouse near Richmond and captured Richard Burns. There is no record of what occurred, but it is believed that a quick trial was held in the woods with Burns found guilty and hanged. Two other named bandits, Andrew Maguire, the man who "ran off with the daughter of old man Deering," and Tom Little, who had ridden with Jesse under Anderson and Quantrill, received the same treatment at the hands of a mob weeks later. Both were lynched near Warrensburg, Johnson County.

Although they were suspected of leading the raid, Jesse and

Frank James presented—through friends—"alibi cards" which were distributed throughout Clay County.

Another former guerrilla who was arrested and then released was Jim Cummins who was to figure prominently in Jesse's later exploits. As Cummins declared some years later after he had voluntarily "come in":

"Conditions at that time in Clay were getting too warm. I took a trip to California."

Three of the four bank robberies had been successful. But from now on Jesse and his gang of outlaws were to be subjected to an ever increasing pressure. They would live in a world of shadows where there was never any peace. They would see their pursuers everywhere: a stranger on horseback; a man in broadcloth stepping from the afternoon train. The innocent remark of a friend could be a death warrant. The nights would be worse: the implacable terror was always crouching there in the quiet darkness—waiting.

The two men who exerted this terrifying pressure were Allan Pinkerton and his son William. Intelligent, incredibly tenacious, physically powerful, fearless, and with an almost fanatical devotion for the laws of their land, they were without a doubt two of America's greatest detectives.

The agency Allan Pinkerton founded in 1850, and which is carried on to this day by his grandson Robert Pinkerton II, can be described as the nation's civilian Federal Bureau of Investigation of the '80's. Pioneers in the field of criminology, the Pinkertons pursued Jesse James and the other outlaws of the West under the most primitive conditions. There was no central fingerprint filing system in Washington, no rogues gallery, no interlocking eight-state alarm system, no teletypes clicking out wanted descriptions to police headquarters in each one of the forty-eight states; no ballistics or modern techniques whereby a criminal can be described even to his habits from a fingernail paring, a smear of clay from a boot, or a few hairs from a pillow.

When Jesse and his outlaws were rampaging across the Middle Border it was a case of strapping on your guns, mounting your horse, and riding to the scene of the crime. There began the endless questioning; the picking up a trail often many days old and following it for weeks, even months, then finally entering the hostile country of the outlaws infested with their kinfolk and henchmen only to have the local peace officer shrug his shoulders and say:

"I'll point out the house but I won't go near it; I have to live here after you're gone."

It was doubly hard for the Pinkertons in their hunt for Jesse James. The only picture of the Missouri outlaw hung in a small gold locket about his mother's neck. There was none for the wanted posters. As long as he lived Jesse James was a man without a face. So complete was his anonymity that in 1882 townspeople in Clay County, Missouri, who had nodded greetings believing him to be a local cattle or horse dealer, were stunned when they gazed down at the bearded face in the casket. To the new generation who had grown up in the Jesse James country, the outlaw was not flesh and blood, but only a legend.

When the first four bank robberies rocked the nation, frightened bankers hired Allan Pinkerton to stop the epidemic of robberies and arrest the perpetrators. Pinkerton was not unknown at the time. His prestige had already been established as head of the Northern Secret Service during the Civil War and also as a private detective. A year before the Liberty, Missouri, bank robbery he had successfully smashed the powerful Reno brothers gang, America's first organized band of outlaws.

"The Eye," as Allan Pinkerton was called, was well known to the members of the nineteenth-century underworld. They knew he was incorruptible and so was his agency. They were also well acquainted with Pinkerton's tenacity; if necessary he would chase you to the end of the earth.

They also knew that no Pinkerton operative was permitted to accept a reward; stool pigeons and the use of liquor to obtain confessions were scorned. But although the outlaws and bandits of the last century hated and feared the Pinkertons they respected them for their fair dealings. The Pinkertons would pursue them relentlessly to put them behind bars, but as Allan Pinkerton declared in his "General Principles" on which he founded his agency, the criminal must not be hunted and persecuted after he had paid his debt to society but "helped to become an honest and reputable character."

In reporting evidence, he insisted that all operatives must report everything favorable to the suspect as well as what was unfavorable to him.

Cases of bank, train, and stagecoach robberies were readily accepted, but Pinkerton steadfastly refused to allow his men to become listeners at keyholes, to trail women for moral evidence, or to become involved in political brawls.

At the time his agency first began to trail Jesse James, Allan Pinkerton was experimenting in new techniques in criminology. He had started a rogues gallery. It included not only pictures and physical descriptions but also a detailed account of each criminal: his habits, his known associates, and his usual haunts.

4.

"YANKEE" BLIGH

FOR a year it was quiet along the border, then on March 20, 1868, the Missouri bandits struck again. This time their target was the quiet little town of Russelville, in the heart of Logan County, Kentucky. The events of that day were to make the names of Jesse James and Coleman Younger familiar to most Kentuckians, and to put on the trail of the gang a persistent Pinkerton operative who was to hound the bandits for years.

His name was A. B. "Yankee" Bligh. Unfortunately Bligh's records were destroyed in the Chicago fire which swept the Pinkerton building. There is no picture, no physical description of the famous Louisville detective, but from the remaining meager records it would appear that Bligh was a persistent, human bloodhound type of detective; he was to become as feared and hated by Jesse and his gang as were Allan and William Pinkerton.

Several days before the robbery, a tall and distinguished man rode up to the local bank operated by Nimrod Long and George W. Norton. Inside he tried to sell a five-hundred-dollar note to Mr. Long.

His name? A "Mr. Colburn" he told the bank official in a soft and drawling voice. A cattle dealer from Louisville. Long examined the note and the attached interest coupons. The banker, sensing something wrong, refused to buy it although the "cattleman" offered to sell it at par with accrued interest thrown in.

A week later Colburn returned. This time he was accompanied by a young man with blinking blue eyes. In contrast to Colburn's neat appearance he was shabbily dressed.

This time Colburn offered a hundred-dollar bill and asked for change. He explained that he had to pay off "one of his hands." Long examined the bill.

"This bill is counterfeit, Mr. Colburn," he said.

Colburn looked shocked. He examined his bill. "I reckon it is," he said after a pause. He apologized and explained that he had "probably received it from another cattle buyer." During the transaction Colburn's companion seemed interested in the physical make-up of the bank. His eyes kept darting here and there, and when they were leaving he held the door open and turned for one last look around.

In a few days seven strangers, all claiming to be traders, drifted into town and divided themselves up among the two hotels. "Four put up their horses at Long's stable and the other three at Brashear's." The seven men visited the saloons "very freely" that night and later congregated in a room at the Forest Hotel "to play a few hands of poker," as they told one bartender.

The next day at about 3 P.M. Long and a farmer by the name of Simms were discussing a loan when Colburn and six men rode up to the bank. Colburn entered with the smaller man who had accompanied him the day before. The "cattlemen" courteously insisted that Long and Simms finish their business and then, nodding a greeting, gave Long a fifty-dollar bank note asking for change.

Definitely suspicious, Long gave it a quick glance.

"I am sorry Mr. Colburn, but this bill is also counterfeit."

Colburn again looked at it and chuckled. "I reckon it is." He tucked the bill inside his coat and quickly yanked out a business-like Colt. He was still smiling. "But this isn't, Mr. Long. Open that vault!"

Colburn's companion also produced a revolver, grabbed the farmer by the coat, and shoved him against the counter. For a moment Colburn's eyes wavered. Long made a desperate dash for the rear door. The blue-eyed bandit yelled and fired. The slug creased the right side of the banker's head and spun him around. In a moment the bandit was upon him, striking him unmercifully with the butt of his gun. But Long was made of stern stuff. With blood streaming down his face he grappled with the bank robber and the two men rolled about on the floor. Colburn, meanwhile, danced around the pair shouting encouragement to his companion and attempting to get an unobstructed shot at the banker.

Long continued to fight back furiously. He at last succeeded in throwing off the bandit. Stumbling to his feet he made a second lunge for the door. Two Colts roared and bullets chewed away at the door jamb just above the banker's head. By a miracle and the miserable marksmanship of the two desperados, he wasn't hit. In a moment he was running down a small alley adjacent to the bank crying out "They're holding up the bank."

Inside the bank Colburn and his companion hastily cleaned the vault of five thousand dollars in bank notes and bags of coins. An additional $9,000 was found and swept into the wheat sack. Some boxes of bonds were quickly examined and tossed aside. At the sound of shots both bandits dragged the sack to the door of the bank.

The shooting had aroused the town and, as the *Courier-Journal* declared: "people ran from every quarter, some bringing buckets of water under the impression that the building was afire."

During the battle, an old man identified by the reporter for the *Courier-Journal* only as "an old man by the name of Lawrence" heard the shooting and ran out into the road as the robbers were dashing up and down the street. One of them—believed to be George Shepherd—rode past, pulled up and shouted: "Old man, we're having a little serenade here and there's danger of you getting hurt. Just get behind my horse here and you'll be out of the way. You needn't be particular about seeing my face so well you'd remember it again if you were asked."

The old gentleman did as the outlaw suggested and escaped injury. But other citizens were armed and had engaged the gang. One named Owen blazed away from behind a tree, but two of the outlaws rode him down.

While some of the community took refuge behind buildings, trees, and fences to bang away at the whooping, firing Missourians, and others ran about helplessly with the water from the wooden buckets spilling into their boots, "Mr. Colburn" and Jesse James dragged the heavy gold-filled sack out of the bank and hoisted it across the saddlehorn of one of their horses.

Wheeling about in good order the freebooters charged cavalry fashion down the main street under the fire of the aroused citizenry. They suffered no casualties.

Before the dust had settled in the road more than fifty men had formed a posse and were galloping out of town. The outlaws were trailed into Allan County where the gang split up into small parties. Some were tracked toward the Red River country where the Hites, Jesse's cousins, lived.

The next day "Yankee" Bligh of Louisville was sent to the scene by Allan Pinkerton. He traced the gang for more than seventy-five miles. At the border of Nelson County, Missouri, he lost the trail. He refused to be stumped and continued the hunt for weeks, going up and down the lonely back roads and lanes seeking information. He finally learned that George Shepherd, "Big George" who had ridden with Jesse in Anderson's band of border raiders, had been a member of the gang.

Shepherd, Bligh discovered, was resting at the farmhouse of the widow Maddox, the same young lady who had "a lock of hair shot from beneath her ear" when the guerrillas fought off the Cherokee Federals in '64. Mrs. Maddox had been widowed rather suddenly a short time after she and her husband, Dick, had returned to Missouri. Dick, who loved to boast he had killed more men than Quantrill at Lawrence, met his match one night in a gun duel and died with his boots on. Big George quickly took his place.

Bligh sent a message in cypher to Pinkerton in Chicago. The agency head dispatched another agent, William Gallagher, with orders to raid the Maddox place. The posse was gathered and they rode up to the weather-beaten farmhouse. From behind a tree "Yankee" ordered George to surrender.

A revolver banged from a window and the shot whistled overhead tearing through the trees.

"Come and get me," was the answer.

Bligh and Gallagher took up the challenge and divided the posse between them to surround the house. A gun battle took place which lasted all through the night. The posse was closing in just about dawn when Shepherd made a desperate dash for freedom. He was quickly brought down with a shot in the leg.

Returned to Russelville by Bligh and Gallagher, he was identified by townspeople as having been a member of the gang. He was indicted for robbery, convicted, and sentenced to Kentucky State Prison for three years. During the trial the old man "named Lawrence" took the stand but said he couldn't identify the outlaw.

Shepherd was escorted to the prison by Bligh and just before the gates clanged shut told the detective:

"I reckon you got me now so I might as well admit I was there."

"Were the Jameses and Youngers there?" Bligh asked.

The convicted bank robber gave him a blank look. "I don't know any of the people who were with me," he said.

After Shepherd's conviction Bligh continued his painfully plodding investigation.

After weeks of riding about the countryside he discovered that the Jameses and Youngers had left Ray County with Ole Shepherd, George's cousin, bound for the comparative safety of Clay County. Bligh, apparently satisfied with the integrity of the county sheriff at Liberty, sent him a confidential telegram to watch out for the arrival of Jesse, Frank, Cole, and Ole.

A few days later a farmer who was hostile to the James gang informed the sheriff that the robber gang had come home to roost. Ole Shepherd, he said, was alone at a farmhouse a short distance from the Samuel place.

A telegram was sent to Chicago and Allan Pinkerton in turn wired Bligh in Louisville. The detective set out at once. In Clay County he selected a posse and raided the farmhouse.

Ole decided to shoot his way out. But he had less luck than his cousin. The guerrilla-outlaw was riddled with bullets before he could leave the door of the house. He was unceremoniously buried and "Yankee" Bligh scratched another name off his list of suspects.

After the Russelville robbery Jesse and several of his gang hid out for a time at the home of his cousins, the Hites, near Adairville, about fifteen miles from Russelville. In the town George T. Hite operated a grocery store. Crippled by arthritis, he was said to have been one of Jesse's closest friends.

Many times after a raid Jesse and his gang would stop off at Hite's place for a few days and describe their latest stage, train, or bank robbery with much guffawing and leg-slapping. After one of the stage robberies Jesse and one of his outlaws "laughed a great deal" as they told how they had forced a Negro preacher to take several drinks of liquor as they relieved the passengers of their watches and cash.

After Jesse's assassination in 1882, Hite sat down with a reporter for the St. Louis *Courier-Journal* and reminisced in great detail about the Missourian and his followers. He gives a wonderfully succinct explanation of how the gang operated.

"They'd decide on going somewhere, and then they'd send word to all the others—they always knew where they were, and then went and done it. That's all there was of it."

After Russelville Jesse stayed at the Hite place until he heard of Ole Shepherd's death. He returned to Clay County but then, like his friend Jim Cummins, decided that the section was getting too warm for comfort.

Before another posse could be rounded up the James boys left on an "extended vacation" in California. Each traveled a different route. Jesse took the long way. First to New York, where he undoubtedly saw the sights; then by steamship to Panama and from there to San Francisco. Frank went by stage and horse.

Both outlaws are said to have stayed for a year at a sanitarium operated by their uncle, Drury Woodson James, at Paso Robles, California. There is no evidence of what they did during that time. Tradition has them searching for the grave of their clergyman-father, who supposedly was buried at Maryville, California.

Meanwhile in Chicago Allan and William Pinkerton were planning their war against the Missouri outlaws. It was a strange and bitter conflict and was to last sixteen years. It was "war with the knife and the knife to the hilt." Its battles would take place in trains, on dark roads and hilltops, in swamps, gullies, and the public squares of small towns. Principals on both sides would fall. For years echoes of the conflict would resound in the convention halls of Missouri's political parties ending careers of fine statesmen. Finally, when the gunfire, the shouting, and the name-calling had died away, the ballad writers would quietly take up their pens and a nation would sing about them.

5

DESPERATE MEN

I T was the seventh of December, 1869, when three men entered the town of Gallatin, in Daviess County, Missouri, and rode up the main street to the door of the Daviess County Savings Bank. It was a cold, windy day and the streets were deserted. At the door of the bank, two of the riders dismounted and entered the bank. The third man remained mounted and held the reins of the other two horses.

Inside the bank a farmer by the name of McDowell was saying good-by to the cashier, John W. Sheets, a former captain in the Union army, when the two men entered. They walked to the counter and one handed Sheets a hundred-dollar-bank note "and requested change." Sheets nodded and returned with a handful of bills. He began to count out the change. Suddenly both strangers yanked out revolvers from beneath their heavy coats and demanded the keys to the inner door of the safe. Sheets stared at them but said nothing. One of the holdup men, a big bearded man, cursed and walked back of the counter. He returned with several hundred dollars in bills and currency which he threw into a wheat sack.

Suddenly his companion grabbed his arm and whispered fiercely. Both men stared at Sheets. Muttering under his breath the smaller one raised his revolver and fired. The blast of the heavy weapon shook the windows and filled the small room. The cashier crumbled to the floor without a sound. The bullet had entered the right eye and emerged from the back of the head tearing a gaping hole in the skull.

Meanwhile, two men had attempted to enter the bank to make deposits but were ordered away by the third man on horseback who kept waving a Colt in one hand and holding the reins of the horses with the other. At the sound of the shot he shouted:

"Hurry boys, they'll be upon us."

Inside the bank Jesse James stared down at the man he had just murdered, glanced briefly to where McDowell stood frozen against the wall, then turned and ran out of the bank followed by the big man, Coleman Younger.

Several citizens had armed themselves at the sound of the revolver shot and were moving cautiously up the street toward the bank. When Frank James saw his brother and Younger run out of the bank he shouted again for them to "hurry" and wheeling about began galloping up the street. As Jesse sprang for his horse the animal reared. The outlaw was thrown with one foot caught in the stirrup. A volley of shots sent the horse off into a loping gallop with Jesse James still dangling from the stirrup. After he had been bounced along the frozen rutted road for about fifty feet the bandit managed to free himself. Apparently stunned he lay on the ground for a few moments and then began to rise to his feet. By then a large crowd of citizens had gathered and was beginning "to open a lively fusillade" when Frank James swung back down the street; Jesse climbed up behind him and away they went together.

Within ten minutes a posse was galloping out of town. They caught sight of the bandits and fired several shots, but the distance was too great.

A mile southwest of Gallatin the Clay County outlaws met "Daniel Smoot, a farmer, riding an excellent saddlehorse." With a pistol "an inch from his nose" Jesse James ordered Smoot to dismount. Smoot dismounted "and took to the brush with great alacrity."

On nearing the village of Kidder, some miles from Gallatin, the outlaws met the Reverend Helm, a Methodist minister, and at gun point forced him to guide them around the community. As they started to leave him, Jesse said:

"I'm Bill Anderson's brother. I killed S. P. Cox who works in the bank back there in Gallatin. He killed my brother in the war and I got him at last."

Jesse's alibi for the cold-blooded murder of Sheets was quick thinking on his part. He knew "Bloody Bill" had been killed by a Lieutenant S. P. Cox in the fall of '64 and decided that Anderson's brother Jim should be the avenger. Safe in Clay County—through friends—he claimed Bill Anderson's brother had visited the Samuel place a few days before the murder and outlined the Gallatin Bank robbery. Jesse pictured himself as becoming indignant and spurning the offer. But at Anderson's plea he loaned him his favorite horse.

Back in Gallatin the sheriff had carefully examined the horse left behind by the outlaw and began a search for its owner. After a nine-day investigation the peace officer announced the name of the horse's owner.

According to the *Kansas City Times* of December 16, 1869, "the horse was fully identified as the property of a young man named James, whose mother and stepfather live about four miles from Centerville, Clay County, near the Cameron Branch of the Hannibal and St. Joe Railroad." The account ended:

"Both he and his brother are desperate men, having had much experience in horse and revolver work."

After the horse had been definitely established as belonging to Jesse James, the people of Gallatin decided to force the sheriff of Clay County to take some action. Two men were selected to visit Liberty. The next day, grim-faced and heavily armed, they rode across the public square and trooped into the office of Deputy Sheriff Thomason, a former captain in the Confederate army with a distinguished war record. The facts were placed before Thomason who agreed that "the Boys" should be brought in. Accompanied by his son, Oscar, he rode off with the Gallatin men for the Samuel place, about twenty miles away. At the farmhouse, the tiny posse was split into two parties, the Gallatin men watching it from the side next to the woods and the Liberty father and son combination dismounting at the gate and walking up the lane to the door.

Thomason and his son were halfway up the path when a Negro boy ran from around a corner of the house to the stable and flung open the door. Mounted on two of their best horses Jesse and Frank came out of the barn "in a rush with drawn pistols and took the lot fence." The Gallatin men fired but missed. Shouting to his son and the other two men to follow him, Thomason mounted and cleared the "lot fence in a gallop." He was soon chasing the two outlaws "riding like the wind."

Behind at the Samuel place, Oscar and the two Gallatin men followed their leader—until they reached the "lot fence." There their horses balked and the three possemen, no doubt cursing all horseflesh and outlaws, dismounted and began yanking aside the rails.

Thomason meanwhile had engaged the bandits in a running revolver duel. While re-loading he suddenly realized that there were no pounding hooves behind him. He drew up and looked about. The road was deserted. Jesse and Frank did the same thing. With a whoop the outlaws turned around . . .

There are two versions as to what followed. The first is Thomason's.

As the outlaws charged down on him he dismounted and pegged several shots. Jesse and Frank answered his fire, and his horse was killed. Satisfied, both robbers wheeled about, waved, and rode off. So, Thomason said, he began walking back to the Samuel place. Somewhere along the way he missed his three possemen. At the farmhouse he collared the little Negro groom and ordered him to fetch a horse. The boy obliged and gave him one of Jesse's better specimens of stolen horseflesh.

As he was mounting, Mrs. Samuel came out on the porch and angrily denounced him for attempting to "arrest her boys." Thomason warned her that her sons would "come to no good" and rode off with the mother of the outlaws shouting, "You people are making my boys bad. Why don't you leave them alone?"

A short time later Frank and Jesse returned to the farmhouse. When Jesse heard that the Liberty peace officer had taken one of his horses, he became furious, denouncing Thomason as a horse-thief and swearing to kill him on sight. Both outlaws took off after the deputy sheriff but missed him in the gathering darkness.

When Captain Thomason reached Liberty about ten o'clock that night he found the town in a high state of excitement. Fred Meffert's saloon seemed to be doing a brisk business in dispensing "Brandenberg's beer of New Jersey—five cents a glass." There wasn't a vacant space at the hitching posts. Clusters of men about the public square, talking loudly and gesticulating among themselves, looked up as he rode by. At the courthouse Thomason hitched his horse and entered his crowded office. The buzz of conversation stopped. His son, Oscar, talking to the two Gallatin men, turned and stared.

"It's Capt'n Thomason!" one of the men said.

The deputy growled that any fool could see that and what was the reason for all the excitement?

His son hastily explained. They had found his dead horse in the road and were just gathering together a posse to go out and bring in his body.

Unfortunately there is no account of Thomason's reply.

The other version of what happened is Jesse's. He later told friends that during the chase he and Frank discovered they were being pursued by only one man. They turned and killed his horse. The deputy leaped from the saddle and fled into the brush. Not wishing to kill him they allowed him to escape and rode back to the farmhouse.

There they discovered Thomason had taken one of the horses and they set out after him but lost his trail in the darkness.

In 1915 Jim Cummins, who was spending his last days at the Confederate Home in Higginsville, Missouri, vigorously denied that he had participated in the Gallatin robbery and murder. Although there were only three outlaws, according to townspeople and McDowell, the farmer, Cummins, insisted that Jesse and Frank James, Wood and Clarence Hite, and Dick Liddell were the raiders. He erroneously told the Kansas City *Star* reporter in the same interview that Frank James was tried and acquitted for the robbery and murder. The elder James brother was indicted, tried, and acquitted for the Winston, Missouri, train robbery which took place on July 15, 1881.

Following the Gallatin robbery William Pinkerton took up the chase and trailed the outlaws across the Missouri River into Clay County. Despite threats and cajoling he found it impossible to enlist the aid of local peace officers to raid the Samuel farmhouse. Realizing it would be suicide to attempt to storm the stronghold of the outlaws singlehanded he returned, embittered and chagrined, to Chicago.

In 1898, commenting on those days before a Chicago convention of police officers from all over the United States, Pinkerton declared:

"When I asked the assistance of the officer in arresting a part of the gang, he said that he would deputize me and aid me secretly, but owing to the relatives and sympathizers of these men residing in the county, he dared not lend a hand openly. He said that I did not have to live there after the arrest had been made but he did."

6.

NEW TERRITORY

T HE Honorable H. Clay Dean was in all his glory. The
public square of Corydon, Iowa, was packed solid this warm
sunshiny day of June 3, 1871. There were farmers in their best,
wives in Sunday-go-to-meetin' clothes, and their children, faces
shining from repeated scrubbings. On the outskirts of the throng
were several buckboards and tassel-topped buggies of the gentry.
The whole town had turned out to hear him speak—as one county
newspaper put it, "There will be plenty of oratory and lager beer
flowing throatward"—and Dean, as he looked over the upturned
faces, promised himself that by the good Lord's grace he was going
to satisfy them. The portly politician had a booming voice and it
was soon rolling over the heads of his listeners, dwelling on
the proposed new school building and the evils of black Re-
publicanism.

Out of the corner of his eye Dean saw several men ride up and
stop on the outskirts of the crowd. One held a small sack slung
across his saddlehorn. After a time one of the men raised his hand.

"A point, sir," he cried. The crowd swung around to look at
the rider curiously.

Dean yielded with a graceful, courtly gesture. "Your question,
my young friend?" he boomed.

"Well, sir," the young man replied, "some fellows were just
down to the bank and tied up the cashier. All the drawers are
cleaned out. You folks best get down there in a hurry."

The bearded rider threw back his head with a wild peal of
laughter. His companions joined in. Then with a chorus of
whoops they spurred their mounts and raced down the street,
disappearing in a cloud of dust.

There was dead silence in the public square. The Honorable
H. Clay Dean stared down the street, his mouth gaping in bewil-

derment. An uneasy murmur rose from the spectators. Then a citizen yelled:

"My God, it's the James gang! They just robbed the bank!"

The crowd churned into a confused mass. Men ran in the direction of the bank; women shouted at their husbands; horses reared and bucked; dogs, sensing the excitement, ran between the legs of the people, yapping and howling. The only one at that moment who was not rushing to the bank was the Honorable H. Clay Dean. Golden voice stilled, he just stood there dumbfounded, looking down the street of the small town.

A few minutes later the first citizens to arrive at the bank found the cashier tied and gagged. The cash drawers were empty. When the gag had been removed and his arms and legs untied, the cashier described what had happened.

A young man with blinking blue eyes entered the bank. Two other men sauntered in behind him. They were the bank's first customers, and the cashier said he was eager to serve them. The stranger handed over a hundred-dollar bill and requested change. The cashier said that when he turned around from opening the safe he looked down the barrel of a revolver. The bandits, after warning him to keep quiet, tied and gagged him. They seemed quite expert in the manner in which they cleaned the shelves of the $45,000, the cashier added as an afterthought.

As the bandits were leaving, a Negro preacher entered the bank and asked one of the gang where he could deposit his life savings. Shoving a revolver into the stomach of the old colored minister, the outlaw exclaimed politely, as he took the money:

"Right in here, uncle."

He tossed the money into the wheat sack.

Later the townspeople learned that the outlaws had first visited the county treasurer's office intending to steal the collected taxes. The bandit chief used the same bill-changing formula. The clerk shrugged his shoulders and threw up his hands in a helpless gesture.

"Sorry, gentlemen, but it is locked," he said, pointing to the safe.

"Why don't you try the Obocock Brothers Bank down the street. It just opened this morning."

"Just opened?" The man grinned, "well I reckon then we'll be their first customers."

Robert Pinkerton, one of the sons who had been summoned from the New York office, was designated by his father to take personal charge of the crime. After studying a few pictures taken about that time of the son of the famed detective, and talking with several retired operatives, it is not hard to picture this grim-faced sleuth, dressed in a dark-blue coat, broad-brimmed hat, and trousers tucked into knee-high boots, jogging day after day from state to state as he followed the cold trail of the freebooters.

Pinkerton's investigation took him from Iowa to the Missouri line, through Mercer County, part of Harrison, Daviess, Caldwell, Clinton—the dread Clay and Jackson Counties—and to the "Blue Mill Ferry," with the chase finally ending at the junction of the Independence and Lexington wagon roads.

It was at this very spot that ten months later, Jesse and some members of his gang brutally murdered Pinkerton detective Joseph W. Wicher.

At the conclusion of his investigation Robert Pinkerton announced that besides Jesse James, the members of the gang which had robbed the Iowa bank were Frank James, Cole, Jim, and John Younger, Jim Cummins, Charlie Pitts, and Ed Miller, brother of Clell and one of Jesse's guerrilla comrades.

The Jameses and Youngers—through mutual friends—presented alibis to the sheriff in Liberty. Several persons came forward and declared that "the boys were in the county" at the time the stick-up took place.

In one last effort Pinkerton arrested Clell Miller and returned him to Iowa. The evidence was too flimsy and the law official reluctantly released the outlaw.

There was nothing more to be done. Robert Pinkerton returned to the Chicago home office. The effrontery of the gang had now become a personal challenge to the agency.

Back in Chicago, dusty and red-eyed from the wearisome miles on horseback, Robert Pinkerton told his father and his brother William as he unbuckled his guns:

"We must smash this gang if it is the last thing we do. They are cold-blooded murderers and brigands and I pray God that I live to see the day that they are put behind bars for the rest of their natural lives."

He did see most of them, but he did not see the leader in his coffin.

7

THE LUCKY DUTCHMAN

ON April 12, 1872, Jesse James murdered again. The victim was a young, unarmed cashier.

It was about 3 P.M. of that mild afternoon when the Missouri bandit led three outlaws into the Deposit Bank in Columbia, Adair County, Kentucky. Outside Clell Miller and one of the Youngers were terrorizing the town as they raced like drunken Comanches around the public square whooping and firing.

At Jesse's command cashier R. A. C. Martin and two other townspeople who were standing in line to make deposits raised their hands.

"Give me the keys to the safe," the bandit leader ordered.

"I'll be damned if I'll do that," Martin replied.

"Dammit! Hand over those keys."

Martin shook his head stubbornly. "No."

Without another word Jesse fired three times. He was so near that the muzzle blast of his revolver burned the cashier's jacket.

Martin crumbled. He was dead before his body touched the floor.

In a frenzy Jesse emptied his revolver at the safe door. It was a futile gesture. Dynamite and not bullets was the only thing which could crack open that tough iron door.

Determined not to leave empty-handed, the three outlaws dumped the contents of a cash drawer into the wheat sack. It had an empty jingle to it as it bounced across the saddlehorn of Jesse's horse when they rode out of Columbia. There was less than two hundred dollars to split five ways that evening.

"Yankee" Bligh followed the trail of the gang into Tennessee but lost it somewhere in the Cumberlands. Rewards were offered, but no trace of the outlaws could be found.

Two weeks later the Missouri freebooters struck again. This

time the stick-up was accomplished without bloodshed, but although the plunder was much more than the few bloody dollars obtained in Columbia, Jesse was bitterly disappointed. He had expected to carry off a hundred thousand dollars. They rode away with only four thousand.

The raided bank was the Savings Association in Ste. Genevieve on the bank of the Mississippi.

Tradition has it that the gang rode out of Jackson County traveling by roundabout routes for a distance of about four hundred miles. First southward, then eastward through the heart of the Ozark ridges, to Bismarck, seventy-five miles south of St. Louis. After resting their horses they resumed the journey, arriving at Ste. Genevieve bright and early on the morning of May 23.

Two new members of the gang, William Chadwell, alias Bill Stiles, and Bob Younger, who had just turned twenty, rode at Jesse's side. The new recruits never served out their apprenticeship. Both died violently of a disease to which early western outlaws were particularly susceptible—lead poisoning.

The gang hit the town as usual, one group sweeping in from the north, another from the south. In one party there were Jesse, Clell Miller, and Bill Chadwell; Cole Younger and his brother Bob composed the other.

The bank was deserted when the outlaws entered. At Jesse's order O. D. Harris, the cashier, opened the vault and the gold jingled into the wheat sack.

It was an easy getaway. But tradition has the wheat sack so weighed down with gold and silver that Jesse's horse bolted and a passing farmer, under the threatening revolvers of the outlaws, chased and retrieved the bandit leader's mount.

The sack was secured and the gang prepared to start off again when the German-American farmer said:

"I catch der horse. Vot do I get for dot, yah?"

"Your life, Dutchy," Jesse answered with a crooked smile. "Vot do you egspect, yah?"

Truth, fiction? After seventy-seven years, who knows? We can only smile and shrug our shoulders helplessly. It is no better or worse than a hundred more stories we have read or heard.

The next holdup attributed to the James-Younger gang took place on September 23 in the same year, when three horsemen "swooped down" on the Kansas City Fair and stole the tin cash box containing almost ten thousand dollars.

The main attraction of the fair was a famous trotter of the time named "Ethan Allen." It is reported that more than thirty thousand fans jammed the fair that day. The race had finished and the mob was streaming out of the exits when the bandits rode down on the messenger, snatched up the cash box, and in a moment disappeared from the scene.

The cashier immediately cried, "It's the James gang," no more certain that it was the Missouri desperadoes than that it was the man in the moon. In a few hours the news spread through Kansas and Missouri that the James-Youngers had successfully raided the fair.

Whether it was the James-Younger gang who committed this holdup will never be known for a certainty. About this time other outlaw bands had sprung up, and nearly every robbery committed throughout the United States was blamed on Jesse and his riders. For example, the bank robbery at Corinth, Mississippi, and the train robbery at Muncie, Kansas, occurred on the same day, but the James-Younger band was credited with both.

However this is certain: no band of outlaws "swooped down," as one newspaper declared, and from the saddle carried off a tin box containing ten thousand dollars. The cost of admission to that fair was probably less than a dollar and there must have been a large amount of small change. How then could a rider on a horse "swoop down" and pluck a box heavily weighted with ten thousand dollars in bills and coins, out of the teller's hands? The *Illustrated Police News* suggested that the officials of the fair might do well to question the teller, who undoubtedly "was the real thief."

Following that raid a letter published in the *Kansas City Times* charged that Cole Younger had led the gang. It was signed "Jesse James." The letter is believed to have been spurious. Jesse's quick temper and audacious plans had provoked more than one quarrel between him and the more conservative—in outlawry—Cole Younger. But it is not likely that Jesse would have stooped to such indirect means to force his chief lieutenant back in line. It would have been more in character for the bandit chief to have yanked out his Colt and filled his follower with lead.

8.

A NEW INDUSTRY IS BORN

J ESSE JAMES has been credited with the invention of the technique of train robbery. This is not true. A more industrious outlaw deserves the dubious honor. His name is John Reno and he headed the first organized gang of daylight bank and train holdup men in America. The Renos—and by a strange coincidence they too were brothers—operated in Missouri, Illinois, Indiana, and Iowa in the years immediately following the Civil War. There were four: John, Frank, "Slim," and William. Each rivaled the other in daring acts of lawlessness. They were a brainy lot and included among their members Peter McCartney, said to have been the first American criminal to remove the ink from bills of small denominations to obtain government paper for the manufacture of counterfeit bills.

It is believed by the Pinkerton Agency that a member of the James gang served time in Missouri State Prison with John Reno and from this inventive outlaw learned firsthand the art of train robbing. Upon his release he hunted up Jesse and described the latest science in outlawry. The imagination of the Missouri bandit chief was fired and plans for the first major train robbery in the world were made.

What followed is conjectural but partially it is based on confessions made by various members of the gang after they had surrendered.

Jesse first sent his brother Frank and Jim Younger to select the train carrying the largest amount of gold. It is said that this is why Frank and Jim were not among the Ste. Genevieve raiders. They were carrying out the more important assignment.

Some weeks after the James gang had returned to Clay County to split up the proceeds of their last robbery, the two traveling representatives returned home. From a bribed railroad employee they had learned that a large shipment of gold would be sent by way of the Chicago, Rock Island, and Pacific Railroad in the latter part of July. The exact date would still have to be ascertained.

In the first part of July, 1873, Jesse led his gang out of Jackson County, heavily armed and well mounted. Near Council Bluffs they made temporary camp while Cole Younger and Frank James pushed on to Omaha, Nebraska.

When they returned the two bandits were jubilant. They had learned that the train with the gold shipment would leave July 21 and would pass through Adair, Iowa, east of the Bluffs, about 8 P.M.

The seven freebooters set out for Adair at once. A spot where the tracks curved was selected. Railroad ties were loosened and the gang disappeared into the brush to wait. It is not hard to imagine the scene; the nervous pawing of the horses, the creak of leather, the savage, low curses, Jesse's final order to slip on the calico masks as they heard in the distance the first clack-clack of the iron-rimmed wheels. There was probably enough light left to see the swaying iron horse come chugging up the narrow-gauge track, the interior of the engineer's cab illuminated with a bloody glow as the door of the fire box was swung open.

There are conflicting stories as to what method Jesse James used. Some say he piled a number of ties across the tracks; others claim some ties were loosened and attached by rope to one of the horses. When the train drew near spurs were put to the horse and the ties pulled free.

No matter what method the Missourians used it was successful. As the train swung around the curve the engine gave a sickening lurch and toppled off to one side. Engineer John Rafferty was scalded to death, his fireman was badly burned, and five day coaches and two sleepers were pulled off the track.

In the gloom broken steam lines hissed, the wheels of the engine spun wildly, and in the cars frightened and painfully bruised passengers crawled over smashed seats to fight their way out of windows. All believed that a serious accident had occurred.

Suddenly from the woods beyond the tracks came a new and more terrifying sound. To the stunned passengers who had lived along the border it was dreadfully familiar; it was the high-pitched yip-yip-yaw of Quantrill's guerrillas as they rode for blood and plunder. A moment later the seven riders dashed from the woods to ride along either side of the train like an attacking band of redskins. Two of them leaped into the baggage car and forced the express clerk to open the safe. The wheat sack was produced and the gold poured into it.

It was plain that it wasn't any hundred thousand dollars, and Jesse snarled at the messenger, "Where's the rest of it?"

"That's all there is," the frightened messenger asserted. "That's the whole shipment."

Satisfied that the clerk was telling the truth, the bandit chief ordered his gang to go through the cars systematically searching each passenger. The bandits soon fell into the swing of this new idea and rings, bracelets, watches, wallets, change, and trinkets clinked into the sack. When the last passenger had been cleaned, Jesse gave the signal and the outlaws fled off into the darkness, their sporadic firing and bloodcurdling yells becoming fainter and fainter.

The gang rode all that night until dawn. At their hideout they counted the loot. It was a trifle more than seven thousand dollars. Jesse was bitterly disappointed and it is said that hard words passed between him and his brother Frank and Cole Younger. What the bandits didn't know until days later was that a second train, twelve hours later, had passed over the spot where the hold-up had taken place. There was seventy-five thousand dollars aboard. Frank James and Cole Younger, it seemed, had made a miscalculation in the time; it wasn't 8 P.M. but 8 A.M.

The news of the train holdup was soon flashed to every paper in the country. Not only in the East but throughout Europe, where, as always, crime news of the United States was eagerly awaited, the story was given great prominence.

Pinkerton's National Detective Agency was engaged by the railroad and the Adams Express Company to track down the bandits. Allan and William took up the chase, which spread throughout the Indian Territory, Iowa, and Kansas. It ended in Missouri where the outlaws vanished into formidable Jackson and Clay counties.

The Pinkertons did determine, however, that the gang was led by Jesse and was composed of his brother Frank, Cole and Jim Younger, Clell Miller, Bob Moore, and Comanche Tony, a petty half-breed outlaw whom Frank James had picked up in Texas.

The detectives also learned that the day following the robbery the gang had stopped at a farm in Ringgold County, Iowa, just above the Missouri line. They were given supper and later that evening sat on the porch of the farmhouse discussing numerous subjects including farming and religion. Their leader was a man about five foot seven inches, with light blue eyes, heavy sandy whiskers, broad shoulders, slightly turned up nose, high forehead, and he appeared to be fairly well educated.

"This," Allan Pinkerton announced, "is a fairly good description of Jesse James."

In April, 1900, a dim echo of the crime was heard when a Marshall P. Wright of Jackson County, Missouri, made an affidavit for a writer who was gathering material on the life of the bandit leader. Wright, who said he was "an old friend of the boys," declared:

In 1873 I was living in Clinton, Missouri, and was there on July 21 when a train was robbed in Iowa, west of Des Moines. The Younger brothers including Coleman and James were charged with the robbery. I knew all the boys well and had known them for years. On the day after said robbery, early in the morning, I met the boys at Monegaw Springs, St. Clair County, Missouri. I had a copy of the paper giving an account of the robbery. Cole and Jim Younger were there and read the account. I read the article aloud to them and remarked on their ability to be in so many places at once. The place where the robbery was committed, Adair, Iowa, was more than 200 miles from St. Clair County, Missouri, which distance— if guilty—they must have traveled in 24 hours. It was stated by people living there whom I know that the Youngers had not been away. There were no cross lines of railroad making it possible for them to cover that distance.

I have every reason to believe and do believe that the charges of that robbery to the Youngers was the work of their enemies who were seeking to drive them out of Missouri.

9

THE FULL YEAR

THE year of 1874 turned. It was to be both a bitter and a full year for Jesse and his followers. Within a few months Jim Younger buried his brother John in the orchard of their home, three Pinkerton detectives died under their bullets, rewards mounted to tempt the many citizen posses, and for the first time the chief official of Missouri came out openly against them as he asked for the aid of the militia to put down the lawlessness of his state. It was also a special year in the lives of Jesse and Frank James. Both outlaws were married. Frank eloped, but Jesse adopted the more conventional method and was married by a preacher relative.

The year which was to be so significant in the lives of the outlaws opened with a heavy snowstorm. It evened off the fields surrounding the Samuel farm outside Kearney, Missouri, making the furrows and the mounds all one in level whiteness. But Jesse and Frank never saw the glaring brilliance outside their front door. At about the time the snow was falling during the afternoon of January 15, 1874, they were lurking in the brush off the side of the road which led from Malvern to the government-sponsored institution of Hot Springs, Arkansas.

Besides the two James boys there were Coleman Younger and at least one of his brothers and Clell Miller. Their object this time was the heavy Concord coach lumbering its way toward them through the dust. Just before the stage reached the spot where they were hiding, the five desperadoes dashed out of the brush to form a human chain across the road.

When the stage braked to a stop, Frank James opened the door and ordered the fourteen passengers to line up in the road. As Jesse, Clell Miller, and Cole Younger began to relieve them of their valuables, Robertus Love would have us believe that this incident took place: One man sputtering with rage surrendered a fine gold watch.

"This, suh, is an outrage," he cried.

Cole Younger studied the protesting victim for a moment.

"Are you a Southerner?"

The victim, surprised at the unexpected question, nodded.

"Were you in the Confederate army?"

Another nod.

"State your rank, regiment, and commanding officer."

Puzzled, the passenger did as the outlaw requested. To his surprise the bandit handed back his watch.

"We are all Confederate soldiers. We don't rob Southerners, especially Confederate soldiers; but Yankees and detectives are not exempt," the burly bandit said.

The other passengers didn't fare so well. One was ex-Governor Burbank of the Dakota territory who lost $840 and a diamond stickpin to the gang. The entire loot amounted to about $4,000.

The best account in the Pinkerton archives of this holdup is an affidavit made by G. R. Crump, one of the passengers. Crump was a representative of Edmunds, Pettigrew and Company, of Memphis, Tennessee, wholesale distributors of cigars. By failing to mention in his account the incident of the ex-Confederate soldier having his watch returned from Coleman Younger, Mr. Crump puts it to rest as pure folklore probably taken from some account of the crime in the *Police Gazette*. If it had happened, the cigar sales representative would undoubtedly have mentioned it. He went to great pains to mention everything else.

Mr. Crump's account of the stickup goes on to say:

> I got out and found three men in front of me with cocked pistols and one more with a shotgun while on the other side of the stage was another pointing his weapon at us.
>
> After we got out we were ordered to put up our hands which we did. The bandits then formed us into a small circle so we all could be covered by their pistols and shotguns. One man then went through us taking all the watches, jewelry and money he could find. From ex-Governor Burbank they obtained $840 in money along with a diamond pin and a gold watch. A gentleman named Taylor from Lowell, Mass. went for $650 in cash. A passenger from Syracuse, N. Y. had $160

and had to give up his last nickle. Johnny Dietrich, the boot and shoe merchant lost $5 and a fine gold watch.

Mr. Dietrich had $50 in his watch pocket which they failed to find. Mr. Charles Moore of the ice house gave up $70 and his fine silver watch but the bandits looked at it and gave it back to Charlie, saying:

"Keep it. We don't want any silver watches, mister."

A Mr. Peoples who lives near the Springs lost $20. Three others were robbed of $15. The express package containing about $450 was also stolen. I had my watch and $45 grabbed up.

After they went through us they opened several mail sacks and tore open the registered letters but did not find any money. While the main party was engaged in robbing us, another closely examined the team of the stage until at last he selected the best horse and threw his saddle on him. Then he rode him furiously up and down the road two or three times. Finally he rode up and said to the rest of the companions, "I think this one will do."

After warning us not to follow, they rode off, whooping and shouting like savages.

Mr. Crump ended his affidavit with this masterful understatement: "There wasn't anything spectacular about the holdup."

After the old-fashioned stagecoach robbery, Jesse and his gang returned to Missouri for another try at the train-robbing technique. They selected Gadshill, a tiny town in the southwestern pine-covered section of their own state, a little more than a hundred miles below St. Louis. Their target was the Iron Mountain Railroad's Little Rock Express which could be stopped at this lonely flag station. Located in the foothills of the Ozarks the wild surrounding terrain was ideal for an easy getaway.

The five bandits entered the town at about 5 P.M. on January 31, 1874, and took over the town lock, stock, and barrel. Coming in from two directions they quietly surrounded the small depot, captured the station agent, the village physician, the blacksmith, and several townspeople who were waiting to witness the big event of the day: the passing of the express bound for Little Rock.

Guns drawn, and wearing calico masks and wide-brimmed hats, the gang forced the stationmaster and his visitors into a small room. Later all witnesses declared the bandits were "big men who wore blue overcoats."

Under Jesse's direction Clell Miller took the trainman's red flag and planted it in the middle of the tracks a short distance from the depot. On the dot of 5:40 P.M. the train chugged up and ground to a stop. The engineer and fireman were escorted at pistol point to the edge of the woods where they were kept under guard by one of the outlaws.

Conductor Alford and a Mr. Morley, the general manager of the line, who happened to be making a business trip to Little Rock that evening, rushed up from the rear car to determine the cause of the delay. They walked right into the guns of Frank James.

"This way, gentlemen," he said politely with a wave of his gun. The conductor and the railroad official joined the other trainmen after Frank had first thoughtfully searched Alford and relieved him of seventy-five dollars.

Meanwhile several other bandits led by Jesse James entered the sleepers and, rousing the passengers, compelled them to toss their valuables into the waiting wheat sack. One passenger, the treasurer of the Clearwater Lumber Company, lost five thousand dollars in cash.

When Frank James, who had joined them, made a move to open the door to the day coaches, Jesse shouted:

"To hell with those Jim Crows, Frank, help us get after the plugged hats."

When one "plugged hat" nervously handed over his silver watch, Jesse blinked furiously and tossed it back to him.

"You're out of our class, mister. Get the hell up in front where you belong."

To two Southerners he returned watches.

"We don't bother our own folks—there's enough Yankees to aid the cause," he said.

After they had cleaned the passengers, including the "Jim Crows," Jesse waved his gang on to the baggage car.

"Rip up Uncle Sam (mailbags)," he shouted. "Let's see what he's got for us today, boys."

"Uncle Sam" yielded a little more than two thousand dollars.

After the bags had been dumped and the registered letters torn open Jesse leaped on his horse and yelled to Cole Younger:

"Give her a toot, Cole."

In the engineer's cab Younger pulled hard on the whistle cord. At the signal, the fireman and engineer were escorted out of the woods. A few moments later, as the train began to move slowly down the track, Jesse James rode alongside the engineer's cab and tossed in a piece of paper.

"Give this to the newspaper," he cried. "We like to do things in style."

The missive is one of the most fascinating pieces of Americana this author has run across.

It was Jesse James's own press release giving an account of the holdup! He even wrote his own headline. It read:

> THE MOST DARING TRAIN ROBBERY ON RECORD!
>
> The southbound train of the Iron Mountain Railroad was stopped here this evening by five heavily armed men and robbed of ———— dollars. The robbers arrived at the station a few minutes before the arrival of the train and arrested (sic) the agent and put him under guard and then threw the train on the switch. The robbers were all large men all being slightly under six feet. After robbing the train they started in a southerly direction. They were all mounted on handsome horses.

Then followed this wonderful postscript:

> There a h—— of an excitement in this part of the country.

The gang were later identified by William Pinkerton as Jesse and Frank James, the Youngers, Arthur McCoy, Jim Cummins, Charlie Pitts, Ed and Clell Miller, and Sam Hildebrand.

As always the Pinkertons took up the chase. The bandits were traced from Piedmont to Black Rock six miles west of Gadshill, then to Shann County sixty miles west of Wayne County. The gang split up after the loot was divided. Jesse and Frank James and the Youngers pushed on steadily until they reached Rock County, a point two hundred miles from Gadshill. From there they traveled by night to Monegaw Springs, near Osceola, the county seat of St. Clair County, Missouri, the Youngers' hideout. Jesse and Frank continued on to Independence, reportedly reaching the Samuel farm sometime in late March. They were just in time for both their weddings!

Jesse James was twenty-seven when he married his first cousin, Zerelda Mimms, who was about the same age. It wasn't a whirlwind marriage by any means. Between holding up banks and railroads and dodging the Pinkertons it took Jesse nine years finally to pop the question.

Outlawry is a fast-moving trade and allows little time for romance. But Zerelda waited. Her mother died and she went to live with her married sister in Kansas City. She was a pretty girl, well mannered and refined. Many young beaux spoke for her hand but were refused. She was determined to wait for her young guerrilla lover with the blinking blue eyes.

In the end she had her wish. On April 24, 1874, in the cold, stiff parlor of his sister-in-law-to-be, Jesse and his faithful sweetheart were married by a clergyman-relative.

Local tradition has Jesse mounted on a sleek, well-groomed horse and dressed in his Sunday best, leisurely riding down the main street of Kearney on his way to the wedding, a Winchester rifle slung across his saddlehorn and two Navy Colts under his carefully brushed black coat.

His sandy beard was trimmed and combed and his knee-high black boots glistened in the sunlight. He was smiling, and many citizens, used to those icy blue eyes and tight face filled with animal shyness and ferocity, were startled when he called out greetings. The ladies, too, received a flourish of his broad-rimmed black hat and a flashing smile. But although he appeared gracious and affable, nearly all the townspeople noticed the sharp glances from right to left and the firm grip on the Winchester. Wedding or not, Jesse was not one to be caught in a crossfire from a hidden posse. However, nothing marred the day and the bandit and his bride rode off that evening on their honeymoon.

Where it was spent nobody knows, but it is interesting to speculate. Was it spent in a hotel room in Kansas City, Chicago, or even New York; in a farmhouse turned over to them for the night by a sympathetic friend or relative; and did she in the warmth of their first intimacy plead with her outlaw bridegroom to hand up his guns; or did Jesse's sharpened senses, like any hunted animal's —a step outside the door, a creaking board, a hoarse voice—destroy the serenity and peace of the first night of his married life...

In the same year Frank James eloped. His bride was Annie Ralston, a seventeen-year-old farmer's daughter of Jackson County.

When her outraged father heard the news he called on the editor of the *Kansas City Times* and the next day there appeared in the paper a letter signed by Ralston in which he disowned his daughter for marrying the outlaw. Later, however, he relented and welcomed his daughter and notorious son-in-law. Mrs. Alexander Franklin James gave birth to one son, their only child, who was named Robert after Frank and Jesse's father.

It is an amazing fact that the married lives of both outlaws were above reproach. There is no account of either bandit engaging in promiscuous affairs. In their own rather warped way both men apparently loved their wives and children. After Jesse's death a reporter for the *Courier-Journal* asked George Hite, "Did Jesse James love his wife?"

Hite, "the best friend Jesse James ever had," thought for a moment then answered: "Yes, I believe he did."

Outside of a few bare facts there is nothing intimately known about the wives of the James boys. All we know is that they faithfully followed their bandit husbands to hideouts from state to state, from Missouri to Maryland on horseback and in jouncing buckboards, loving them and caring for them and bearing their children. Like the women of every century who fell in love with men outside the law, they led bleak and strenuous lives, enduring much, forgiving much.

Mrs. Frank James saw happier days. She was still in middle life when her husband "came in" and was acquitted of the charges against him.

It was Mrs. Jesse Woodson James who was to witness tragedy piled on tragedy: the murder of her husband; the horror of formally identifying his body to incredulous peace officers; the coroner's inquest and the crowds of curiosity seekers who stood below her window; the shocked faces of her two small children; the long, sad journey back home and the burial in the yard of the weatherbeaten old Samuel farmhouse under a dull and dripping sky.

The list of Jesse's crimes is long and bloody, but the blackest of all are the ones he committed against those he loved.

19. Dr. D. C. McNeill attended Louis J. Lull, the Pinkerton Detective Captain, fatally wounded in the gun fight with the Younger brothers near Monegaw Springs. (*Courtesy Pinkerton's National Detective Agency, Inc.*)

20. Thomas T. Crittenden, who, elected Governor of Missouri in 1881, vowed to rid the state of Frank and Jesse James. (*Courtesy Pinkerton's National Detective Agency, Inc.*)

21. Jesse James. One of the reasons for his elusiveness was that he rarely had his picture taken. This daguerreotype was made in 1875 at Nebraska City, Nebraska. (*Courtesy National Archives*)

22. Jesse James with a full beard. *(Courtesy Pinkerton's National Detective Agency, Inc.)*

GOOD BYE, JESSE!

The Notorious Outlaw and Bandit, Jesse James, Killed at St. Joseph

BY R. FORD, OF RAY COUNTY,

A Young Man but Twenty-one Years of Age.

THE DEADLY WEAPON USED

Presented to His Slayer by His Victim but a Short Time Since.

A ROBBERY CONTEMPLATED

Of a Bank at Platte City—To Have Taken Place Last Night.

JESSE IN KANSAS CITY

During the Past Year and Residing on One of the Principal Streets.

KANSAS CITY EXCITED

Over the Receipt of the News—Talks with People— Life of the Dead Man.

THE DEAD OUTLAW

Fully Identified by His Mother and Others Who Have Known Him.

RESULT OF THE INQUEST.

Jesse James Came to His Death at the Hands of Robt Ford.

WHAT THE SLAYERS SAY.

Interviews with the Two Fords, Dick Liddil and Gov. Crittenden.

JESSE'S HOME IN THIS CITY.

Interesting Reminiscences of the Bandit and His Family.

23—24. Headlines announcing Jesse's death in the Kansas City *Daily Journal,* the 4th and 5th of April, 1882. *(Courtesy James D. Horan Western Americana Collection)*

10

THE FIRST YOUNGER FALLS

IN 1874 Jesse James and his outlaws rode into Missouri's complex political picture. They stayed there for more than ten years, shooting down careers of honest statesmen, robbing men of hard-earned reputations, and fanning the hates and feuds which still glowed with a fierce white heat although almost a decade had passed since Appomattox.

When Jesse and his riders first appeared on the political horizon their crimes threatened to split the Missouri Democratic party, which was divided into two factions: those who had either fought in the Union army or were sympathetic to the Abolitionists during the Civil War and the ex-Confederate soldiers and violently anti-northerners. With each new robbery or murder the southern faction of the party would insist that "the Boys" were only misguided champions of the Confederacy who had been driven into a life of banditry by the war. But the northern section would loudly declare that the Jameses and Youngers were nothing but common thieves and murderers who should be hanged to the nearest tree. The leading newspapers of the state added fuel to the controversy by taking sides. The powerful *St. Louis Democrat* thundered that the James-Younger reign of terror had halted immigration into the Middle Border and had shut off the flow of untold millions of dollars into the state's industries. That same year, 1874, the *Democrat* coined the phrase "Poor Old Missouri," which echoed down through the years in the nation's press and resounded in the convention halls of both parties and in the legislature at Jefferson City.

The Republican party of Missouri, meanwhile, took a dim view of the situation. According to the *People's Tribune* of September 20, 1874, the Republicans adopted a resolution condemning the policies of the Democrats which had led "to the insecurity of persons and property, the prevention of immigration, the utter prostration of business and the ruinous depreciation of all values of property."

The political cauldron boiled over on March 23, 1874, when Missouri's Democratic governor, Silas Woodson, mounted his rostrum to face a full legislature. For days it had been rumored that Woodson was preparing a special message in which he would discuss "the Boys," and as he cleared his throat and adjusted his spectacles, there wasn't an empty seat in the house. In a cold and bitter voice, Missouri's chief executive denounced the Jameses and Youngers for their lawlessness and warned the intent lawmakers that the time had now come to put down the reign of terror. Admitting that the authorities were powerless to deal with the outlaws, he asked for an appropriation of ten thousand dollars to form a group of "secret service men" to hunt down the Clay County freebooters.

In a voice which echoed in every corner of the domed hall, Woodson declared:

> There exists in this state a certain band of outlaws who, in disregard of all social and legal obligations to God and to country, have been murdering and robbing with impunity and defying the peace officers in this locality.
>
> These desperadoes one day enter and rob a bank and cold-bloodedly murder a cashier. The next day they visit an agricultural fair in the most populous part of the state and in the midst of thousands of men, women, and children rob the safe and make good their escape.
>
> Anon they enter another town, rob a bank, and shoot down in cold blood its officers. Then they deploy murderously and feloniously into our sister states. Soon they return to Missouri and rob a railroad train.
>
> The law is inadequate. The authorities are powerless to deal with these outlaws. Life and property are unsafe.
>
> The time has come to put an end to these conditions of affairs that have become uncontrollable.

In Kearney, Jesse James, when he heard the news, told friends with a cynical brightness: "Tell them to come in and get us."

Two days after Woodson's message the legislature overwhelmingly authorized ten thousand dollars for a secret body of investigators to purge the state of the outlaws. The bill, however, was declared "out of order" by the presiding officer of the legislature. Governor Woodson's action was loudly criticized by the Missouri newspaper editorial writers. As usual, a battle of the editorial pages followed. Republican organs blasted the Democrats and the Democratic papers in turn cried out against the Republicans.

In Jefferson City, the *Democrat,* voice of the Missouri Democratic party, denounced Woodson for his message, indignantly pointing out:

"If the reputation of our state is bad it is the Republicans who have made it so."

In his fine study of Frank and Jesse James in Missouri politics, written for his master's thesis, William A. Settle, Jr., graduate assistant in the history department of the University of Missouri, declares that the James-Younger issue had become so grave in state politics that in their 1874 state convention the Republican party did not nominate a ticket. Instead the delegates "almost to a man" voted to support the candidates of the People's party for the office of governor, William Gentry of Pett's County.

According to the *Missouri Statesman* of September 11, 1874, the platform of the newly organized People's party was suppression of outlawry in Missouri, "in order that capital and immigration can once again enter our state." This plank was the highlight of Gentry's acceptance speech.

The Democratic convention meeting a short time later carefully ignored the issue of Jesse and his hard-riding outlaws and their effect on the state's settlement and finances.

During the bitter political rows, the Pinkertons sent one of their finest operatives to Clay County in an attempt to try to find a breach in the seemingly impenetrable Jesse James country.

The man selected for the task was Louis J. Lull, unknown to any of the outlaws. Lull, who used the name of Allen on this mission, was a fine-looking man just under six feet tall. Born in Montpelier, Vermont, in 1847, he was appointed to Annapolis in 1862. A year later he resigned from the academy to enlist in the Vermont brigade. He became an officer and left the Union army at the end of the war with a gallant war record. He joined the Chicago police force and by 1866 had attained the rank of captain. He resigned a short time later to join Pinkerton's National Detective Agency. On his last and most dangerous assignment into Missouri, Lull was accompanied by another operative, James Wright, also one of the agency's ablest men.

Both detectives began their investigation immediately after the Gadshill robbery. At Piedmont they joined the posse who set out after the gang. Discouraged and weary, the posse returned home after several days, but both detectives continued to search the Ozarks. They discovered that the bandits were heading into the direction of Monegaw Springs, known haunt of the Youngers. Acting on the theory that one or more of the Youngers were in the band, they set out for the rural watering place in St. Clair County.

At the county seat of Osceola the Pinkerton men hired Edwin B. Daniels, a former deputy sheriff of the county. It was agreed that the two detectives would pose as cattle and horse buyers. On the way Lull and Wright stopped at a farmhouse owned by a farmer by the name of Theodore Snuffer. Why they stopped is not known. Snuffer is said to have been related to the Youngers and both operatives may have learned this from Daniels and placed the house down on the list of possible hideouts.

They walked up to the front door and knocked. When Snuffer answered they inquired how they could reach the Widow Simms place. The farmer gave them directions and both men thanked him and rode off.

Unknown to Lull and Wright, Jim and John Younger were visiting Snuffer at the time. After listening to the conversation they watched from an upstairs window as the operatives jogged down the road.

The following conversations and events are based on newspaper accounts of the time and the deathbed statement of Captain Lull.

As the Youngers watched from the window, Snuffer joined them. The farmer grunted as the two men turned down a fork in the road.

"That's funny they took the left fork instead of the right," he said.

"I don't like their looks, Jim, let's go after them," John declared, turning to his brother.

Jim Younger shrugged his shoulders. The ride from Gadshill had been long and weary and he was still tired.

"Oh, hell," he replied, "they're gone, John, let them go."

His brother insisted. He walked to where his two guns were hanging from a hook. "I'm going after them. I'd just as soon be killed now as the next day—if it's got to be. Nobody will catch me lookin' through a gratin'."

Still reluctant, Jim strapped on his guns. Both bandits mounted and set off after the law officers. About a mile past Snuffer's farm they caught up with them on the crest of a small, stony hill. Wright was riding in front and Daniels and Lull a short distance behind. It was half past two on the afternoon of March 16, 1874.

John Younger carried a double-barreled shotgun, his brother, two revolvers. John called out and the detectives drew over to the side of the road and waited.

What happened in the next violent few minutes is best told in Lull's own words, taken down as he lay dying in the Roscoe Hotel in nearby Roscoe. At that time he was not known to have been a Pinkerton detective and the clerk of the Coroner's Jury swore him as W. J. Allen.

The deposition, taken the following morning, reads:

Yesterday, about half past two o'clock, the 16th of March, 1874, E. B. Daniels and myself were riding along the road from Roscoe to Chalk Level, which road runs past the house of one Theodore Snuffer and about three miles from the town of Roscoe in St. Clair County, Missouri.

Daniels and myself were riding side by side and Mr. Wright, a short distance ahead of us. Some noise behind us attracted our attention and we looked back and saw two men on horseback coming towards us. One was armed with a double barreled shotgun and the other with revolvers; don't know if the other had a shotgun or not. The one with the shotgun had it cocked and ordered us to halt. Wright drew his pistol and put spurs to his horse and rode off. They ordered him to halt and shot at him and shot off his hat, but he kept riding.

Daniels and myself stopped standing across the road on our horses. They rode up to us and ordered us to take off our pistols and drop them in the road, the one with the gun covering us all the time with the gun. We dropped our pistols to the ground, and one of the men told the other to follow Wright and bring him back but he refused to go saying he would stay with the other. One of the men picked up the revolvers we had dropped and looking at them remarked they were damn fine pistols, and they must make them a present of them. One of them asked me where we had come from, and I said Osceola. He then wanted to know what we were doing in this part of the country. I replied: just rambling around.

One of them then said, you were up here a couple of days ago. I replied that we were not. He then said we had been at the Springs. I replied that we had been at the Springs but had not been inquiring for them, that we did not know them.

They said that detectives there had been hunting for them all the time and that they were going to put a stop to it. Daniels then said: "I am no detective and I can show you who I am and where I am going." One of them said he knew him and then turned to me and said; "what in the hell are you riding around here with all them pistols on for?" and I said, Good God! is not every man wearing them that is traveling, and have I not as much right as anyone else?" The one with the shotgun said, "hold on young man, we don't want any of that," and lowered his gun, cocked in a threatening manner; then Daniels had some talk with them and one of them got off his horse and picked up the pistols; two of them were mine and one was Daniel's; the one mounted had his gun on us and I concluded that they intended to kill us.

I reached my hand behind me and drew a No. 2 Smith and Wesson pistol and cocked it and fired at the one on horseback. My horse frightened at the report of the pistol and turned to run, and I heard two shots and my left arm fell, and then I had no control over my horse, and he jumped right into the bushes and the trees checked his speed, and I tried to get hold of the rein with my right hand to bring him into the road; one of the men rode by and fired two shots, one of which took effect in my left side, and I lost control of my horse and he turned into the brush, and a small tree struck me and knocked me out of the saddle. I then got up and staggered across the road and lay down until I was found. No one else was present.

The affidavit was attested to and signed by a James St. Clair, the clerk of the Coroner's Jury of Roscoe.

From a physician's report it was decided that the dying John Younger administered the ghastly wound in Captain Lull's neck with a shotgun blast after the Pinkerton man's bullet tore through his chest. Jim Younger killed Daniels and rode past Lull, firing two more bullets into the body of the wounded operative.

As Lull fell from his horse and crawled off to one side of the road, Jim Younger, described "as half-demented by his grief," slung his brother's body over the saddle of his horse and rode back to Snuffer's place. The remains were buried that twilight in the orchard. Jim carved the rough slab of wood which served as a temporary tombstone. Years later the remains of the outlaw were removed to the Younger's burying place on the Osceola and Chalk Level Road.

Lull lingered for six weeks at the Roscoe Hotel. After his identification had been established, William Pinkerton and Mrs. Marian B. Lull rushed to Missouri. Lull was conscious but in great pain. His wife never forgot those bitter days and nights. When the Youngers were desperately fighting for their freedom in 1892, with powerful interests pleading in their behalf, Mrs. Lull wrote Governor David M. Clough of Minnesota opposing the granting of an executive pardon to the outlaws:

"James Younger murdered my husband."

Lull was buried in Chicago with masonic honors. Daniels was interred in the Osceola cemetery. The *Missouri World* recorded: "There was a large turnout to honor this brave man."

At about the time Lull and his two companions were approaching Snuffer's farmhouse, John W. Whicher, another Pinkerton operative, was leaving Chicago bound for Clay County. Whicher, who had persistently volunteered for the dangerous assignment, was finally given permission by Allan Pinkerton to try to "arrest Jesse James, Frank James, or other members of their gang."

Whicher's record in the Pinkerton archives describes him as an "excellent operative." When he left for his mission to the "Robber State" he was just twenty-six years old. He was a six footer with blue eyes, light brown hair, a smooth, boyish face, "and just the trace of a mustache." He was born in Des Moines, Iowa, and went to sea after his school days. His first trip was aboard a fruit freighter sailing to the Mediterranean. Before the cruise was ended he had been made first officer. Whicher followed the sea until 1871 when he fractured his leg in a fall and was forced to miss his ship. When his leg had mended he cast about for a new livelihood. The adventures of the Pinkertons as they chased the James gang about the Middle Border were in the Chicago papers almost every day, and the stories caught the imagination of the young seaman. He applied for a position in the agency and was accepted. He attended the detectives' vigorous course, conducted by the Pinkertons, and was given several trial assignments which he completed successfully. Gradually he was given more important investigations and in 1874 was put on the staffs working on bank, train, and stage robberies. Whicher insisted that he be allowed to try to penetrate the Jesse James country but was refused.

In Clay County, while the furious political battle on the issue of outlawry raged, harassed citizens began to band together. A cautious correspondence began with the Pinkertons. When Whicher again approached his superiors he was granted permission.

"It was a dangerous assignment," the Pinkerton archives point out. "Instead of being harassed and hounded by their neighbors into a life of banditry and murder, the outlaws had the support and assistance of many persons throughout the countryside to keep them well informed of the arrival of strangers and their identity."

"After memorizing the names of our friends in Clay County," Whicher departed for Missouri. He first stopped at Liberty and contacted a Mr. Adkins, the head of the Commercial Savings Bank.

When the banker heard the detective outline his plan, he threw up his hands and cried:

"My God, man, do you know what you are doing? A gang of devils would be easier to arrest than these scoundrels."

Whicher persisted and the banker launched on a long discourse of the power wielded by the Jameses and Youngers in the district.

"Thank you for your interest, Mr. Adkins," Whicher replied, "but I'm going in after them anyway."

"Very well, young man," Adkins said. "I will do what I can to help you," and then he told Whicher to see a Colonel P. P. Moss, ex-sheriff and open foe of the James gang.

"He is one man I can trust and who I can safely say is a reliable and trustworthy citizen," Adkins said.

The reaction of the ex-sheriff, however, was that of the banker. "By God, this is the most foolhardy thing I ever heard of. You are going to seek out two men who wouldn't trust their own mother. These scoundrels will see through your disguise before you are within ten miles of the Samuel place. If not, one of their sympathizers in town here will send them word. Strangers in this town stand out like a sore thumb."

Whicher listened politely but refused to take Moss's advice and return to Chicago. Like the banker, the ex-sheriff finally yielded. For the next few hours he carefully briefed the operative on the terrain and names of the few law-abiding persons in the county who refused to be intimidated by the terrorist tactics of the outlaws.

"Pray God you succeed," Moss said in parting, "but should it fail it will be on your head alone."

Whicher thanked him and returned to the local hotel. That afternoon he placed his valuables and credentials with Adkins for safekeeping, discarded his city clothes, and purchased a complete outfit of clothes such as were worn by farm hands. Before dawn he slipped out of the hotel and left the town by side streets. At sunup he was on the road to Kearney.

Unknown to him the wheels of Jesse's flawless counter-espionage system had begun to turn. Every move of the detective had been followed by a lanky man in rough work clothes and an out-of-shape black hat. His name was James Latche, a hanger-on of the gang. Before Whicher left, Latche was on his way to the Samuel place with news of the stranger and his queer doings.

When Whicher arrived at Kearney he set out immediately for the bandit's hideout. On the way he stopped at several farmhouses asking for work. He posed as an easterner whose business had gone broke and who now wanted to turn to farm work. The story was plausible; Black Friday was only five years past and unemployment was still widespread in large eastern cities.

Near twilight Whicher came up to the Samuel place. He was about to turn into the road which led to the house when a man slipped from behind a large clump of bushes and stood in front of him. At his command Whicher raised his hands. The man carefully opened the detective's coat and removed the revolver from inside the waistband. His eyes blinked as he stared at it.

"Who are you?" he asked.

"I'm a farm hand looking for work," Whicher answered.

Jesse James sneered. "Damn fine gun for a farm hand to be carrying around."

"I'm looking for work," Whicher said quickly, "maybe you can give me some."

The bandit menaced the detective with his gun. "You got a job already with those goddamned Pinkertons," he said savagely. He called out and two more men stepped from behind the bushes.

"Look at his hands," Jesse ordered.

One of the men examined Whicher's outstretched hands. "He's no farm hand," he said.

"I just came from the east," Whicher began. "I am . . ."

"Shut up," Jesse growled.

"Let's finish him here, Dingus," said the man who had examined the detective's hands.

The bandit shook his head. "Too near the house. We'll take him over to the other side of the river."

What followed after the bandit and his three followers—one was Latche, the other is said to have been Clell Miller—has never been known. The story picks up on the following morning at about 1 A.M. when the ferryman on the Owens Ferry which crossed the Missouri between Clay and Jackson Counties was aroused by three mounted men. The faces of all three were half concealed by woolen mufflers.

"We're deputy sheriff Jim Baxter's posse," one said. "We caught a horse thief and we're going to take him to Jefferson City where we'll get his mate."

When the ferryman protested that his assistant was on the other side of the river and to ferry the boat across alone was no job for one man, one of the men grabbed him by the coat he had thrown over his nightclothes and snarled: "If you don't want your goddamned boat cut loose tonight, get started and be quick about it."

The frightened ferryman agreed, but as the men rode aboard he saw that Sheriff Baxter was not among them. During the journey one of the outlaws untied the bound and gagged man and said in a low voice to get down "and get the needles out of your feet." When the boat docked at the south bank one of the muffled men paid the fare and, leading the horse of the man who had been again tied, they rode away.

At 3 A.M. the same morning a Mr. Botts, who lived "eight rods from the fork where Liberty, Independence, and Lexington Roads diverge" heard several pistol shots and the sounds of galloping horses. Two hours later a farmer from Independence met a man leading a riderless horse. A buckboard driver meeting the early train also saw this man and the riderless mount. However, when they were later questioned they both insisted he was "a stranger."

At 10 A.M. a laborer walking down the road found the body of a man, a rope wound about his neck, lying in a pool of blood. There were several wounds in his head, shoulder, neck and stomach. The last two shots were fired at such close range that the clothing, skin, and hair had been blacked and burned by the muzzle blast of the revolver. Part of the face had been chewed away by wild hogs.

The body of the stranger was removed to the county morgue and a coroner's jury quickly returned a verdict of a death "at the hands of some unknown party." Days later diligent reporters from Kansas City identified the detective through the tattooed initials "J. W. W." a few inches above the right wrist. The body was shipped back to Chicago.

The Tuesday night following the murder, the James boys and some of their followers were seen near Kearney for the first time since the Iowa robbery. On Thursday night, heavily armed, they rode into Kearney and stopped off at the homes of several citizens who had been heard to discuss the murder and who indicated that the James brothers had more than a little to do with it.

They were told:

"Keep quiet if you don't want your goddamned head blown off."

Apparently they kept quiet because the same week there appeared this story in the *Missouri World* from a correspondent writing from Appelton City, Missouri:

"So great is the terror that the James and Youngers have instilled in Clay County that their names are never mentioned save in back rooms and then only in a whisper. Clay County has a population of 15,000."

11

THE NIGHT OF BLOOD

YELLOWING, fifteen-page letter in the historical archives of the Pinkerton Detective Agency perhaps gives the best clue to the personality of Allan Pinkerton, who chased Jesse James and his outlaws for so many years. The letter, written in the careful Spencerian handwriting of a stenographer in the post-war years of the Civil War, is dated December 31, 1868, and is a review of the work accomplished by the New York branch of the rapidly expanding agency. It is Allan Pinkerton at his best. The letter is brutally frank, every paragraph a shoulder blow. It is amusing to try to visualize the spreading dismay on the face of "Mr. Bangs, the New York Superintendent" who received the letter, as he learns that a new superintendent is coming along to take charge and that, in regard to the "incompetents who have brought disgrace and infamy" upon his office, he is to "give them your boot. Show your fist and let them be kicked downstairs as quickly as possible."

One important paragraph gives a fine glimpse of this determined man. In it Pinkerton could have been speaking of the Missouri outlaws.

> I shall not give up the fight with those parties until the bitter end and the last die is cast whatever that may prove to be; life or death, prosperity or adversity, the present life or the eternity of darkness...I have told Mr. Davies (the new superintendent) how we stand and what his course must be; it must be war to the knife and the knife to the hilt.
>
> You know my policy in such cases, it is no delaying the fight; if a fight has to come, let it come and let it come soon; the sooner the better for all concerned—at all events for me. Delay no fight one moment; make all the attacks you can;

keep yourself right upon the attack and with hands clean and with clear conscience you are sure to win....

The long letter ended on this note:

...and you know that I do not know the meaning of the word "fail." I know no such thing as being beaten in any fight that I go into; going into it as we do and coming out of it as we do with clean hands and a conscience as clear and bright as the sun which rises out of the ocean upon a clear July morning...no power in hell or heaven can influence me when I know that I am right. Remember, sir, that the right is mighty and must prevail and all we have to do is to manage our affairs with discretion, with honor, with integrity and we must and we shall win....

It is clearly the letter of a man equipped with an indomitable and enormous tenacity. A man, too, who once he has begun to fight will never yield and even though beaten to his knees will continue to bring the war to his enemy. The traits found in Allan Pinkerton were handed down to his sons.

Thus, it is not hard to imagine the bitter rage which filled both Allan and William Pinkerton as they gazed down at the body of their operative, James W. Whicher, lying in the cheap pine coffin from the Clay County mortuary.

In one month three Pinkerton operatives, one by special service, had been killed. The score must be evened, the fight must be brought to the enemy's door again and again. Plans were made and another Pinkerton detective courageously volunteered to go into the James country. His name was John "Jack" Ladd.

This operative apparently was a real man of the soil. By slow degrees he worked his way into the Clay County farm district and was soon employed as a hand on the farm of Daniel Askew, near the Samuel place. He was a hard worker, and old Dan Askew probably thanked the fates which led Jack Ladd to his doorstep. After a time Ladd became a member of the Askew family circle, attending church with the family, bowing and passing the time of day after services with Dr. and Mrs. Samuel. There is no record of it, but it was said that the Pinkerton man many times nodded to Frank and Jesse as the outlaws passed the Askew farm.

In January, 1875, the plot was ready to hatch. It was to be the most elaborate yet to wipe out the James gang. Ladd had seen the outlaws in the vicinity of the Samuel place and had been told they were going to "visit the old lady" for a week or two. The detective slipped away from the farm and sent an urgent message to the Pinkerton office in Chicago. Allan and William immediately set out for Kansas City where they set up secret headquarters "at a north end hotel." The local sheriff was taken into their confidence and promised his complete co-operation.

Meanwhile several other operatives and, as one account in the *Kansas City Times* disclosed, "several trusty Clay County men" scouted the Samuel farm home.

Reports were wired daily to the Pinkertons by a leading Liberty, Missouri, attorney who headed the secret committee of townspeople who had grown weary of the brazenness of the gang and the indifference of local peace officers. Later the attorney was forced to flee from Liberty, but he returned after the death of Jesse James.

On January 5, 1875, a message in cipher was sent to Kansas City. Both outlaws had been seen entering the Samuel place. The hour for the attack on the James stronghold was set at 10 P.M. A telegram came back to the Liberty attorney. It read: "Attack Castle James."

An arrangement had been made with the superintendent of the Hannibal and St. James Railroad for a special train to take the posse through Clay County from Liberty. The conductor in charge of the train was a Mr. Westfall. By a coincidence he was to meet and be killed by Jesse James in another train holdup years later.

The day coaches were darkened, and as the *Times* story stated, "The members of the posse boarded five minutes apart."

The train crept over the Hannibal Bridge and into the Clay County forests. The track was perfectly clear; it was a bright, moonlit night and bitterly cold. At the zero hour the posse surrounded the Samuel place.

The men in the lead went to the west side of the house. A window was forced open and a "ball of fire" tossed inside the room. In the house were Dr. Samuel, Mrs. Samuel, and three Samuel children. Outside, the posse stood with pistols cocked. What happened then discredited the Pinkertons in the eyes of the public and switched sympathy to the side of Jesse James. "That night of blood" as it was termed by the Missouri papers, made him a martyr. The "ball of fire" was poked into the hot embers in the fireplace by Dr. Samuel and a terrific explosion occurred. The posse outside could hear Mrs. Samuel issuing orders in a calm voice. When they rushed in they found Archie Samuel, Jesse's eight-year-old half-brother, lying in a pool of blood and Mrs. Samuel's right arm hanging in shreds. Dr. Samuel was wounded slightly in several places. A colored servant was also injured. The little boy's side had been torn open and he died that night.

Ironically, neither Jesse nor Frank were captured. Both outlaws had sensed the danger and fled.

The "bomb throwing" episode rocked the nation and newspaper editorial writers leaped upon the Pinkertons. The two detectives were denounced as being guilty of an "inexcusable and cowardly deed."

Forgotten, of course, were Jesse and Frank James. Nor was it pointed out that both outlaws, knowing that they were fair prey for peace officers, had drawn the posse to the farmhouse by deliberately seeking refuge there. Nor was it recalled that a man had died a frightful scalding death in the cab of his engine when Jesse and his gang overturned the train at Adair, Iowa; an unarmed cashier had been murdered in cold blood; three peace officers had been shot down, one riddled with bullets as he kicked out his life at the end of a rope and his body left for the wild hogs.

The Pinkertons immediately denied that any of their operatives had tossed "a bomb" into the Samuel place. But the denial was lost in the hue and the cry.

What was thought to be a "bomb" was an iron cylindrical flare called "Grecian fire," the type posted today as warning signals about excavations. The flare's contents were either kerosene or turpentine. When it came in contact with the hot embers gas was created and an explosion followed. The Pinkertons knew that the Samuel farmhouse would be a bolted and shuttered fortress and that after a window had been jimmied open some illumination would be needed to silhouette the outlaws whom no one expected to surrender. The explosion occurred when the flare was pushed into the hot coals of the fireplace by Dr. Samuel.

In 1925, William E. Lewis, a well-known newspaper man and a personal friend of Frank James and Sheriff Timberlake, who chased the outlaws for years and who helped to plan Jesse's

assassination, made an independent investigation of the tragedy.
After interviewing the principals still living and residents of the
county, Lewis wrote a series of articles for the *Morning Telegraph*.
He said in part:

There was no bomb. Frank James himself, supported by
Timberlake, stated that there had never been a bomb exploded in his mother's house. The James boys were believed
to have been in the house, but they were not. They had been
there, but the instinct of the partridge had sensed the hunter
from afar and they had fled. The house was surrounded by
detectives who were decidedly anxious to get any members
of the train robbing gang, for several of their number had
been assassinated and one or two killed in open fights with the
outfit.

Mrs. Samuel, mother of the James boys, who was extremely
gifted in an executive and practical way, was in the house
with two children of her husband, Dr. Samuel, when the
detectives and the posse surrounded the house. Mrs. Samuel
extinguished what few lights there were, and what conversation was held with the besiegers was carried on in the darkness.
The law officers and members of the Pinkerton staff who
surrounded the house had prepared for an emergency in the
Samuel house. They carried with them what was known as a
flare. It was a lamp with a hemispherical bottom of cast iron.
The top was of brass and two tubes about six inches long carried the wicks. It was just such a flare that snake doctors and
Tonka bean vendors used on street corners in those days.

The specialty and peculiarity of this lamp which made it
valuable was that it could be relied upon not to tip over.
The heavy weight and the circular iron bottom made the lamp
right itself from whatever position it might be placed. It was
similar to a species of oil can now highly esteemed by plumbers
and automobile men, which will not tip over and waste oil.

This flare, then, the detectives lighted and tossed through
a window. Immediately the interior of the living room was
illuminated and the occupants were palpable targets. Dr.
Samuel who found himself measurably aided in his daily
coming and going with a cane, beat out the light with his cane
and then pushed the light into an open fireplace full of dying

embers. The attack on the house had been made about two and a half hours before midnight when the family was preparing for bed. The so-called "bomb explosion" was the explosion of the flare lamp.

An interesting statement on the incident was given earlier by Luther James, a cousin of Frank and Jesse, in an interview in the *St. Louis Daily Globe Democrat* of July 4, 1902, in which he said that "William Pinkerton had nothing to do with that [explosion]. But the man who did that destructive work to my relatives on that stormy night is dead and buried at his home in Lawrence, Kansas."

Who that mysterious "man" was James never made clear nor did the reporter writing the interview think the point important enough to question him on it.

After the "bombing" Jesse swore eternal vengeance against the Pinkertons. Legend has him going to Chicago to kill Allan Pinkerton. But it is more than legend. Jesse James did go to Chicago and for months stalked the detective. More than once he had Pinkerton or one of his sons in his gun sights but did not fire because: "I wanted him to know who did it."

Jesse told the story to his close friend, George T. Hite, the grocery store owner in Adairville. The Clay County outlaw was not a boastful man and he undoubtedly told the truth. After Jesse's death Hite disclosed the story for the first time as he sat in a barrel seat and interrupted the interviewing by a *Courier-Journal* reporter to sell onions and shovels.

> He [Jesse James] went to Chicago to kill Allan Pinkerton and stayed there for four months but he never had a chance to do it like he wanted to. That was after the Pinkertons made a raid on his mother's house, blew off her arm and killed his step brother. He said he could have killed the younger one (either William or Robert) but didn't care to. "I want him to know who did it," he said. "It wouldn't do me no good if I couldn't tell him about it before he died. I had a dozen chances to kill him when he didn't know it. I wanted to give him a fair chance but the opportunity never came."
>
> Jesse left Chicago without doing it but I heard him often say: "I know that God will someday deliver Allan Pinkerton into my hands."

THE AMNESTY BILL AND
ITS AFTERMATH

WITH public sentiment swinging over to the side of the outlaws following the "bomb throwing" incident, Missouri's celebrated "Outlaw Amnesty Bill" was introduced into the state legislature in the spring of 1875. The author and sponsor of the bill was the Honorable Jefferson Jones, a fighting Missouri Democrat from "the Kingdom of Callaway County," and a powerful friend of the bandits.

Jones, like many Missourians, was quick to apologize for the acts of the gang as stemming from their wartime experiences. The popular attitude was that the bandits were not men of evil or murderous intentions, but were simply men who had been forced by uncontrollable circumstances to commit their transgressions. If society would forgive them and allow them to live normal lives they would become respectable, upright citizens.

Jones' amnesty bill asked just that. It said in part:

WHEREAS, under the outlawry pronounced against Jesse W. James, Frank James, Coleman Younger, James Younger, Robert Younger and others, who gallantly periled their lives and their all in defense of their principles, they are, of a necessity made desperate, driven as they are from the fields of honest industry, from their friends, their families, their homes and their country, they can know no law but the law of self-preservation, and can have no respect for and can feel no allegiance to a government which forces them to the very acts it professes to deprecate, and then offers a bounty for their apprehension, and arms foreign mercenaries with power to capture them; and

WHEREAS, believing these men too brave to be mean, too

generous to be revengeful, and too gallant and honorable to betray a friend or break a promise; and believing further that most if not all of the offenses with which they are charged have been committed by others, and perhaps by those pretending to hunt them or by their confederates; that their names are used to divert suspicion from and thereby relieve the actual perpetrators; that the return of these men to their homes and their friends would have the effect of greatly lessening crime in our state by turning public attention to the real criminals; and that common justice, sound policy and true statesmanship alike demand that amnesty should be extended to all alike of both parties for all acts done or charged to have been done during the war; therefore, be it resolved by the House of Representatives, the Senate concurring therein:

That the governor of the state be, and he is thereby requested to issue his proclamation notifying the said Jesse .W. James, Frank James, Coleman Younger, Robert Younger, and James Younger and others, that full and complete amnesty and pardon will be granted them for all acts charged to or committed by them during the late Civil War, and inviting them peacefully to return to their respective homes in this state and there quietly remain, submitting themselves to such proceedings as may be instituted against them by the courts for all offenses charged to have been committed since the said war, promising and guaranteeing to them and each of them full protection and a fair trial therein, and that full protection shall be given them from the time of their entrance into the state and his [governor's] notice thereof under said proclamation and invitation.

Jones first submitted the bill to Attorney General Hockaday, who approved it. The bill was later introduced. It was promptly ridiculed by the Republican papers, who wept editorially, "Poor old Missouri," while the Democratic press advocated the bill in guarded tones. The *Kansas City Times* boldly endorsed the Outlaw Bill with Major John N. Edwards, who shared the honor with Jones of being the state's chief defender of the outlaws, even going to Jefferson City to lobby for it.

The bill came up near the end of the session. The debates were long and furious. Fifty-six Democrats and two Republicans voted for it and twenty-six Democrats and nineteen Republicans voted against it. It was obvious who were Jesse's friends. The resolution, however, according to the records of the Missouri legislature, "was declared out of order by the presiding officer, for concerning business not embodied in the call for that session."

Before his death Jeff Jones declared that both outlaws were anxious to "come in" and face the charges pending against them. Despite Jones' statement it is doubtful that any of the named bandits would have surrendered. The list of their crimes was too long and bloody. To give themselves up to the authorities meant hanging or life imprisonment. The defeat of the bill now gave them a permanent lease on outlawry from their own state. They made good use of it. In less than a month they struck back, and in badly battered Clay County tragedy piled upon tragedy. Daniel H. Askew, who unknowingly had hired Jack Ladd, the Pinkerton detective, was murdered only a short distance from his own front porch.

After the raid on the Samuel place, Askew, a well-to-do farmer and highly respected citizen of the county, was accused by friends of the outlaws of having been a member of the Pinkerton posse. The farmer heatedly denied participation or even knowledge of the purpose of his farm hand, who had disappeared the night of the tragic raid.

On April 12, Askew walked from his front porch to a nearby spring for water. It was a bright moonlit night. The time, according to the coroner's inquest, was eight o'clock. As the farmer lifted the bucket three shots rang out. All were in the back and he was killed instantly. As his wife and daughter ran out of the house, three horsemen galloped down the road. Although there is no positive evidence, it is said that the assassins were Frank, Jesse, and Clell Miller. A short time later these three outlaws called at the farmhouse of Henry Sears, a short distance from the Samuel place. As Sears came to the door one of the men called out:

"We just killed old Dan Askew, and if any of his friends want to know who did it tell them the detectives did it."

The brutal murder of the old farmer caused widespread indignation, and the fickle tide of public sentiment swung back to the cause of law and order. Editorial writers who had damned the Pinkertons only a few months before now thundered indignantly against the outlaws declaring:

"If this well known and respected farmer can be shot down in cold blood in the dark for his opinions, who then is safe. . . ?"

13.

MUNCIE

AFTER the defeat of the Amnesty Bill the James-Younger gang split up and departed for parts unknown to wait until, in the parlance of the modern underworld, "the heat was off." Frank drifted down to Texas and Jesse to Kansas City. Apparently friction was beginning to develop among the outlaws because from his hideout Frank James sent a long and rambling letter, addressed "to a friend" who thoughtfully sent it on to the editor of the *Pleasant Hill Missouri Review,* who published it. The photostatic copy in the Pinkerton archives covers thirteen and a half pages. It is the typical "I was framed" cry of the criminal.

In it James disclosed for the first time the breach existing between him and his younger brother whom he so affectionately called "Dingus." He wrote:

"We were not good friends at the time [the robbery at the Kansas City fair grounds] nor have been for several years."

The letter goes on to denounce those who had "hounded" poor John Younger "like a wild beast." Not mentioned, of course, were the dead Daniels and Lull.

Before listing his various alibis, Frank James—whom Jim Cummins in later years contemptuously declared "was always sproutin' Shakespeare to us"—sanctimoniously prophesied that "the day is coming when the secrets of all hearts will be laid open before the All-Seeing Eye and every act of our lives will be scrutinized, then will his soul be white as the driven snow, while those of the accusers will be doubly dark. . . ."

After this bit of claptrap he takes up the robberies one by one, with this businesslike preface:

"I will now come to the Ste. Genevieve robbery."

For the rest of the letter he lists each crime and his alibi.

On December 12, 1874, the feud between Jesse and his brother was apparently patched up. On the afternoon of that day, the Missouri outlaw led his gang—with his no longer repentant brother riding at his side—into the town of Muncie, Kansas, eight miles west of Kansas City. It was to be another train robbery. The gang was heavily armed with revolvers and carbines. They dismounted and entered Purdee's general store. The *Missouri Sunday Sun* said the outlaws "chatted pleasantly for a time about the weather" then ended the social call by producing revolvers and tying up the storekeeper. Six other customers who came in were also bound. One was a schoolteacher. After he was searched, one of the outlaws laughed and warned him against "going out with only a shin plaster and a knife." Another tried to escape and was shot in the leg. The bandit examined the wound and casually informed his victim, "It ain't serious. I reckon you won't die from it."

While waiting for the train, "the robbers dressed themselves up in best clothes, selected hair brushes and perfumery, took all the money, silks, laces and then filled their flasks and cigar cases."

When it came to looting, the ex-guerrillas were obviously experts.

While their companions were "dressing themselves," the rest of the gang had taken over the town. Men, women, and children were pushed into commandeered buckboards and driven to the depot where they were put under guard. Several of the men were ordered out and forced to lay ties across the tracks.

At 4:45 P.M. the train rounded a bend and came to a stop, as Engineer Robert Murphy later declared, "about a hundred feet from the ties piled across the tracks."

The train was quickly surrounded by the whooping bandits. One of the outlaws, later identified as Jesse James, ordered Murphy and conductor Brinkerhoff down from the train. Brinkerhoff, ignoring the menacing revolvers, swung off the coach and began to walk back up the tracks.

Jesse rode alongside him. "Where the hell do you think you're going? Get back," he shouted.

Brinkerhoff looked up at the bandit and answered calmly: "I am going to plant a flag a short distance up the tracks. There is a freight due and they might crash into us."

After a moment or two Jesse nodded and waved the conductor on. Brinkerhoff planted the red flag and returned to take his place among the other prisoners.

In the meantime the bandits had uncoupled the express car and forced the engineer to move the engine up to the ties. The door of the baggage car was opened and the messenger, Frank Webster, was slugged and beaten with gun butts. About twenty-five thousand dollars in gold and jewels were dumped into the wheat sack. There were a number of silver bricks in the car, but the bandits left them behind, declaring that they'd "be too heavy for the horses."

The gang were experts in train robbery technique by this time and the passengers were smoothly and efficiently bone-picked of their cash and jewels. Satisfied, Jesse ordered Clell Miller to the engine to blow the whistle. At the signal the passengers were allowed to return to the cars and the gang gathered about their leader in front of the depot. Two of the outlaws were assigned to go through the town killing all horses which could be used by pursuers. When they had returned, the townspeople were forced to remove the ties. The track clear, Jesse ordered the engineer to "get going, and give our love to Kansas City."

As the train pulled away through the dull wintry twilight, the bandits raced through the town howling their rebel cry and firing their revolvers. The total loot was estimated as sixty thousand dollars in cash, jewels, and other valuables.

When the train arrived later at Kansas City, Missouri, with whistle going full blast, the Pinkertons and local police hurriedly organized a posse and raced back to Muncie. The gang was traced to the Missouri state line; there, as usual, it disappeared in Jackson County, where questioners were received with blank looks and shrugging shoulders.

The first break in the investigation came a few weeks later when Bud McDaniels, one of the gang, was arrested by the marshal of Kansas City, after he had started to shoot up the main street. Searched at the jailhouse Bud, who was well in his cups, was found to be carrying more than a thousand dollars in his rough jeans. After a grilling by Pinkerton agents and local authorities, he admitted participation in the Muncie robbery and named his companions. Bud sadly explained that he had returned to Kansas City after he had promised "my girl that I would return with a fortune."

"She was out so I got drunk," he added sadly.

Bud was sentenced to two years in prison but escaped while on his way to jail. He was later killed in a gun duel.

14.

CHOIR BOYS WITH
NAVY COLTS

AFTER Muncie, Jesse, following the guerrilla tactics, broke up his gang until he would summon them for another strike. Jesse and Frank probably rode back into Clay County, but Cole, Jim, and Bob Younger set out for Texas where several out-of-the-way ranches were used by the gang as hideouts. One was in Collins County, northwest of Dallas and conveniently near the Scyene ranch owned by John Shirley, father of Belle Starr. On August 6, 1874, Jim Reed, a Texas bad man and the so-called "husband" of Belle Starr, was shot fifteen miles northwest of Paris, Texas, by Deputy Sheriff John W. Morris of Collins City, Texas. Before he died Reed confessed to taking part in the Gadshill robbery and named Jesse, Frank, and the Youngers as his accomplices. With Reed out of the way, Cole probably had ideas of resuming his courtship.

There is no record of their travels, but it is known that the Youngers finally settled for a time in Dallas. Cole immediately became the pillar of the community, singing with his brothers in the choir of the Dallas Baptist Church and assisting the local marshal in arresting "desperate characters."

The activities of the three brothers in Dallas are outlined in an affidavit, a copy of which is in the Pinkerton archives, signed by

E. G. Bower, who was district attorney of Dallas County from 1874 to 1876 and who later served as a county judge.

Cole Younger, Bower declared, "was a man of kindly nature, entire truthfulness, and heroic gallantry." He added: "Cole, Bob, and Jim Younger sang in the choir of the Baptist Church in Dallas where they were on the side of law and order. The boys were often called on by the sheriff to assist in the arrest of desperate characters and they always responded."

All three bandits were civic-minded, too, Bower disclosed. "They not only sang in the choir," the district attorney said, "but they also assisted in taking the scholastic census of Dallas in 1870."

One can see the huge, solemn-faced Cole and his brothers side by side sharing a hymnbook under the admiring eyes of Dallas' fair sex, while underneath their neat broadcloth coats rested well-oiled and much used Navy Colts—and the three outlaws gently knocking on the door of a Dallas household, sweeping off their broad-brimmed hats and saying:

"I'm Cole Younger, ma'am, taking the government census. Could you tell me how many children you have—your husband's business—?"

One wonders if Mr. Bower ever read the wanted posters. An explanation for his obvious dereliction of duty could probably be explained by his statement:

"I was a war comrade of Cole."

It was the same in other states. The gang could kill and plunder as much as they wanted as long as their victims were banks, railroads, and express companies. These three institutions at the time were popularly regarded as robbers of the people. When they were raided by the outlaws the public generally shrugged their shoulders. Many peace officers, like Bower, were ex-soldiers, and to arrest a "war comrade" was unthinkable—unless of course that comrade had raped your sister, insulted your mother, or stolen your horse. But because he robbed an express train or bank? Never!

William Pinkerton, meanwhile, was slowly organizing a secret intelligence system, employing farm hands, trainmen, itinerant peddlers, trusted law officials, citizens, and businessmen of Clay and Jackson Counties, who were eager to rid the state of the outlaw stigma. The grapevine snaked through the Jesse James

country and linked cities and towns in other states frequented by
the gang to the Pinkerton offices in Kansas City and Chicago.

Thus, in the spring of 1875, William Pinkerton was not surprised to learn that the Youngers were in Dallas and that Frank
James was reported spending his time at a nearby ranch. He
ordered one of his operatives to Dallas to verify the report. In
the interim Jesse rode down to Texas.

On May 12, the James-Younger gang held up the San Antonio
stage, twenty-four miles outside of Austin, Texas. Two of the
five masked men grabbed the bridle reins of the four-horse team
and the others covered the driver and ordered him to "throw
down the box." The eleven passengers, three of whom were
women, were forced to line up alongside the big coach.

There is an amusing, if not probable, tale of one of the passengers, a Bishop Gregg of the Protestant Episcopal Church, in
Austin, protesting against giving up his watch. The bandit, who
held a big Colt uncomfortably close to the parson's stomach,
replied solemnly:

"The Good Book says, parson, when traveling take neither
purse nor script. Therefore we propose to put you back into the
good graces of the Lord. Shell out."

Needless to say the Bishop shelled out. Another passenger,
George Breckenridge, president of the First National Bank of
San Antonio and a well-known Texan, surrendered a thousand
dollars. The total proceeds of the robbery, including cash taken
from the registered mail, amounted to approximately three
thousand dollars.

The outlaws had no sooner disappeared in a cloud of dust than
the grapevine began to hum. The Pinkerton operative in Dallas
trailed the gang to one of its hideouts and wired his Chicago
office. William Pinkerton ordered a raid on one of the known
hideouts of the outlaws. But the luck of the Missourians still held.
While the Pinkertons and local law officers were crashing in the
door, the gang was riding toward Clay County.

For months the border was quiet. After Muncie the Republican
papers again denounced the Democrats for not suppressing the
gang, but the issue soon died. There were more ominous rum-
blings heard in Missouri's political world. The famous "Whiskey
Ring" which controlled nearly every distiller in the state was
crumbling. The scandal, one of the worst in the nation's history,

was to rock the state. Repercussions would reach the very inner offices of the White House. The ring, controlled by a powerful newspaper publisher, a United States Army General, and the St. Louis United States Internal Revenue Collector, defrauded the government of hundreds of thousands of dollars in whisky taxes.

The Missouri press was filled with accounts of the scandal and Jesse must have read them with interest. One can see the outlaw tossing the evening paper aside as he indignantly snorted to his mother, "And they call *me* a thief."

Some time in the spring of the following year Jesse visited St. Louis to check a report he had received that a large shipment of gold was due to leave. It was a bustling city and the Clay County outlaw must have taken in the sights. The community was still buzzing with the dramatic appearance of President Grant at the courthouse, where he had testified in the trial of General Babcock accused as one of the leaders of the Whiskey Ring. On the strength of the presidential testimony Babcock was acquitted. During the afternoon, along with the rest of the male members of the community, the outlaw probably took a position along the main street to watch Louise Hawkins, "the most beautiful woman in Missouri," take her afternoon ride in her buggy. It was a daily and stirring event in the city when "the Sylph," as she was called in St. Louis, took her outing. When General Grant attended the St. Louis Fair in 1874 and was entertained by the leaders of the Whiskey Ring, Louise showered her attention on the President's secretary. To get an idea of what Jesse and the community's males saw, "the Sylph" was described by one of her admirers in his memoirs as "a woman whose plumpness makes her tempting, luscious, delicious, and totally irresistible."

Although he took in all the sights St. Louis had to offer, Jesse stuck close to business. Through some means, probably a bribed railroad employee, he found out that the Adams Express Company and the United Express Company were shipping a large amount of gold on the Missouri-Pacific on Friday evening of July 7. One estimate had the gold valued at a hundred thousand dollars.

Jesse rushed back to Clay County. Riders pounded along the back roads as the outlaws gathered. Some reports have the gang meeting in Clell Miller's shack in northwestern Missouri; others say the plot was hatched in the Samuel farmhouse.

With his gang about him Jesse spread "a state map" on the table and with a grimy fingernail traced the route of the Missouri Pacific Railroad. His finger stopped at a place called "Rocky Cut" on the Lamine River. Here, he told his gang, the tracks crossed a rickety wooden bridge. The spot he had selected was just east of Otterville. With its high bluffs it was ideal. There was only a watchman on the western end of the bridge, Jesse explained, and it would be a matter of minutes to overpower him.

How those rough, bearded faces must have tightened and the eyes glistened in the yellow lantern light when he announced that the cargo of gold was worth about a hundred thousand dollars!

Although it was a beautiful moonlit night the passing scenery had become boring and monotonous to Louis Peter Conklin, of Chicago, the baggage master of the Missouri Pacific train. After the last stop at Sedalia, thirteen miles west of Otterville, where an additional express car had been coupled onto the baggage car, Johnny Bushnell of St. Louis, who was guarding the two safes in the car, one belonging to the Adams Express Company, the other to the United Express Company, had gone back to pass the evening gabbing with the conductor. "Pete" Conklin yawned. He wished now that he had gone along with Johnny. He gazed out at the black forests of Cooper County. Soon the ageless hypnotism of the clicking wheels overpowered him and he dozed. The screeching wheels grinding to a sudden stop brought him awake with a start. He started to rise to his feet when the train gave a sudden lurch, sending him spinning across the car. He looked up into the masked faces of three men who were entering his car.

"Give us the key to the safe, young fellow," one snapped.

"I haven't got it," Conklin said. "I'm only the baggageman."

"Where's the messenger?"

Conklin jerked his head. "Back in the train."

The bandit spokesman grunted. "Come on and we'll find him."

With a gun at his back Conklin found Bushnell. The messenger turned over the keys and they all marched back to the baggage car. By this time several of the bandits outside the train were racing up and down whooping and firing their revolvers.

Bushnell opened one safe and the cash poured into the wheat

sack. Then the leader—later identified by his own men as Jesse James—turned to the other safe and gestured with his gun.

"I can't open it," Bushnell protested. "It's going locked all the way through."

Jesse turned to Bob Younger. "Get an ax, Bob."

Younger returned a few minutes later with a fireman's coal pick and began to hammer at the top of the safe. It barely made a dent in the tough metal. After he had watched impatiently for a few moments, Cole brushed his brother aside.

"Here, let me have it."

With two hundred pounds behind each swing, sparks flew as the pick bit into the metal. Finally a small ragged hole was made in the top of the safe. Cole tried to squeeze his big hand through the opening but it was useless. He was starting again to use the pick when Jesse stopped him.

"Let me try."

Jesse carefully worked his smaller hand into the jagged opening and began to lift out the leather pouch. The hole was too small, but while he held it one of the other bandits slit open the pouch and removed the currency, stack by stack.

When he had finished, Jesse ran a sleeve across his dripping face.

"Damn, but that's hot work," he said. Turning to Conklin he asked: "Where's the water, young fellow?"

Conklin indicated the water bucket and one by one the bandits refreshed themselves.

As they started to drag the heavy wheat sack across the car floor one of the gang said to Jesse:

"Let's get the plugged hats now, Dingus, I need a new super [watch]."

"To hell with your super," the bandit chief snarled, "help with this sack and let's get out of here."

The sack was quickly tied across the back of one of the horses which had been brought to the entrance of the baggage car. As he mounted, Jesse looked back at Conklin and laughed: "If you boys see any of the Pinkertons tell 'em to come and get us."

With a wave of his hand Jesse and his gang disappeared into the darkness. The high bluff banks threw a faint derisive yip-yip-yaw, then all was still. A moment later the serene moonlit night was shattered by excited shouts of the passengers and crewmen as they tore down the barricade of logs and railroad ties. Then, with a series of resounding toots, the looted train chugged off into the night, while in the cars excited groups of men with sideburns and plugged hats discussed the robbery and cursed "that damn James gang."

Several weeks later Hobbs Kerry was arrested and readily confessed to having participated in the holdup. He named the members of the gang and detailed to the authorities how it had been planned and staged by Jesse James. Hobbs, described as an illiterate, was sentenced to the Missouri State Penitentiary for two years, receiving, as the Pinkerton records succinctly state, "a reasonable sentence for aiding the state with his confession."

15.

THE NORTHFIELD BANK
ROBBERY

IT was only sixty minutes after the James-Younger gang stormed Northfield, Minnesota, that an outraged citizenry blasted them out of existence with rifle fire, ancient and rusty firearms, and just plain rocks. Not in five hundred years since the death in 1381 of Wat Tyler, who organized London's mob rule, had there been such an uprising by the defenders of law and order against pillagers and robbers. It demonstrated that peculiar quality of peace-loving citizens everywhere: they will allow themselves to be pushed so far and no further—then God help their antagonists.

What happened on that drowsy afternoon of September 7, 1876, at Northfield, is the stuff from which are made the ballads and songs of a people. The full story, as told here, is based, even to the curses, on the voluminous file on the crime in the historical archives of Pinkerton's National Detective Agency, along with a memorial to Joseph Lee Heywood, the murdered cashier, printed in Northfield more than half a century ago. Compiled by George Huntington, this rare and tiny volume of Americana is thoroughly reliable.

The eight-bandit gang was led by Jesse James. His followers were Frank James, Coleman, Jim, and Bob Younger, Clell Miller, Charlie Pitts, alias Sam Wells, and William Chadwell, alias William Stiles. The outlaws were divided into three divisions: Jesse and Frank James, the three Youngers and Miller, and Pitts and Chadwell. During the actual robbery the gang split up into two trios and one couple. One trio was assigned to the robbery of the bank, the second trio was posted as rear guard to aid in the retreat, and the remaining pair of riders stood in front of the bank to fight off any possible interference. It was the most elaborate robbery the gang had ever planned.

There are two theories as to why the First National Bank of Northfield was selected by the outlaws. The first has Chadwell, who hailed from Minnesota, suggesting it and selling Jesse James the idea that it was the richest bank in the territory; the other, that Cole Younger had received information that General William Butler and a son-in-law, W. A. Ames, of Mississippi, both violently hated by the Confederacy, were the principal stockholders in the organization. The first is probably true.

In August, 1876, the James-Younger gang assembled at Fort Osage Township in Jackson County, Missouri. Guided by Chadwell, they set out for Minnesota. Nearly all of them were well dressed and imposing in personal appearance, well mounted and equipped. Each man carried a carbine strapped to his saddle and two Colts hidden under a long linen duster. They traveled leisurely, passing through cities, towns, and small hamlets. All were well supplied with money and spent it freely. Their procedure was to split up when they entered a town, some putting up for the night at hotels, the others at boarding houses or nearby farmhouses. When asked their business they said they were civil engineers, railroad men, cattle merchants, or horse buyers. They introduced themselves under various names. Three that can be recalled were: James C. King, Jack Ward, and Ira Miller.

The gang traveled as far north as St. Paul and as far east as Red Wing. Pinkerton detectives, later retracing the route, declared that the bandits were on a grand tour of crime, selecting new victims and in each case carefully familiarizing themselves with roads and back lanes, lakes, bridges, and fords. Among the communities visited were St. Peter, Mankato, Lake Crystal, Madelia, St. James, Garden City, Jamesville, Cardova, Waterville, Millersburg, Cannon, and finally Northfield. The tour took approximately three weeks. At the end of this elaborate survey the gang selected the First National Bank of Mankato, at the great bend of the Minnesota River, as their first victim.

Five of the desperadoes rode into Mankato at about nine o'clock on Saturday morning, September 2. They made several small purchases and entered the bank where Jesse James tendered a five-dollar bill for change. It was given him and James left. A few minutes later an excited townsman rushed into the office of the sheriff.

"Jesse James is in town," he cried, "and it looks like he and his gang have an eye on the bank."

The sheriff looked incredulous. "Jesse James?"

"I come from Missouri and know him by sight," the man said. "He's probably got his whole gang with him waiting out of town."

The sheriff grabbed his hat. "By God, there'll be no robberies in this town—let's go to the bank."

Both men hurried to the bank where the employees were alerted and armed and warned of the expected raid. The next night, Sunday, two of the five men who had visited the bank were seen entering a local saloon, described as "a rendezvous for the lowest criminals" and located on the opposite side of the river. This was reported to the sheriff who had the men followed when they finished drinking and rode off.

At noon the next day the gang rode back into town ready for the attack. They had seen the streets at that hour and knew that the force of the bank employees would be considerably reduced. As they rode up the street, Jesse noticed a large group of citizens gathered on the street a short distance from the bank. As they drew nearer, the bandit leader saw one of the men in the group point to him and say something to his companions. The crowd turned to stare. Convinced that they were suspected and might be walking into a trap, Jesse quickly ordered his gang to keep riding. In a few minutes they were galloping out of town.

Unknown to Jesse, the men near the bank were simply "sidewalk superintendents" watching workmen repairing the founda-

25. Bob Ford, cousin of Jesse's, who pulled the trigger to shoot Jesse in the back on April 3, 1882, at St. Joseph, Missouri. The gun he is holding is reportedly the assassination weapon. *(Courtesy National Archives)*

26. H. H. Craig, one of the law officers whom Bob Ford telegraphed to collect his reward after his shooting of Jesse James. *(Courtesy Pinkerton's National Detective Agency, Inc.)*

27. Ed O'Kelly, the man who shot Bob Ford in 1892. O'Kelly, his life sentence commuted, was himself murdered in 1904. *(Courtesy Fred M. Mazzulla)*

28. Mrs. Jesse James, the former Zerelda Mimms and first cousin of Jesse's, pictured with Jesse's armory after his death. (*Courtesy Pinkerton's National Detective Agency, Inc.*)

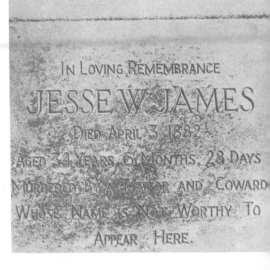

29. Jesse James' tombstone. He was buried in his mother's yard at the edge of a coffee-bean tree. (*Courtesy Pinkerton's National Detective Agency, Inc.*)

IN LOVING REMEMBRANCE
JESSE W JAMES
DIED APRIL 3 1882
AGED 34 YEARS 6 MONTHS 28 DAYS
MURDERED BY A TRAITOR AND COWARD
WHOSE NAME IS NOT WORTHY TO
APPEAR HERE.

30. Frank James, the Shakespeare and Bible-quoting member of the James-Younger gang, in his later years. (*Courtesy Pinkerton's National Detective Agency, Inc.*)

31. William H. Wallace, prosecuting attorney of Jackson County, Missouri, who bravely, but without success, tried to buck public sentiment and convict Frank James of murder when he surrendered to the law. (*Courtesy Pinkerton's National Detective Agency, Inc.*)

32. Jesse and Frank's mother lived to see Jesse assassinated and to bury him. During her sons' long careers in outlawry she never expressed anything but love for her "boys." Many times she berated law officers who came searching for them for "persecuting" her sons. (*Courtesy Pinkerton's National Detective Agency, Inc.*)

tion of a building; the one who had pointed was calling attention to the Missouri outlaw's excellent mount. Ironically, the bank officials had refused to believe that Jesse and his gang were in the vicinity and had failed to take any precautions.,

Out of Mankato, the gang headed toward Northfield. They reached Jamesville that night, eighteen miles east, and late the next afternoon stopped at Cardova, eighteen miles north of Jamesville. After resting their horses they moved northwest to Millersburg, only eleven miles from their goal. There, on the afternoon of September 6, the gang split, four staying in a hotel in Millersburg and the rest pushing on to Cannon City, ten miles away.

Northfield in 1876 was a beautiful and quiet little town in the heart of Minnesota's rich agricultural region. It had excellent railroad facilities and the Cannon River flowed through it supplying the small manufacturing mills with power.

You came across a wooden bridge into Bridge Square from the west. Across the square is Division Street, the main business thoroughfare. At the southwest corner, to your right, is a building called the Scriver Block, with an outside staircase to the second floor. The stores of Lee and Hitchcock and H. Scriver were on the ground floor to your left and the First National Bank in the right half.

On the western side of this building is a narrow alley, with rear entrances to the stores and the bank. West of the alley and fronting the square are the two hardware stores owned by J. S. Allen and A. E. Manning.

On the eastern side of Division Street and facing the square were a number of retail stores. One, equipped with a faded green awning, was the drugstore of Wheeler and Blackman. Overlooking the square was a fifty-foot bluff dotted with residences, churches, and public buildings. Among them were Carleton College and the towering spire of St. Olaf.

It was a few minutes after two o'clock when Bob Younger, Charlie Pitts, and Jesse James clattered over the bridge, crossed the square, and dismounted in front of the bank. After hitching their horses they sauntered up the street to the corner and sat on some dry-goods boxes in front of Lee and Hitchcock's store. Pitts removed a bowie knife from a sheath under his linen duster and

began to whittle industriously at a piece of kindling. His companions talked in low tones. Five minutes later, Clell Miller
and Cole Younger walked their horses down the street. At a mut-
tered command, Bob Younger and Pitts followed Jesse into the
bank. Miller rode up, dismounted, and tied his horse alongside
the other three. He opened the door of the bank, peered in, then
quickly closed it. Cole Younger, meanwhile, had dismounted in
the middle of the street, where he made an elaborate pretense of
tightening his saddle girth.

The activities of the strangers in the hush of the square attracted the attention of Henry M. Wheeler, a nineteen-year-old
medical student home on summer vacation from Michigan University, and of J. A. Allen, owner of one of the hardware stores.
Allen was leaning against the door of his store and young
Wheeler, sitting under the awning of his father's pharmacy, was
idly looking across the square in the bright sunlight. Curious,
Allen began walking down the street. As he made a move to walk
into the bank he was grabbed by Miller who poked a revolver
into into his stomach with a warning to "keep your goddamned
mouth shut."

Allen, grasping what was happening, pulled away and ran
across the square shouting at the top of his voice, "Get your
guns, boys, they're robbing the bank."

Young Wheeler, who had leaped to his feet when he saw Miller
grab Allen, ran out into the square yelling, "Robbery! Robbery!
They're at the bank!"

Cole Younger shouted an order to Miller and both outlaws
sprang into their saddles. Miller jerked his horse about and sent
a bullet whistling over Wheeler's head. He missed, and the boy
ran back to the drugstore.

Up to this time there had been only five outlaws on the scene,
but now three more—Frank James, Bill Chadwell, and Jim
Younger—appeared. Joining Miller and Cole, they began to shrill
their wild cries and ride furiously up and down Division Street
crying, "get in . . . get in. . ."

It was an indescribable scene: heavy Colts slammed, glass windows shattered, bullets whistled through the air, choking clouds
of dust mixed with acrid gunpowder smoke filled the square,
while above everything was the blood-curdling cry of Quantrill's
riders coming in for the kill.

Meanwhile, inside the bank the robbery had misfired with tragic results. At the time of the stickup the bank was housed in temporary quarters. The banking room was in one large oblong space, divided two-thirds of the way back by a railing extending from the south wall to the vault. The rear room, proudly termed "director's room," had a door leading to the alley. It also contained the vault. A counter, similar to a store counter, extended along the side of the space to the director's room. A high railing of clouded glass surmounted the counter. There was a small entrance just wide enough for one person to pass through.

Present at the time the three bandits walked into the bank were Joseph Lee Heywood, the bookkeeper acting as cashier, F. J. Wilcox, assistant bookkeeper, and A. E. Bunker, teller. The three men were busy at their books when the door opened. Heywood smiled and started to rise from behind a desk as the robbers pulled their revolvers. As he slumped back, smile frozen, the Missourians moved in behind the counter. One motioned with his gun to the employees to raise their hands. The order was promptly obeyed.

"There's forty men outside this bank, so don't holler," Jesse snapped.

Turning to Heywood he asked: "Are you the cashier?"

Heywood shook his head. The outlaw turned to the others questioningly. All shook their heads. The revolver swung back to Heywood.

"Open the safe goddamned quick or I'll blow your head off."

"There's a time lock on it," Heywood protested. "I can't open it."

Enraged at the cashier's refusal Pitts struck him across the head with the butt of his revolver. As Heywood fell to the floor the outlaw jerked out his bowie knife and shouted, "Let's cut his damn throat." Leaning over the bandit he slashed at the throat of the helpless man inflicting a slight wound. Pitts and Bob Younger then dragged the dazed man across the floor and propped him up against the bank vault. There they kept thrusting their revolvers into his stomach and demanding that he open the door. The courageous bank cashier steadfastly refused. Had he wanted to he could not have opened the vault. It was already open! The bolt was in place, but someone had neglected to spin the dial.

As a last measure of intimidation Pitts placed his revolver a few inches from the head of the semiconscious Heywood and fired. The heavy slug grazed his ear and tore into the vault, shattering a tin box containing jewels.

Bunker and Wilcox meanwhile were being manhandled by Jesse, who was joined by Bob Younger. When the two employees insisted that they couldn't open the vault, the two outlaws kicked them to their knees and forced them under the counter. As Younger began to search for the cash box, Bunker inched in the direction of a drawer hiding a derringer, but Pitts noticed the sudden move and grabbed the weapon.

"You couldn't do anything with that little gun anyway," the bandit said contemptuously as he pocketed the gun. When Pitts turned away Bunker rose again to his feet intending to make a dash for the rear door. Before he could take a step Younger suddenly turned and clutched his arm, shouting: "Where's the money outside the safe? The cashier's till?" Bunker pointed to a box on the counter which held a few dollars in change. Almost at his elbow at the time was a second drawer containing six thousand dollars. Younger unrolled a wheat sack and jerked open the drawer Bunker had indicated. The small amount seemed to infuriate him and he turned again to the teller.

"There's more money—where is it? Where's the cashier's till? And what in the hell are you standing up for? I told you to get down."

Seizing Bunker by the shirt Younger forced him to his knees. Pressing the revolver against his head the bandit snarled:

"Show me the money you son of a bitch or I'll kill you."

Bunker shook his head but did not answer. Younger cursed again and then Pitts joined him in searching for the cashier's till. Seeing his chance the undaunted teller leaped to his feet and ran into the director's, or rear, room. With a yell Pitts fired. The bullet whistled past Bunker's ear. As he neared the door— more like two large shutters or blinds than a solid door—Bunker flung himself through the air. He crashed through the door, rolling down a small flight of concrete steps leading into the alley. He scrambled to his feet and was a few yards from the entrance to the next building when Pitts stuck his head out of the shattered door, aimed, and fired. The bullet tore through Bunker's right shoulder barely missing the giant subclavian artery and coming out below the collar bone. The teller stumbled but kept on his feet and safely turned the corner of the building.

Pitts ran out of the bank shouting, "The game's up. Pull out or they'll be killing our men."

Bob Younger and Jesse scrambled across the counter and made for the front door. The last one—it is not known which—turned toward the dazed Heywood who was struggling to his feet and fired, killing him with a single shot in the head.

After he had made that wild dive for cover when the bandits had fired at him, young Wheeler, the medical student, scrambled to his feet and made for the drugstore where he had only that morning placed his gun under the counter. But suddenly recalling that he had taken it home at lunch and had forgotten to bring it back with him, he ran through the store without stopping and headed for the Dampier Hotel a few doors away. Hanging on a wall in the lobby was an old army carbine and some cartridges. He loaded the gun and dashed up to the second floor of the hotel, where he took his station.

Meanwhile the merchant, Allen, ran to his hardware and gun store and began loading every rifle in his shop, shouting to the men crouching in nearby doorways and windows to come and get them. One citizen, Elias Stacy, grabbed the first gun, to make good use of it within the next few minutes.

When young Wheeler and Allen had first shouted that the bank was being robbed Manning, the other hardware merchant, had stepped outside his door to inquire as to the cause of the excitement. He quickly found out when one of the bandits pounded past, sending several shots through his window and door. Manning ducked and, when the outlaw had turned back up the street, snatched a breech-loading rifle and some ammunition from his window and hurried up the street, loading as he ran.

The square by this time had been turned into a battleground. Clouds of dust filled the air as the bank robbers raced up and down Division Street and about the square; Colts banged, the outlaws high yip-yip-yaw rose and fell; glass tinkled into the street and bullets ricocheted off the sides of the stone building. After the first few shots, stores and offices were shut and bolted. The postmaster, Captain H. S. French, locked his registered mail in his safe and barricaded the doors of the post office. From the

whooping and shouting and rapid firing the townspeople believed
at first that a large force had taken over the community. One of
the first casualties of the day was a Scandinavian, Nicholas Gustavson. Unable to understand English, he became frightened and
started to run across the street when one of the gang rode him
down. He died in the dust, riddled with bullets.

After the first few bewildered minutes the people of Northfield,
now fighting mad, struck back. The first blood was drawn by Elias
Stacy. As he dashed out into the street he saw Clell Miller. Stacy
took careful aim and fired. The fine birdshot shredded the outlaw's face but failed to inflict a fatal wound. Blood streaming
down his face and half blind, the bandit remained in his saddle,
still slinging lead.

Meanwhile Manning, the other hardware merchant, joined the
battle. When Stacy hit Miller, Jesse and Bob Younger ducked
behind their mounts still tied at the hitching post. Judging that
a dead horse would effectively cripple the gang, the merchant
shot one of the animals in the head, then leaped back behind the
corner of the building. To his chagrin he found the breech lever
had stuck and he was forced to run back to his store for a ramrod
to dislodge the empty shell. In a moment he was back. As he
peered about the corner, Cole Younger saw him and fired. Manning answered, wounding the bandit slightly. Dodging behind the
corner he ejected the shell with the old-fashioned ramrod. Loading, he looked about for another target. Seventy-five yards away
Chadwell had swung his horse around. Manning coolly took aim—
local tradition insists that he took so long those who were watching him kept crying: "Shoot! Shoot!" But the hardware merchant
took his time. His aim was perfect. An autopsy disclosed later
that his bullet caught Chadwell square in the heart.

As the outlaw dropped from his saddle like a poled ox, his
horse dragging him in the dust for several feet, young Wheeler
was poking his ancient army carbine out of the window of the two-
story hotel building. He fired his first shot at Cole Younger who
was racing by. The ball jerked off the bandit's hat as if it had
been attached to an invisible string. As he reloaded, Clell Miller,
swaying in his saddle but still firing his revolver, passed beneath
the window. Wheeler took careful aim. The heavy slug entered
the bandit's breast severing a large artery. Blood gushing from

his mouth, the Missourian slid from his horse. He flopped about in the dust for a second or two, then lay still.

The street battle had now reached its peak with the desperadoes rapidly losing ground. Charging like cavalry the gang rode across the square, reins in teeth and guns blazing. Bob Younger, now horseless, crouched behind the hitching post seeking a target. He spotted Manning reloading and pegged a shot at the hardware store owner. He missed. The merchant jumped behind the corner of the building and Younger, in a crouching run, reached the outside wooden staircase. For several tense minutes it became a deadly personal duel with each man carefully stalking the other. But the outlaw had either forgotten or was not aware of young Wheeler above him in the hotel window. As Younger took aim, the carbine roared. The bullet tore along the robber's right hand shattering the elbow. Coolly changing the Colt to his left hand, Younger fired at Manning but missed.

There was a lull for a moment. Manning left his bullet-chipped post and began to run toward the corner, hoping to trap Younger from behind. Before he started he shouted his plan to Wheeler. The student took this opportunity to reload. Other citizens, armed and unarmed, now began to appear on the streets. The town's ex-policeman, Elias Hobbs, and a Justice Streater began to shout: "Stone 'em ... let's stone 'em." Several citizens adopted the idea and rocks began to fly through the air. It was too much for the gang. They threw in the towel. One of the gang waved his guns and shouted:

"It's no use men—let's go."

After milling about for a moment the Missourians charged down the street. As they came abreast of the bank Bob Younger jumped from behind the staircase, waving his hands. Cole drew up and his brother mounted behind him. With a final burst of revolver fire they fled from the town. The battle was over. The allegedly professional sharpshooters had been outfought, outgunned, and outgeneraled by a handful of amateurs.

The gang was in desperate straits. Chadwell, who knew the territory, was dead, one horse was carrying a double burden, and behind them a posse was gathering. They were less than a half mile from the town when they heard the church bells begin a wild clanging. Through the dust they could see the figures of

horsemen filling the square. But their luck still held. They rode
for Dundas, three miles south of Northfield, ahead of the news.
Telegraph wires were humming, but at Dundas the key ticked
in vain; the operator was at home eating lunch! At Millersburg
it was the same. A few citizens paused to gaze in wonderment as
the five horses galloped past them, but no one raised a challenge.

The gang pushed on steadily all the rest of that afternoon.
They rode five abreast, forcing everyone else on the road into
the ditch. A short time after they had left Millersburg they
stopped a farmer and stole his horse; later they stopped another
farmer and stole a saddle. But toward twilight the saddle girth
snapped, spilling Bob Younger into the road. For the second time
the wounded bandit, now in severe pain, scrambled up behind
his two-hundred-pound brother.

The next morning the weather turned cold and drizzly and
continued like this for days. After the first hue and cry the hunt
became more systematic. From the state's capital telegrams were
sent to almost every town and hamlet in Minnesota. Sheriffs,
posses, Pinkerton men, and vigilante committees began to be
organized into one vast bandit-hunting army. By Friday night
five hundred had reported and were in the field. Two days later
more than a thousand were swarming about the countryside.

On Thursday afternoon the first contact was made with the
outlaws. The encounter was with two scouts who saw the gang
robbing the farmer of his horse. Later, at Shieldsville, fifteen
miles west of Northfield, a small posse had gone indoors, stupidly
leaving their rifles outside, as the gang rode by. Acting under
Jesse's orders the outlaws surrounded the posse and held them
under guard while they rested and watered their horses. Less than
an hour later the same posse exchanged shots with the robbers
in a ravine four miles west of the town, but the Missourians escaped into a thickly wooded area.

On Friday afternoon, September 9, two days after the attack,
at about two o'clock, three possemen exchanged shots with the
freebooters as they were crossing a small ford on the Little Cannon River. There were no casualties and the gang escaped.

They continued to push on. Around Elysian Township they
found themselves in a wild country filled with lakes, swamps,
ravines, and gullies. It seemed ideal to hide in. From an isolated
farmhouse they stole two horses and later that same day stole

two more. Between Elysian and German Lake they made camp, stretching their blankets over the dripping bushes in the form of a crude Indian tepee.

The next day, Saturday, they abandoned their horses and continued their journey through the rugged country on foot. That afternoon they selected a high camping ground built on the lines of a small fort, and here they remained until nightfall. They marched all night and at daybreak again halted near the village of Marysburg. As they stretched out on the wet ground under the dripping trees, they could hear in the distance the solemn tolling of the church bells. That evening they circled the town and spent the night, all Monday, Tuesday, and Tuesday night at a deserted farmhouse. In five days they had covered less than fifty miles.

On Tuesday afternoon they had called on a German farmer near Mankato and purchased some food. On their return to the farmhouse they intercepted a farm hand by the name of Dunning. Upon a promise of secrecy they released him. It was a serious mistake. Dunning immediately notified his employer who in turn called on the authorities of Mankato. The army of manhunters again reorganized. Roads, bridges, fords, and all avenues of retreat were blocked off and a separate force under General Pope of Mankato began a systematic search of the countryside.

It was then that the gang divided, Pitts and the three Youngers forming one branch, and Jesse and Frank James the other. Cole and Bob were wounded; Chadwell and Miller had died in the dust at Northfield.

The decision to split up into two parties was a wise move and was said to have been Jesse's idea. There is a tradition that the split was decided upon when Jesse, haggard and savage, proposed that they cold-bloodedly kill the wounded Bob Younger so that their escape could be expedited. It may be only folklore, but it makes a thrilling scene—the six bearded, red-eyed men sitting in one of the dark rooms of the rickety, deserted farmhouse: Jesse, snarling and ready to claw for his gun; Cole, big and bearish and ready to spring; Bob Younger, burning with fever and clutching his shattered elbow bound with a blood-crusted strip of blanket; Frank James, solemn-faced, ready to quote the Bible or Shakespeare.

On the night of Wednesday, the thirteenth, the Youngers and

Pitts crossed the Blue Earth River bridge. Jesse and Frank, mounted on a single horse which they had stolen from a farm-house, attempted to cross a picket line spread across the road near Lake Crystal. A guard, Richard Roberts, hearing the hoof-beats, fired blindly. A chance shot killed the horse, thus throwing both of the bandits. But their luck still held and they managed to crawl away safely through the darkness.

After they had escaped in the darkness Jesse and Frank stole a span of grays which they rode bareback. Assuming the role of members of a posse chasing the outlaws, they successfully passed through several lines of pickets. The one stop they made for food was at a farmhouse off the main road. The farmer and his family later told peace officers that while the two Missourians were eat-ing they spun a thrilling tale of how they had chased the bandits and engaged them in a vicious gun battle. What a wonderful picture of the two outlaws attacking with relish the heaped dishes as they described their furious clash with the outlaws to the open-mouthed farmer and his family.

On Sunday, September 17, the two outlaws passed the Minne-sota line into what is now South Dakota. In the last forty-eight hours they had covered eighty miles through hostile country. That night they stole a pair of bays and left the weary grays behind in payment. It was one horse deal in which Jesse took the short end. His mount, he soon discovered, was blind in one eye. The nag Frank James rode was even worse; it was blind in both eyes!

They turned southward to Sioux Falls. A driver of the Yank-ton stage hailed them and they returned his greetings. A doctor they passed was not that fortunate; he was forced at gun point to exchange his neat, black, professional-looking suit for Jesse's mud-smeared and travel-worn clothes. The physician later said that the bandit chief was gruff and nervous and his eyes kept blinking. It was just as well that the doctor did not protest too much; that was Jesse's killing mood.

That was the last seen of the James brothers in action. To all appearances they had disappeared from the face of the earth. Large posses and trained Indian scouts hunted for days without uncovering a sign. As a last measure the bordello outside of Mankato, which was the meeting place for the gang before the attempted robbery of the Mankato Bank, was raided by a posse.

There weren't any bank robbers to be found, but two horse thieves were nabbed. There is no record of their names or what happened to them, but one wonders if the frustrated citizens didn't form a necktie party, then and there.

On Thursday morning, September 21, fourteen days after the abortive robbery, telegraph wires began to hum with the news that some of the James-Younger gang had been trapped in a small village of Madelia, twenty-four miles southwest of Mankato, in Watonwan County, Minnesota.

The area was wild and rugged with a chain of beautiful lakes. Five miles southwest of the lake region ran the fork of the Watonwan River.

Earlier in their crime survey the gang had visited this small town and Cole Younger and another of the gang had spent the night at the Flanders Hotel. Sitting in the lobby that night Cole closely questioned Colonel Thomas L. Vought as to the geography of the district, especially the lake region to the north. When he heard the news of the Northfield robbery Colonel Vought surmised that his guests had been the bandits. On his recommendation he and two other men from the town guarded a small bridge between two of the lakes.

The nights were cool and Oscar Suborn, also spelled Sorbel, the son of a nearby Norwegian farmer, made several visits to the three men, bringing them food and coffee and news from the town. Young Suborn seemed particularly interested in the bandits and made the hotel proprietor go over their description again and again. After several nights of huddling before a small fire in their blankets, the volunteer vigilantes packed up and returned to town. Suborn saw them off and promised to keep a sharp lookout for the gang.

On the morning of September 21 four strangers posing as fishermen appeared at the Suborn farm trying to buy food. Oscar gave them a few eggs and, after they had disappeared down the road, mounted the best horse he had and booted it into Madelia. He was a frontier Paul Revere. As he passed each farmhouse he yelled at the top of his voice: "The robbers! Look out! They're about!" Farmers milking their cows looked up and grinned. That Oscar was a one. The boy just couldn't make anyone believe that the Jesse James gang was lurking in the neighborhood.

Less than a mile outside Madelia, Oscar's farm plug stepped into a hole and the boy went flying. Bruised but still determined, he remounted and kicked his nag into town. His first stop was at the Flanders House. There a crowd gathered about the gesturing and stuttering boy. When Colonel Vought calmed him down and heard the story he turned to Sheriff James Glispin and nodded. The lad's description fitted Coleman Younger.

As the news spread, men, women, and children crowded the main street outside the hotel. Most of the townspeople were incredulous and refused to believe the news. A posse slowly formed; Dr. Overholt, W. R. Estes, and S. J. Severson were the first to join Colonel Vought and Sheriff Glispin. C. A. Pomeroy, G. A. Bradford, and Captain William W. Murphy soon came pounding up on horses when they heard it. A telegraph warning was sent to nearby St. James, but the townspeople laughed it off as just another false alarm. G. S. Thompson and B. M. Rice were the only two who would join the men of Madelia.

The posse rode out of town with young Oscar trailing in the rear, pounding the belly of his plow horse with his heels. Within an hour the four strangers were sighted passing through what was then known as Hanska Slough. Sheriff Glispin made a megaphone of his hands and shouted a command to halt. The strangers turned and ran out of sight behind a knoll. Several shots were fired, but the long range made them ineffective.

The posse separated, some going up Lake Hanska and the remainder searching for a crossing. As the two sections of the posse closed in they saw the strangers again. One was hobbling with the aid of a stick. Again they ignored the command to halt. Both Dr. Overholt and Colonel Vought fired, one shot breaking the stranger's makeshift cane. Several more shots were fired, but the men disappeared.

A short time later the bandits appeared on the bank of the Watonwan River opposite the farmhouse of Andrew Anderson. Seeing Anderson in the field they called out that they were possemen hunting the bandits who were reported in the neighborhood and would he dispatch a horse or two across the river? The trick failed. Anderson, suspicious of the rough, bearded men, drove his horses away from the river bank into the opposite direction. The Missourians, no doubt heartily cursing Farmer Anderson, moved up the river to a shallow ford where they crossed. They came down on the opposite bank and ran across Anderson's field to a granary. It appeared that they might make a last stand here, but for some reason they abandoned the idea and fled. A few minutes later Horace Thompson and his son, who were out hunting, came down the road with two livery teams they were returning to Colonel Vought.

The four outlaws ran out of the brush and started to rush toward them, but the hunter and his son pulled their shotguns and the gang turned off the road and scrambled back to the river bottom. The fugitives were now hemmed in on all sides. South of them was a towering, unscalable bluff. On the north, the river blocked their way, touching the bluff on the left and then swinging away from it in a double curve and then back to the bluff again. The erratic course of the river formed a rough triangle, nearly five acres in width and covered with a thick and almost impenetrable undergrowth of willows, wild plums, and grapevines strung about like strands of wire.

Captain Murphy, a former Union officer who had been wounded three times in the Civil War, and a man of great coolness and daring, now assumed command of the tiny force. Picket lines were secured across all possible routes of escape and the best marksmen placed on guard. Then the former army officer called for volunteers to go in and flush out their human game. His plan, he said, was to form a line four paces apart and advance rapidly, drawing the fire of the gang. This way they could discover the hideout of the outlaws and concentrate their fire upon it.

Six men answered within a few minutes. They were to march upright across flat land, overgrown with wild brush, with every step measured by desperate men hiding somewhere in front, their .45 Colts leveled at head, heart, or guts. The names of these six: Captain W. W. Murphy, Sheriff Glispin, Colonel Vought, B. M. Rice, G. A. Bradford, C. A. Pomeroy, and S. J. Severson.

At a signal from Murphy they advanced rapidly across the eastern end of the triangle from the bluff to the river and then, turning to the left, followed the river's course. They had covered about fifty yards when a revolver barked. The bullet struck Captain Murphy in the side, smashed a briar pipe, and lodged in his pistol belt.

The shot was a signal for the battle to begin. Advancing slowly, the six-man posse poured a deadly fire into the clump of bushes

where they could now see that the outlaws were hiding. The firing
was rapid. At thirty feet several rounds were exchanged. In the
brief fusillade Bradford's right wrist was grazed by a bullet and
Severson's side was slightly creased by a passing ball. In a lull
Sheriff Glispin called out:

"Do you men surrender?"

There was silence for a moment or two. Then a weak voice
answered "I surrender." From the brush Bob Younger rose, his
hands held high. "They're all down except me," he called out
helplessly. He threw his revolver in front of him, but a guard
posted on the bluff misunderstood the move and fired, the bullet
wounding the bandit slightly in the cheek. Captain Murphy
shouted a cease-fire order and moved in on the outlaws. The
six volunteers discovered that the remnants of the once powerful
James-Younger gang had been almost torn apart by their deadly
fire. The three Youngers were severely wounded: James Younger
had five wounds, Bob Younger two, and Coleman Younger was
riddled with eleven from chin to ankle. Charlie Pitts, still clutching his Colt, had died with his boots on. Five holes were counted
in his breast. The bank's derringer—"the little gun"—was found
in his pocket.

The posse gave first aid to the bandits and a rider was dispatched to town for a wagon. An hour later the vehicle rumbled
down the road to Madelia. Less than a mile out, it was met by a
large posse the members of which had arrived by a special train
from the nearby and now no longer incredulous community.
They greeted the Madelia victors with a cheer and formed a triumphant escort. The town was packed solid with the curious by
the time the wagon moved down the main street. When the crowd
shouted and waved hats and handkerchiefs, all three bandits,
including the big, bearded Coleman Younger, blood-soaked from
his eleven bullet holes, waved their hats in response.

The three live bandits and the one dead one were removed to
the Flanders Hotel which was turned into a jail and hospital.
Local physicians found the three brothers suffering from exhaus-
tion, exposure, and hunger in addition to their wounds. After
their wounds had been dressed, they were given new clothes and
placed in the best rooms in the hotel.

A heavy guard was posted that evening when some jubilant

celebrants began to turn ugly and shout in the crowded saloons to "string 'em up."

The day following the capture of the desperadoes great crowds filled the town and from dawn to dusk filed past the room where the prisoners lay on cots. The Missourians talked freely, Coleman Younger insisting, "We were victims of circumstances" or "We were drove to it, sir."

In the Pinkerton historical archives, in the dusty file containing the records of the aftermath of the Northfield Bank Robbery, is included a brown and brittle newspaper clipping from the St. Paul *Pioneer Press*, dated September 22, 1876. It is three columns in length and is an account of a visit with Coleman, James, and Robert Younger at their hotel-prison in Madelia.

The author, a working newspaperman, takes off his hat to as fine a piece of reporting as he has ever read. That frontier reporter had all the opportunity in the world to lapse into purple phrases and high-flown dramatics, but he presented rather a dramatic but lucid account of his visit and interview with America's most famous outlaws. He wrote:

> ... both brothers are under heavy guard in the Flanders Hotel and share a bed. Both are terribly wounded and their faces much disfigured. They certainly do not look like the dangerous desperadoes they are. Coleman Younger is a large man with bright red whiskers. He had his right eye bandaged and said that he was suffering from many wounds. James Younger has a frightful looking mouth, with the lower jaw-bone shattered.
>
> I told them I represented the *Pioneer Press* and asked them if they had anything to say to the public.
>
> Coleman said that he was obliged and asked if I would kindly express their thanks to the citizens of Madelia who had treated them with such kindness. He expressed his surprise at such treatment and declared that he was grateful for it. The doctor who was present would not allow them to talk much, and as curious persons were going in and out of the room I left them to call on their brother, Bob.
>
> These two men suffer much and their talk is sometimes delirious. They are brave, never moaning, and are receiving every possible attention.

I found Bob—as he asked to be called for short—lying in bed shackled, suffering from wounds in the breast. He was pleasant, cheerful and communicative. He is a six foot boy, 23 years old, and as fine a specimen of manhood as I ever saw. He has a kind expression and speaks in a low voice using the best of language. During our interview he did not use oaths or slang. He was willing to talk about himself but declined to say anything of the movements of the other men.

I gave him a cigar for which he was very thankful and he smoked it while we conversed. He said that he had tried a desperate game and had lost. He said that he and his brothers were rough boys and used to rough work and therefore must abide by the consequences. He was inclined to think Heywood, the cashier, was more frightened than brave.

He said the shooting was an impulse of passion on the part of the man who shot him. He said they all deeply regretted it. He declared that they could have picked off many citizens, as they were dead shots but did not desire to do murder. He would not say who shot Heywood. He said that the witnesses undoubtedly knew.

This was in answer to my question:

"Did the robber killed yesterday shoot him?"

Of course, he said, he regretted his situation but all chances had been weighed before starting in. He had looked over the other banks before deciding and knew all about those in the larger places. He said he wished now he had taken one of them as the chance to retreat was much better than a small place.

At Shieldsville they had frightened the posse badly but did not shoot to kill anyone. He said they could have easily shot several.

He said they stayed in the woods about Kilkenny Thursday night when they crossed the ford at Little Cannon. They knew the guards had guns but did not know how many. They moved back into the woods but started to make a crossing before the guards were reinforced.

They camped Thursday night where the horses were found. They left about midnight, made a little headway and stopped on a sort of a peninsula, probably half a mile from the German Church. They made a fire there and took comfort.

They shot a pig and a calf in the head but both refused to die and they dared not fire again. They pushed on Saturday night until about midnight and camped. They heard church bells strike and thought it was about a mile away.

They made a fire there and had a good meal of corn and potatoes. Monday they made good headway and at night camped in some bushes in a field. Twice they were alarmed by people passing. They did not go to Indian Lake as proposed by Sheriff Davis.

He said that Dunning, the farm hand they took prisoner, took a solemn oath not to reveal having seen them. He said they would not have shot him under any circumstances and said they did not tie him to a tree from human feelings, as they feared he would not be found and would die there.

While passing through Mankato, the steam whistle of the old mill blew at midnight and startled them. They hid for a while and then passed on, and did not hear or see any guards on the bridge.

After crossing, he said they got four watermelons and had a feast. He said they intended to call around someday and pay the gentleman for them. Then they got two old hens and a spring chicken at a house nearby and in fifteen minutes would have had a good breakfast but they were alarmed by shouting men on the railroad or by pursuers. He said they saw one man looking for boot tracks and then they ran up a bank. It was the closest call they had. They did not cross the Blue Earth River at that time but he said they did later. They kept on through the woods.

Two of the men in their party left (Frank and Jesse James) and as the pursuit was after them, had an easier time.

Bob Younger blamed himself for their capture, as he said he was overcome with drowsiness and insisted to the others on remaining in the field while the others pleaded to go on. He said they would not leave him; had they gone a half mile further they would not have been caught.

He declined saying anything about his previous life. He said they had no regular leader, that every man was expected to do his work, whatever it was.

His wound is in the elbow joint of the right arm, the joint being fractured. He cannot straighten the arm or contract the fingers. He is polite when questioned and is so mild mannered that he would make a good impression on anyone.

He shows much gratitude for his good treatment and said that he fears to give trouble. He says they were all tough and could have endured much longer. He insisted again that it was his own fault that they were captured, as his lagging gave them away.

He said the men who captured them were brave fellows and deserving of much credit.

The dead bandit (Charlie Pitts) is a man of marked physiognomy, coal black whiskers, mustache and eyebrows. His face shows great determination. He must have been killed instantly. On his body were found a compass, a state map, a derringer and a pocketbook containing five dollars. Two of the others had the same amount. James Younger had $150 and Coleman Younger had a pocketbook and compass. No one had a watch. Their clothing was terribly used up. All were well supplied by local citizens. Bob says the coat found in the camp at Mankato belonged to him. They were making due west as near as possible. He would not say where to.

Around the face of the dead man flowers had been placed by some lady in the town and others scattered on his breast. The swollen features present a horrible sight.

Sheriff Barton will proceed to Faribauly by way of Mankato, leaving here at 5:45 A.M. The body of the dead robber goes on the same train to be embalmed. The trip will be hard on these wounded men particularly the one shot in the jaw. He suffers much. The doctor here objected this morning to moving him but the men are plucky and said they will go alright.

The town is filled with people, but all are quiet. One is not admitted to the hotel which is heavily guarded.

When found the robbers had pieces of underwear in place of stockings. Some of Cole Younger's toenails fell off when his boots were removed. He told doctors he did not care for himself, that if he were dead all would be over in five minutes. He was anxious about his brother and told him repeatedly to cheer up. One time he asked the doctor if he would die. While his wounds were being dressed he did not flinch or move a muscle.

He said that when their two comrades left they gave them most of the money, watches, rings and valuables. He said that he thought their chances were best. . . .

The capture of the Youngers was soon humming over the telegraph wires to almost every part of the United States. William Pinkerton and several operatives from Kansas City rushed to Madelia. When questioned, the outlaws admitted their identity to Pinkerton as they did to other law officers but steadfastly refused to divulge the names of their companions living or dead. Meanwhile at Northfield the two robbers killed by the sharpshooting citizens were identified by other Pinkerton detectives as Clell Miller and Bill Chadwell, alias William Stiles.

As the editor of the St. Paul's *Pioneer Press* had disclosed, the wounded prisoners were delivered into the custody of Sheriff Barton of Rice County on September 23 and then taken to Faribault and lodged in the county jail. There were threats of lynching, "but these were quickly squelched by law officers who completely surrounded the jail with a heavy guard and maintained a strict discipline upon those who entered it," as the *Pioneer Press* declared.

In the county jail the Youngers freely gave interviews, insisting again and again that "they were victims of circumstances" and "they drove us to it," and Bob saying quietly, "We are rough men and are used to rough ways." There is no evidence that they boasted of their life of outlawry. In fact all the interviews and stories written about the famous desperadoes pointed up their regret and contrition.

Before many weeks had passed the more seriously injured of the brothers were able to leave their bunks and walk about the cell block. On November 9, sixty-three days after their guns had shattered the quiet of Northfield, the three bandits, still recovering from their wounds, were heavily shackled together and escorted to the nearby county courthouse to stand trial. Four indictments were handed up to Judge Samuel Lord by public prosecutor G. M. Baxter. They were:

1. Accessory to the murder of J. L. Heywood.
2. Attacking of A. E. Bunker with intent to do bodily harm.
3. The robbery of the First National Bank of Northfield, Minnesota.

4. Coleman Younger, as principal, and Robert and James Younger as accessories of the murder of Nicholas Gustavson, a citizen of Northfield, while the three defendants were participating in the robbery of the bank at that place.

Under the Minnesota law a person charged with murder and entering a plea of guilty could not be sentenced to capital punishment. Each of the Youngers took advantage of this statute and pleaded guilty. They were immediately sentenced after receiving a delay of two days in which to make their decision. Judge Lord gave the three Youngers life imprisonment in the state prison at Stillwater, Minnesota.

A few days later the three members of the now shattered James-Younger combination who had blazed their way across the midwest for so many years entered the state penitentiary.

All three stood for a few minutes outside the grim walls talking to the editor of the St. Peter, Minnesota, *Tribune*. According to this interview with Bob Younger:

> He is a man fully six foot tall and well built, sandy complexion, whiskers and a pleasant face. He could be picked out of any crowd as a kind hearted man whom one would expect to readily grant a favor. He conversed freely and answered all my questions without apparent resentment. He admitted that the party was engaged in the Northfield Bank Robbery, and in reply to our question why they had killed the cashier, he replied:
>
> "It was a d--d fool trick."
>
> We asked if he hadn't had a rough time of it in Minnesota and he replied:
>
> "I had never been in anything like that before."
>
> We also asked why they had selected Northfield in preference to any of the other banks, and he said they thought there was much more money to be had there. He said that in Mankato there were three banks and the money was too much divided. In St. Peter they thought they wouldn't have gotten much.

A Madelia lady called to see Cole and told him "she was glad he fell into Christian hands and that he would be well taken care of." The big handsome outlaw replied that he "was grateful for it but could not say that he deserved it."

"Circumstances, ma'am," he said, "sometimes make men what they are. If it had not been for the war I might have been something, but as it is I am what I am."

A few minutes later, with a final wave of his hand to the *Tribune* editor and the lady from Madelia, Cole Younger and his two brothers entered the Stillwater penitentiary.

The final chapter of the James and Youngers was rapidly drawing to a close. Robert Younger, the quiet-spoken well-mannered desperado and a model prisoner, died in prison September 16, 1889, from tuberculosis. He was buried in the old family plot beside his mother and other brother at Lee's Summit, Missouri.

After Northfield, Jesse and Frank fled for Kentucky and Tennessee. They evidently reached Clay County and from there Tyler Burns, a kinsman, drove Frank James and his wife in a covered wagon. At a town Frank took one of the horses, circled the town, and rejoined the wagon later. The wagon with Jesse and his wife was driven by John Samuels, a stepbrother.

They made Nashville, Jesse under the name of Howard and Frank as Woodson. There Bill Ryan, under the assumed name of Tom Hill, and Dick Liddell, as Charles Underwood, joined them. Jesse disliked Ryan and called him on numerous occasions "that damn Irishman." It was here, Cummins said, that the outlaw tried to pick a quarrel with his brother and later with Liddell.

In Nashville Jesse's disguise was so complete that on one occasion he entered his horse at a state fair and rode it himself to win a prize. No one recognized him, though detectives thronged the fair grounds. He was still a name without a face to the Pinkertons and the law officers hunting him.

After an interval in Nashville, Jesse pulled up stakes and left with his family for Kansas City where he vanished. However, the records of the Pinkerton's National Detective Agency later showed that he had taken his family to California from Kansas City where he lived quietly, still using the name of Howard.

For a year there was silence. The Pinkertons expanded their pressure and their operatives were everywhere. Like an exhausted fox with the horns loud in his ears, Jesse knew the end was drawing near. He must keep moving...moving...

It was a harried existence of suddenly telling his frantic wife that they must leave at once; of hurriedly putting the bewildered children in a rickety wagon with the mixed and vague explanations and moving off in the dead of the night. Then, as the inexorable pressure mounted, there were nerve-shattering moments of jerking awake and listening in the night; of groping for the pistol under the pillow at the creak of an ancient floor board; of feverishly asking himself the same questions—who was that man in the sorrel gray who rode past at noon—the man who stepped from the train—a goddamned Pinkerton detective? And what of the members of his gang? Were they still loyal, or were they studying with greedy eyes the reward posters? Could he ever return home? Where were they hunting for him now?

And then he had to go back to Missouri, where the word went out that Dingus was back. Then mysterious horsemen began to make their way toward the secret hideout. The rifle fire and rocks at Northfield had shattered the old gang and Jesse, the lost leader, formed a new one. There were five recruits: Ed Miller, brother of the dead Clell; Wood Hite, a first cousin; Bill Ryan, "that damn Irishman"; Dick Liddell, comrade of the Quantrill days; and Tucker Basham, a simple-minded Jackson County farmer.

They struck first at Blue Cut near Glendale, a small station in Jackson County on the Chicago and Alton Railroad. Here old "Uncle" Herndon, who "knew him well," claimed Jesse met the widow and returned her money because her husband was lying stiff and cold in his coffin in the baggage car. It was near Jeb Crabtree's place where Capt. Harrison Trow said: "Quantrill always stopped for news and food."

At twilight on October 7, 1879, Glendale was roused by the old alarms, the shouting, the tumult of the horses, the firing, shattered windows and lamp lights. Three men on duty at the depot were herded into a storeroom. The incoming train was flagged down and the bandits leaped aboard.

In the express and baggage car the messenger, William Grimes, attempting to hide the thirty-five thousand dollars in his care, was brutally beaten with gun butts. The bandits galloped off with the money and left no clues.

The Pinkertons began again their weary way on horseback through the rough country with the endless, dogged questioning of witnesses whose eyes looked over their shoulders at the name of Jesse James. Enough information was obtained for William Pinkerton and Marshal Liggett of Kansas City to make the joint announcement that the gang had been led by Jesse James with Miller, Hite, Ryan, Liddell, and Basham. Three years later when they surrendered, Liddell and Basham confirmed these identifications to William Wallace, Missouri's fighting prosecutor and racket buster of his day.

And now a familiar face reappeared. He was a big man with a dark beard and a loud voice. Under "Bloody Bill" Anderson he was known as "Big George" Shepherd. His last exit had been at the gates of the Missouri state penitentiary when he said to "Yankee" Bligh, the Pinkerton detective, "I don't know any of the men who were with me."

On his release from prison Shepherd tried for a different part. His outlaw friends saw nothing of him. Marshal Liggett of Kansas City saw a great deal. There were many hush-hush conferences. Reporters for the *Kansas City Times* and other papers, seeking desperately to find what it was all about, were told to stand by for a "sensational announcement." Weeks passed and the earth-shaking bulletin was never given out. Then one day the press was hurriedly summoned and Liggett proudly announced:

"Jesse James is dead. George Shepherd killed him in his camp at Short Creek."

Liggett went on with the story of how he had hired Shepherd as a thief to catch a thief. Armed with a specially prepared newspaper clipping, telling how he was the subject of an extensive police hunt, Shepherd went off in search of the gang in the vicinity of Granby, Missouri. The outlaws "welcomed him with open arms." At an opportune moment, Shepherd said, he killed James but was shot in the thigh by one of the gang who escaped.

The Pinkertons were openly doubtful of Shepherd's story. It was a question of first seeing the corpus delecti. But Liggett was jubilant. He swallowed Shepherd's story, hide and tail, and proudly insisted to the world that Jesse was dead.

Many who knew Jesse joined with the Pinkertons in scoffing at the tale, but when months slipped by with no sign of the gang some of those who scoffed began to waver.

"Maybe he did shoot Jesse," they said. "After all, George Shepherd was known to him and he might have welcomed him as a member of the new gang." But in his Chicago office William Pinkerton refused to believe that the man he had hunted for

so many years was dead. He waited, and while he waited he
plotted.

The year turned, and in early March of 1881, Jesse, his brother
Frank, and the rest of the gang rose from the brush along the
road at Muscle Shoals, Alabama, to rob a stagecoach. Four months
later, on July 10, they swung off their lathered horses outside the
Davis and Sexton Bank in Riverton, Iowa, and robbed it of five
thousand dollars. On their return journey the gang stopped off at
the nearby ranch of Burks and Parsley where they stole "two
fine horses."

The Pinkertons rushed to Iowa but the gang, traveling by horse
relays, left the posses far behind. William Pinkerton now knew
that George Shepherd's story was a fabrication, and messages began to hum along the telegraph to all branch offices "for every
man to be on the alert." The detective declared that Jesse, realizing that the forces of law and order in his own state were now on
the move, was attempting in a series of swift and far-flung raids
to gather together as much loot as possible with the probable
intention of quitting the game for good.

The pressure expanded. The Pinkertons fanned out from
Kansas City and Chicago to cover Missouri, Iowa, and parts of
Texas and Tennessee. Some operatives shadowed friends of the
outlaws, the Samuel farmhouse, weather-beaten ranch houses
nestling in canyons or off lonely roads; others rode trains and
express cars and guarded banking houses in remote farm areas
likely to be struck next.

Five days after Riverton a train was held up outside Winston,
Missouri, and Jesse James killed two men in cold blood. That
night in the hot, dusty express car the disintegration of his band
began. The horns of the hunters were now loud and clear. Soon
there wouldn't be any place left to hide.

Passenger train Number Two of the Chicago, Rock Island and
Pacific Railroad had pulled out of Kansas City at 6:30 P.M., July
15. The train ran over the southwestern division of the road, a
branch of the main Omaha line from Kansas City. It was due in
Davenport, Iowa, at 8:00 A.M. the following morning.

The train had a combination baggage and express car, a smoker,
two day coaches, and a sleeper. The cars were unusually crowded,

and as the train puffed its way through the warm night the idle talk of tired travelers the world over began. There was much to chat about: the disappearance of the James gang during the past year, the shooting of President Garfield, the murder of that foreigner, the Czar of Russia, and the story the Kansas City papers had printed on page one that a street in New York had been illuminated by electricity.

There was some grumbling among the men in the smoker. Two young ladies had invaded it and settled down in one of the faded plush seats. They sat there neat and prim, wrinkling noses and delicately coughing behind bits of lace whenever a male passenger snipped off the end of a stogie with tiny scissors and, lighting up, began exhaling clouds of strong smoke.

At Cameron station, sixty-four miles from Kansas City, where the Rock Island meets the Hannibal and St. Joseph's Road, three men entered the smoker and took seats across from where the ladies sat. Later one of the females said they had been attracted to the men because they were "funny looking as though they wore false whiskers."

The strangers were husky, bearded men dressed in plain black clothes, boots, and wide-brimmed black hats. They spoke in low tones for a moment or two then slumped back in their seats jerking their hats over their faces.

The 6:30 rattled along, stopping at Gallatin, sixty miles from Cameron, and puffing on toward Winston, eleven miles beyond. As he approached the depot town the engineer yanked the whistle cord and the sharp toots echoed and reechoed across the dimming countryside. At 8:30 P.M. the train rolled into the station.

As the train ground to a stop one of the men did a curious thing. He took out a large white handkerchief and, holding it to the window, peered out as if he were trying to get his bearings. As the conductor swung aboard, two men slipped out of the shadows and grabbed hold of the railing of the "blind end" of the baggage car next to the tender. In a few minutes they were crawling along the roof of the car toward the engine.

Inside the smoker the conductor, a smiling, affable man wearing a regulation hat, long-skirted blue coat with a maroon vest beneath, began to collect his tickets and stick his "tabs" into the hatbands of new passengers. As he threw back his head to laugh at the rough pleasantries, his coat swung open showing a heavy watch chain, from which dangled one or two lodge emblems. Suddenly the three bearded men leaped to their feet, heavy Colts, Navy type, in hand. "Up . . . up . . . get them up," one began shouting and firing. An oil lamp shattered.

Then suddenly he stopped firing and stared at the conductor standing white-faced in the middle of the aisle holding his sheaf of tickets. The gunman leaned forward as though he were about to spring. Then, after snarling something over his shoulder to his two companions, he raised both guns and fired. The conductor moaned and staggered back up the aisle. Almost at his heels followed the outlaw, calmly firing at the stumbling man. At the heavy door the conductor fumbled for the knob with bloody hands. By some superhuman effort he swung it open, lurched across the platform, and leaned against the railing swaying with the motions of the car. More shots rang out. Slowly, almost reluctantly, the dying man crumbled to his knees and tumbled down the iron steps into the darkness.

The three outlaws ran up the aisle and looked out. Satisfied they came back into the car, closing the door behind them. Still firing and shouting their order to "up . . . up . . . keep 'em up . . ." they walked through the smoker into the next car.

The disappearance of the three bandits was a signal for a mad exodus of passengers from the car. The first two to reach the rear platform were Frank McMillan, a burly stonemason from Kansas City, and a passenger by the name of Penn. Both men clung to the iron railing asking each other, "What should we do?"

Before the rest of the passengers could leave the car, however, one of the bandits returned and flung open the front door. He fired several wild shots and shouted again for them to put up their hands. For a moment there was a lull as the bearded man, with his unwavering smoking guns, stood in the open doorway glaring down the length of the car at its frightened occupants.

On the rear platform Penn took this opportunity to peer through the heavy glass window of the door. A gun crashed. The glass showered Penn, inflicting a deep gash on his left wrist. At the same time a man's shrill cry came from inside the smoker.

"That's Father," McMillan cried. He sprang for the door and yanked it open. There was a burst of gunfire. McMillan screamed and staggered back across the platform. Before Penn could grab him the stonemason spun about and plunged down the steps.

Meanwhile another conductor, John Southworth, had given the alarm in the next car and ordered all windows locked and both doors bolted. On the rear of the platform at the time of the shooting was C. F. Chase of the Topeka, Kansas, Police Department and Harry Thomas, the brakeman. When the first shots rang out Chase grabbed a lantern.

"I'm going to signal the engineer," he shouted to Thomas and swung out as far as he could waving the lantern. There was no response. The police officer ran back into the car and yanked on the emergency cord. The train ground to a bone-shaking stop as the big wheels skidded on the rails. Passengers and bandits alike were swept off their feet as the cars slammed into one another.

But the gang, no novices at the technique their leader had perfected, soon had the train covered from the locomotive to the last car. Up in the locomotive the fireman, guessing at what was taking place, leaped from his cab and hid himself in a ditch. Two of the bandits leaped into the cab and one fired a shot over the head of Engineer Walcott.

"Pull ahead, damn you. Pull ahead."

Walcott said that he would try.

According to the engineer's story the two bandits shouted that they were going to find the fireman and ran off into the darkness. Walcott took this opportunity to extinguish the lantern hanging over the steam and water gauges and put out the headlight, thus plunging the whole engine into darkness. He later said that he could hear the train robbers cursing loudly as he crawled to the top of the pilot.

Four of the bandits by this time had forced open the door of the express car. Inside were Charles Murray, the United States Express Company messenger, and Frank Stamper, the baggageman. One of the men grabbed Stamper and, beating him with the butt of a revolver, forced him from the car.

"You ain't needed here," he shouted.

Murray made a dive for some packing boxes. A bullet splintered the wood just above his head. Suddenly, from up ahead, a fusillade of shots rang out and the four desperados ran from the car. Murray jumped from the boxes and bolted the rear door. Several bullets crashed through as he swung it shut. As he was closing the side door a bandit on guard outside shouted and fired. Splinters flew. The door quickly rolled shut. Murray now turned his attention to the forward door. As he was about to bolt it the door was flung open. The force flung Murray across the car. Five men poured through the door. Two dragged him to where the safe was located. Another unrolled a wheat sack. After a beating with gun butts Murray painfully opened the safe. Eager hands ripped open the paper coverings. There was only six hundred dollars and a nonnegotiable bond.

"Damn it, where's the rest of the money," the bandit leader demanded furiously.

"That's all there is besides the silver bricks...."

The outlaw shoved his revolver into Murray's face. "We know you have twenty-five thousand dollars. Give it to us or by God I'll blow out your brains."

"That's all there is besides the bullion," the messenger protested desperately. "I..."

The robber slashed him across the face with the gun butt. Grabbing him by the collar he began forcing Murray to his knees. The express company messenger fought back savagely.

"No...no," he cried. "I won't do it...you'll have to kill me on my feet."

For a long, heart-stopping second Murray stared into the gun barrel.

Then, with a curse, the outlaw flung him across the car. Bleeding and dazed Murray slumped to the floor.

Turning to his companions the bandit leader shouted: "Get out boys, there's nothing more for us here."

The side door was rolled open and the gang leaped to the ground. A minute or so later there were several scattered shots and wild shrieking yells, then silence. The holdup was over.

Less than half an hour later the body of the murdered conductor, found in the ditch into which it had rolled, was lifted into the baggage car and placed alongside the riddled corpse of the stonemason. One of the passengers who had helped to search for the conductor's body turned to the engineer:

"What is the name of this poor man?"

"Westphal—Bill Westphal," Walcott answered bitterly.

Conductor William Westphal—the man who had been in charge of the special train which had rolled into Kearney the night of the tragic raid on the Samuel place. Seven years later a strange fate had pushed him into the sights of two Colts held by Jesse James.

That's the story of the robbery and the McMillan and Westphal murders, for which Frank James was to face trial a few years later. No one knows whether or not Jesse recognized Westphal or if he even had a way of knowing him. It is curious that, in Frank James's trial, such a strange coincidence, if it was that, was not brought out.

Governor Thomas T. Crittenden, who had taken office in 1881, accepted the latest outlaw challenge. A Democrat, he had defeated General Marmaduke at the Democratic convention for the nomination and had been elected by a majority of fifty-four thousand. He was a brave and conscientious executive who told his legislature in his message that he had "three well-defined purposes and plans. First the building and establishing of the financial security of the state; second, a broader and far-reaching system of education for our children. Third, a solemn determination to overthrow and to destroy outlawry in this state whose head and front is the James gang."

They were also Crittenden's campaign vows. He now took steps vigorously to fulfill the last one.

There was no law in Missouri which would allow the state's chief executive to offer more than a three-hundred-dollar reward, so Governor Crittenden summoned representatives of Missouri's railroad companies to a secret meeting at the state's capitol in Jefferson City. On July 28 he called the press into his office.

"A reward of $5,000 for the capture of Frank and Jesse James and $5,000 for the conviction of each" had been posted, he told reporters. "It was understood that the railroads would supply the funds."

Curiously, Democratic newspapers immediately approved the plan, but the Republicans denounced it.

The first shot had now been fired in this strange war between the chief executive of Missouri and the Clay County outlaw. It was to be, as Allan Pinkerton once said, a war with the knife and the knife to the hilt.

16.

THE CURTAIN COMES DOWN

T HE curtain was brought down on the long and bloody melodrama on the evening of September 7, 1881, exactly five years after the original gang had been blasted out of existence by the outraged citizens of Northfield, Minnesota.

It was another train robbery with the technique now stereotyped. Even the scenes were familiar: Blue Cut near Glendale and the ties piled across the Chicago, Alton roadbeds, the train halted and the bearded man with the blinking blue eyes poking the revolver in the back of the engineer. "I'm Jesse James," he said, and they took the engineer, Foote, with them to the express car.

There in his peculiar way Jesse formally introduced the members of his gang to Foote and the express messenger, H. A. Fox. "This is Frank James," he said, and then went on down the line of the grinning bearded men: Wood Hite, showing his prominent decayed front teeth; Clarence Hite, Dick Liddell, and Charlie Ford. The introductions finished, the gang set to work. The safe was opened and six hundred dollars tossed into the Missouri wheat sack. The passengers were lined up and relieved of an estimated $1,500 in jewels and cash.

The gang went to their hideout at the home of Frank James on the High River Pike, three miles outside of Nashville, Tennessee. The fighting cocks had come home to roost.

Pinkertons were everywhere; the pressure was terrific and the gang had begun suddenly to be afraid of their leader and of one another. Their evil loyalties were cracking. Faces began to disappear. Almost overnight the gang crumbled and Jesse turned back to Missouri with Ed Miller. Somewhere along the trail James killed him.

The only version we have of the murder is from Jim Cummins.

Near Norborne, Carroll County, Missouri, a man named Sam Burton saw Jesse and another rider pass. The second man was riding a brown horse. Burton took him for Jim Cummins. Later Burton heard that a dead man had been found in a blackberry patch and he rode over to help bury him.

"Burton thought he was burying me," Cummins said in later years, "and plenty of other folks thought so too. It was Ed Miller Burton buried. Jesse had shot him. He soon showed up at Charlie Ford's hiding out place in Ray County leading the brown horse. Charlie asked Jesse where Ed was and Jesse said Ed was seriously ill and had to go to Hot Springs and he didn't believe Ed had long to live."

Meanwhile, a brother of Charlie Ford, Robert, an occasional rider with the Jameses, went to see Governor Crittenden at the St. James Hotel in Kansas City. It was their first meeting. A few months later Ford told a coroner's jury what followed the meeting.

"The Governor told me that ten thousand dollars had been offered for Jesse and Frank James, dead or alive. I afterward told Charlie of the conversation and told him I would like to go with him. He said if I was willing to go, alright. We started that night and went up to Mrs. Samuel and put the horses up." Thus laconically were betrayal and assassination planned.

Charlie and Bob met Jesse in the barn in back of the Samuel place. John Samuel (Jesse's half-brother) had been wounded at a "neighborhood dance" and was expected to die that night, and the clan had been summoned to his bedside. There were some relatives to whom Jesse did not want to speak or to reveal his whereabouts, and he and the two Fords slept that night with the horses. Before dawn they started out and "had supper at one of his [Jesse's] brother-in-law's." From there they journeyed to St. Joseph where Jesse joined his wife and two small children. He spent little time on reunion and with the Fords began a new survey of vulnerable banks. Elias "Cap" Ford, a brother, was now in touch with Sheriff Timberlake of Clay County. Timberlake organized a posse and had a train "with full steam" ready to depart at a moment's notice. The circle was tightening, and Charlie and his brother Bob, with a reward of ten thousand dollars dangling before them, "discussed the matter again and how we could kill him." With an air of a careful and conscientious workman, Bob Ford so testified to the coroner's jury later.

Elsewhere the rats were leaving. Wood Hite, the gangling, stoop-shouldered man with the decaying front teeth which were to be so vividly remembered by the witnesses at the murder trial of Frank James, fled to his father's home in Logan County, Kentucky.

"Old man George Hite's place" was two miles outside of Adairville. A *Courier-Journal* reporter described it at the time:

> A dirt road leads away from the pike through the woods to a lane that reached old man George Hite's. The lane is narrow and lined with stumps, and very rough riding in a vehicle. Great oak trees guard as silent sentinels the whole day and tilled fields face on one side; woods and underbrush the other side. A mile and a half of this and the famous hostelry of the most royal robbers that any land or any people ever knew comes into view. It nestles in a clump of cedars on a grass-browed knoll 100 yards from the lane. It is a modern two-story house and is painted white, looking neat and well kept with its broad porch on the L and green shutters.

Until 1877 George Hite was a wealthy man owning about six hundred acres "of the best land" in Logan County. The property was reputed to have been worth a hundred thousand dollars. He was finally forced into bankruptcy and his wife died. Some time later he married "the prettiest widow in the county."

The *Courier-Journal* called her "plump and handsome and the old man gave her, if not his heart, the keys to the Hite homestead and she took them and she used them."

The reporter added: "She was a fine looking woman and she led the old man a dance that was rapid."

The young widow was rumored to have been the cause of many of the gang's violent disputes. It was said that she fell in love with Jesse James and "that was the cause of disaffection among the Hites, the Jameses and other members of the gang."

For some reason she hated Wood Hite. A short time after his return Hite shot and killed a Negro. One story has Wood killing the Negro, John Tabor, because he found him delivering messages between the young widow and "a young man in the neighborhood"; another has Hite killing the Negro as he sat on a fence "for insulting him as he passed." The latter explanation would seem to be more likely. All the outlaws were suffering from a bad

Courteously Yours

Jos. G. McCoy

33. J. G. McCoy, the founder of the first cow town, Abilene, Kansas, in 1887.
(Courtesy James D. Horan Western Americana Collection)

34. Hole in the Wall, the mountain stronghold in Wyoming which sheltered a community of the lawless. *(Courtesy Condit Collection, Archives and Western History Dept., University of Wyoming Library)*

35. Dugout home of Nathan Champion and Nick Rae. *(Courtesy Peter Decker)*

Chicago 1670
No. 41131

36. Bob Lee, cousin of the Logans, who joined them in the Wild Bunch. (*Courtesy Pinkerton's National Detective Agency, Inc.*)

37. Thomas O'Day, known to the gang as Peep O'Day. (*Courtesy Pinkerton's National Detective Agency, Inc.*)

38. [LEFT] Red Angus, sheriff of Johnson County, Wyoming, in 1892. He was one of many law-enforcement officers who rode with Champion and helped keep the members of Champion's gang from being convicted in Wyoming courts. *(Courtesy Archives and Western History Department, University of Wyoming Library)*. 39. [RIGHT] Cattle Kate, who was hung by cattle barons for refusing to stop trading her favors for stolen cattle. *(Courtesy Fred M. Mazzulla)*

40. The cabin where Butch Cassidy was born. Part of the original ranch it is located about a mile south of Circleville, Utah. *(Courtesy Frank T. Jensen, Cedar City, Utah)*

41. Butch Cassidy, born George Leroy Parker, took the alias by which he is
known in Western outlawry from the man who taught him how to shoot, ride and
rustle, Mike Cassidy. *(Courtesy Pinkerton's National Detective Agency, Inc.)*

42. [LEFT] Butch Cassidy's rogues gallery picture taken in the Wyoming State
Penitentiary on the first and only time he was ever imprisoned. *(Courtesy Victor
Hampton).* 43. [RIGHT] O. C. Hanks, alias Deaf Charley, was the court jester of
Cassidy's Train Robber's Syndicate, the early version of the Wild Bunch. *(Courtesy Pinkerton's National Detective Agency, Inc.)*

44 Elza Lay, "the educated outlaw," who became Cassidy's close friend after Butch was pardoned from the Wyoming State Penitentiary. (*Courtesy Pinkerton's National Detective Agency, Inc.*)

45. [LEFT] Sheriff Frank M. Canton, of Johnson County, Wyoming. Canton a Texan, was in turn a law officer, line stock detective and deputy United States Marshal. He played an important part in the Johnson County War. (*Courtesy Frontier Pix*). 46. [RIGHT] Pinkerton detective Charles A. Siringo, the famous cowboy detective. (*Courtesy Pinkerton's National Detective Agency, Inc.*)

case of the jitters. A curious look was enough to make any of them paw for his gun.

Mrs. Hite declared she witnessed the murder and swore out a warrant. Hite was arrested and taken to Adairville by a Marshal Jeter who threw him into the lockup and posted a guard. Hite escaped and the *Courier-Journal* gives us a delightful account of what followed.

"An hour afterward he [Hite] returned to town and offered in the public square a $100 reward for the return of his guard. He [the guard] couldn't be found; even the $100 had failed to resurrect him and Hite rode out of town without molestation."

Suspecting that a foul deed had been perpetrated upon the commonwealth, the reporter added:

"The $100 may have been given to the guard beforehand. There are a number of people in Adairville who are brave enough to believe so."

Hite, probably out of hundred-dollar bills for police guards, left Kentucky for Missouri. He stopped off at the Ford's farmhouse in Ray County, where Mrs. Martha Bolton, the young and widowed sister of the Fords, was keeping house for them. Also present was Dick Liddell. Hite was there for only a few days when he was killed by Liddell and Bob Ford. In his confession Liddell later told what took place that morning:

> I came down to breakfast and Wood Hite, who had come in from Kentucky three or four days before, was there and Bob Ford came down a few minutes afterwards. When Wood Hite first came in he spoke to me and I told him I did not want him to speak to me as he had accused me of stealing $100 at the divide in the Blue Cut robbery. I told him he lied; he said he could prove it by Mrs. Bolton, and I wanted him to prove it. He then denied ever saying anything of the kind. I told him he did say it and we both commenced drawing our pistols.
>
> We fired about the same time. He shot me through the right leg between the knee and the hip and I shot him through the right arm. He fired four times at me and I five times at him and then I snapped another barrel at him. I drew my other pistol when he commenced falling.
>
> Bob Ford fired one shot at him. I did not know this until afterward when he exhibited the empty chamber. The wound

that killed Hite was through the head. It struck him about two inches above the right eye and came out in front and a little above the left ear.

Bob claimed that his shot was the fatal one. Hite lived about fifteen or twenty minutes but did not speak. Cap and Bob dug a grave in the woods about a mile from the house and buried him. My leg was too sore to help. We did not use a coffin.

When the body was exhumed by the authorities later it was found that Wood Hite's shroud was only a foul horse blanket and his grave a scooped-out hole.

A few days after Hite's death Jesse arrived at the Ford farmhouse with Charlie Ford.

"They tried to get me to go with them," Liddell declared in his confession. "They claimed to have come from Nebraska. I declined to go. I mistrusted Jesse and believed he wanted to kill me. I refused and they left."

James had killed Miller. Hite was dead. Dead men tell no tales. Liddell was afraid of the bearded face and blinking eyes of the man he had followed.

At last when he could stand it no longer he sent his sweetheart, Mattie Collins, to Governor Crittenden. The plump woman in gingham, more at home in her rough farmhouse kitchen than the office of the state's chief executive, perched on the edge of the leather chair and nervously inquired under what condition any of the outlaws could surrender.

"If any of the James brothers wish to surrender, ma'am, it must be unconditionally," the Missouri governor replied firmly.

She whispered, "And the others, sir?"

Crittenden answered, "If any of the others wishes to surrender and assist the authorities in apprehending their leaders, his services will be amply rewarded."

It was enough for Liddell. On the night of January 24, 1882, he "came in." His confession of March 29 was long. For days he gave names, dates, and plans of nearly every holdup the gang had pulled.

Liddell not only sang loud and long but helped to arrest Clarence Hite, Wood's brother, who was one of Jesse's riders at the Winston and Blue Cut robberies. On the night of February 11, Liddell, with police Commissioner Craig of Kansas City and

Sheriff Timberlake of Clay County, rode up to the Hite home and said "they were on the lookout for the James boys." They searched the house and found "Jeff," as Clarence was called, and "after handcuffing him they rode away."

On the morning of February 13, the St. Louis *Globe-Democrat* reported "a mysterious stranger shackled and ironed and heavily guarded was hustled out of the cars and conducted to the Second Street Jailhouse. There he was immured and no one permitted to question him while the officers were as dumb as oysters about the identity of this stranger."

The shackled stranger about whom the jail officers were as "dumb as oysters" was Clarence (Jeff) Hite. Taken to Cameron, Missouri, he confessed to having been a member of the gang which staged the Winston robbery and was sentenced to serve twenty-five years in the Missouri penitentiary at Jefferson City. But the outlaw was in the last stages of tuberculosis. A short time after he entered the penitentiary he was released. He died a few weeks later in the house with the road "guarded by the big oaks."

The sands were running out in other lives. In St. Jo, Jesse, with Charlie and Bob Ford apparently in agreement, selected the Platte County Bank for his next robbery.

Shortly after eight o'clock on the morning of April 3, 1882, Bob Ford killed Jesse James as the nation's most storied outlaw was dusting a picture. For the first time in sixteen years, Ford says, James took off his holsters "with four revolvers" and placed them on a bed. Ford declared he feared for his life and knew he must kill the bandit chief. Only that morning Jesse had learned that Liddell had surrendered. Bob tells how with hammering heart he saw Jesse start as he read the headline.

"I knew then I had placed my head in the lion's mouth. How could I safely remove it?" Ford declared.

James got up, incongruously, to straighten a picture. He liked targets in line. Ford fired and killed him. But the tragic figure that day was Zerelda James, "a pleasant faced woman with light hair and blue eyes" who sobbed bitterly as she knelt in the sun-splashed room to cradle the bloody head of her dying husband. The Fords, with Bob mumbling, "The gun went off accidentally," and Mrs. James, between sobs, answering, "Yes, I guess it did go off on purpose," left the house and hurried to a telegraph office where they sent telegrams to Crittenden, Craig, and Timberlake:

I HAVE KILLED JESSE JAMES. ST. JOSEPH. BOB FORD.

The Fords turned leisurely back from the telegraph office through the morning quiet of St. Jo streets. The reward was sure and their own skins safe. *Their job was done.* The posse, alerted already, probably by the startled telegraph clerk, were racing ahead of them to the "little house on the hill." The Fords had to run for it if they were going to be there in time to be sure of the reward.

They caught up with the posse only at the door with Bob gasping, "I killed Jesse James."

With the Fords at their heels the police posse entered and found the sobbing widow. It is recorded they stayed there for some time and that the newly made widow made dinner for all hands!

At three o'clock the officers and the hired assassins and Zerelda James left for the "old circuit court room" where the inquest was held. The news of Jesse's murder raced through the city and hundreds gathered at the Sidenfaden undertaking establishment, the city hall, and on street corners. There was wild excitement everywhere with report counteracting report and rumor piling on top of rumor: Jesse James was in Texas; Jesse James had a double; Jesse was not killed; he was killed; he had only been wounded; he was a prisoner at the courthouse.

The news was page one. The headlines were bold and black.

The St. Joseph *Gazette* cried:

"Jesse By Jehovah."

The St. Joseph *Evening News* solemnly declared in its black banner: JUDGMENT FOR JESSE—THE NOTORIOUS BANDIT AT LAST MEETS HIS FATE AND DIES WITH HIS BOOTS ON.

The *Kansas City Journal* wept: "Goodbye Jesse!"

The accounts of the assassination ran for columns. No twentieth-century metropolitan newspaper could have covered the story more completely and more competently. It was all there, from the first report of the bullet to the last sob of the widow.

One of the most dramatic moments of the day was the appearance of the Ford brothers and Liddell all "heavily armed" at the coroner's inquest. A wave of sound rolled from the courtroom out into the street when the clerk called "Charles Ford."

On the witness stand he testified that he was about twenty-four years old and had lived in Ray County near Richmond "for about three years." He met and became acquainted with Jesse James soon after his residence began, and last November left the farm and went to Kansas City. While there he again met Jesse James.

"Did he ask you to join him?"

"Jesse James asked me if I did not want to take a trip with him, and we would go and make a raise somewhere. He was living in Kansas City then. We left Kansas City on the fifth and arrived in St. Jo on the eighth, and went to Twenty-first and Lafayette streets where we lived until the day before Christmas, when he rented the house where he was killed and we lived there ever since. He said he wanted to take a trip out through Kansas and see how the banks were situated and said he would get the men, and wanted to know if I knew of anyone we could get to help us. I told him I thought I could get my brother to help if I could go down and see him. So we went down there and we went to his mother's and stayed there until Friday night, and then we went to my brother's and stayed until Saturday and started to St. Jo, where he said for us to stay until night and he went on in. He said there was going to be a murder trial in Platte City, and we would go up there and if the bank was all right we would rob it. He said when they were making the speeches everybody would be up to the courthouse and we would rob the bank."

"Well, now, explain how it was you came to kill him?"

"Well, we had come in from the barn where we had been feeding and currying the horses, and Jesse complained of being warm and pulled off his coat and threw it on the bed and opened the door, and said that he guessed he would pull off the belt as some person might see it. Then he went to brush off some pictures, and when he turned his back I gave my brother the wink and we both pulled our pistols, but he, my brother, was the quickest and fired first. I had my finger on the trigger and was just going to fire, but I saw his shot was a death shot and did not fire. He heard us cock our pistols and turned his head. The ball struck him in the back of the head and he fell. Then I went out and got our hats, and we went and telegraphed Captain Craig and Sheriff Timberlake what we had done. Then we went to the marshal's office and asked a policeman that was there if he knew where the marshal was. He said that he did not, but that he would go with us to look him up. I asked a gentleman up town if he knew where the marshal was, he said he had just seen him get on a car going down in that direction. I said that that was probably where they were going, and that we might as well go down there, and I told them who it was in the house and who it was that killed him, and how it took place and where his pistols, gun, and jewelry could be found and from there we came up here."

"How did you know it was James when he came to you?"

"He came to my house two years ago last summer; he was a sporting man and so was I; he gambled and drank a little, so did I. I was acquainted with Miller, and he came with him and introduced him as Mr. Johnston. He stayed until the next day and he left, and after that Ed Miller told me it was Jesse James. I did not see him any more for some time, and when I did see him I asked him where Miller was, and he said that Miller was in bad health, and that he did not think he could live long. Then I did not see any thing more of him until the next spring. He was there two or three times last summer. Then he came down last fall."

"He asked you to do what?"

"To help rob trains and banks. I have been with him ever since."

"Had you any intention of leaving St. Jo soon?"

"Jesse said he would like to rob a bank and look around a little beforehand and I started out with him. He went first to Hiawatha, then to Pawnee City, from there to Forrest City, then to White Cloud, Kansas, from there to Forrest City to see how the bank at that place was situated. He said that he liked the way the bank at Forrest City was situated, and said he wanted to take that bank, but I told him I did not want to go into that as I was sick then. We came up to Oregon. He said that he wanted to look at that bank, and from there we came down here, and that is the only trip I ever made with him. He would go into a bank with a large bill or several small ones to get changed and while the cashier was making the change he would take a look and see whether they were caged up, what sort of looking man it was, and whether they had a time lock or not."

"How did you get your living?"

"I was not at any expense. I did not spend any money. He had a good deal of money. He had some $1,500 or $1,600."

"Where did he keep it?"

"I don't know."

"Where did he get it?"

"I have no idea where he got it. I guess he must have got it robbing."

"Did Bob, your brother, come here to assist in robbing a bank?"

"Jesse had looked at a bank at Platte City. He said they were going to have a murder trial there this week, and while everybody would be at the courthouse, he would slip in and rob the bank, and if not he would come back to Forrest City and get that."

"What was your idea in that?"

"It was simply to get Bob here where one of us could kill him if once he took his pistols off. To try and do this with his pistols on would be useless, as I knew Jesse had often said he would not surrender to a hundred men, and if three men should step out in front of him and shoot him he could kill them before he fell."

Robert Ford, "the young man who did the shooting," was then called, and as the man who shot Jesse James walked forward, he was the center of every eye in the room. He gave his evidence clearly, and stated that when he went to Ray County to live he heard about the James boys, but did not meet Jesse until three years afterward. He came with Ed Miller. He testified that he had known Miller and he knew they were talking and planning "a train robbery." Last January, he said, he went to Kansas City and had an interview with Governor Crittenden about capturing Jesse, at the St. James Hotel.

"Did the governor tell you anything about a reward?"

"He said $10,000 had been offered for Jesse or Frank dead or alive. I then entered into arrangements with Timberlake and Craig. I afterward told Charlie of the conversation I had with the officers and told him I would like to go with him. He said if I was willing to go, all right. We started that night, and went up to Mrs. Samuel and put the horses up.

"John Samuel [Jesse's half-brother] was wounded, and they were expecting him to die. There were some friends of the family there whom Jesse did not wish to see him, so we stayed in the barn all night until they left, and that was pretty nearly daylight, and we stayed in the house all next day, and that night we started away. That was on Thursday night; Friday night we stayed at his brother-in-law's. We left Mrs. Samuels' and went about three miles into the woods for fear the officers would surprise us at her house. We started from the woods and came up to another of his brother-in-laws and got supper there and started from there here."

"This was last week?"

"Yes. We came at once to St. Joseph and then talked over the matter again, and how we could kill him."

"What have you been doing since you came here?"

"My brother and I go down town some times at night and get the papers."

"What did you tell Jesse you were with him for?"

"I told him I was going in with him."

"Had you any plans made to rob any bank?"

"He had spoken of several but had made no particular selection."

"Well, now will you give us the particulars of the killing and what time it occurred?"

"After breakfast, between 8 and 9 o'clock this morning, he, my brother and myself were in the room. He pulled off his pistols and got up on a chair to dust off some picture frames and I drew my pistol and shot him."

"How close were you to him?"

"About six feet away."

"How close was the hand to him which held the pistol?"

"About four feet I should think."

"Did he say anything?"

"He started to turn his head but didn't say a word."

"How often has Charlie been at home since he first went to Jesse's house to live?"

"Once during Christmas."

"Has he not been home since then?"

"No, sir; he came to my uncle's."

"How often has he been at your uncle's?"

"I saw him twice; once when he was there, I was in Kansas City."

"Was Jesse James unarmed when you killed him?"

"Yes, sir."

"Do you remember ever hearing any of the Samuel family calling him by name?"

"They always called him 'Dave'; that was the nickname. They never called him anything but Dave."

"Did any one speak to him and call him by name?"

"Yes, I heard his mother speak to him and call him Dave and he called her Mother."

"Do you know any one that can identify him?"

"Yes, sir, Sheriff Timberlake can when he comes; he was with him during the war."

This closed the testimony on Monday, and court adjourned to meet at 10 o'clock the following day. At that hour, the St. Joseph *Gazette* reported, "an immense crowd filled the room. There was great excitement to see Little, Mrs. Samuel, and Mrs. James, both of whom entered the court after the testimony was about half over."

Mr. Henry Craig, police commissioner of Kansas City, was the first witness examined. He testified:

"I was not acquainted with Jesse James personally, but am positive the body of the dead man is the outlaw, as it corresponds with the descriptions I have heard. I know Robert Ford, and for two months he has assisted Sheriff Timberlake and myself in the endeavor to capture Jesse James. He was not employed regularly by us, but acted in good faith, and according to our instructions, and assisted in every way he could to aid us. Charlie Ford I have never seen until I came to St. Jo, but understand he and Robert had some understanding."

Sheriff Timberlake of Clay County was next called, and said he was sheriff and was acquainted with Jesse James "during life" and recognized the body as that of Jesse. He testified he had known him since 1864, and "saw him the last time in 1870. Knew his face as well as any one. He had the second joint of his third finger shot off by which I also recognized him. Ford was acting under my instructions and said if he could see Charlie Ford we could accomplish our end the sooner, and he acted squarely to all agreements."

Dick Little, or Liddell, was then called. "I have seen the body of the dead man and recognize it; I was with him a good deal last summer and know him perfectly; I also recognize him from the wounds on hand and on the right side."

Charles Alderman, who kept a livery stable in St. Joseph, was the next witness. He testified that "he was a trader; was not acquainted with Jesse James in life; have seen the body and recognize it as that of a man I traded horses with but did not know who he was, and last Saturday I got it back from Charles Ford, who has been at my place several times. He said he wanted a horse for his uncle, who I now presume was Jesse James."

Deputy Marshal Finely of St. Joseph followed the liveryman: "I was not acquainted with Jesse James; went to the house where he was killed in answer to the telephone where the man was killed; found him on his back, and from Mrs. James got a description of the two men who killed the man and started out in search of them. She said one was her nephew and the other a young man, both named Johnson, but no relation. As we were going out we met the boys coming back. Bob said: I am the man who killed the person in the house. He is the notorious outlaw, Jesse James, or I am mistaken, and I can identify him. He described the wounds on Jesse James' body. He told us there were two watches and some diamonds in the house. We could not find them at first, but did find a necktie and a gold ring with the name of Jesse on the inside. Afterward we found two watches in the trunk. There was some small change in an old pocketbook, which I gave to Mrs. James. On a one-dollar gold piece as a scarf pin were the initials J. W. J. Most of the property is now in the hands of the city marshal."

When the name of Mrs. Zerelda Samuel was called "every man in the courtroom stood up for a good look at the mother of the dead bandit, and as she passed up the center aisle with the wife and the children of Jesse and a Mrs. Turner, the crowd parted right and left" and the party passed the reporters' table and took seats directly in front of the coroner.

Her testimony was as follows: "I live in Clay county, and am the mother of Jesse James." Here she broke down and moaned several times, "Oh, my poor boy. I have seen the body since my arrival and have recognized it as that of my son Jesse; the lady by my side is my daughter-in-law and the children hers." (Mrs. Samuel again broke down at this point.) "He was a kind husband and son."

Mrs. Jesse James was asked if "any valuables" had been taken from the house at the time the officers arrived and she detailed the articles found by the city marshal.

This concluded the testimony. It was announced that a recess would be taken, and the courtroom began to empty. Mrs. Samuel arose as did Mrs. James, and as Jesse's mother turned and faced the crowd she spied Dick Liddell. Raising the stump of her right arm, she shouted: "Traitor." Liddell, white faced and shaken, hurriedly left the courtroom.

The coroner's jury returned for deliberation, and in about half an hour returned the following verdict:

STATE OF MISSOURI ⎫
                   ⎬ ss.
COUNTY OF BUCHANAN ⎭

An inquisition taken at St. Joseph, in the county of Buchanan, on the third day of April, 1882, before me, James W. Heddens, M.D., coroner of the county aforesaid, upon their view of the body of Jesse W. James, then and there lying dead, S. H. Sommers, W. H. Chouning, J. W. Moore, Thomas Norris, William Turner, W. H. George, good and lawful householders of the township of Washington, who, being duly sworn and charged diligently to enquire and true presentment make, how and in what manner, and by whom the said Jesse W. James came to his death, upon their oaths do say:

That the body of the deceased is that of Jesse W. James and that he came to his death by a wound in the back of his head, caused by a pistol shot fired intentionally by the hand of Robert Ford, in witness whereof as well as the jurors aforesaid, have to this inquisition put their names at the place and on the day aforesaid.

> James W. Heddens, coroner
> S. H. Sommers, foreman
> W. H. Chouning,
> J. W. Moore,
> Thomas Norris,
> William Turner,
> W. H. George.

That night there was more excitement when Missouri's chief executive, Clay County officials, and close friends of Jesse James arrived on the Missouri-Pacific to identify the body. There were Governor Crittenden, Clay County's outlaw-busting prosecutor William Wallace, Mattie Collins, Mr. Mimms, at whose house Jesse had first fallen in love, and James Wilkinson. The last man off the train was a slender, grim-faced man in a business suit with the pants legs stuffed into knee-high black boots. Of all those who had come, Jesse would have given him the warmest welcome. His name was Harrison Trow. "Captain Trow"—who had ridden many long and weary miles at the side of the outlaw leader under

Quantrill, Anderson, and Todd. After James had been killed, Crittenden had sent an urgent telegram to Trow requesting him to come at once to St. Jo and identify the body.

"I wired I would, providing I could go armed," Trow said in his memoirs. The Missouri's chief executive answered that "it was perfectly satisfactory" for the guerrilla fighter to return with his six-shooters.

Trow arrived with several ex-guerrillas, "for I did not know how I stood with the people of St. Jo," he explained. "I was just playing safety first."

17.

GOOD-BY JESSE

EVEN after death Jesse was wanted by the police. There was a dispute between Police Commissioner Craig and Clay County's Sheriff Timberlake over the body. Craig refused to release it and the special train was forced to wait from 10 A.M. to 6 P.M. Timberlake wired the executive mansion at Jefferson City:

"What must I do? The officers won't either turn over the body of Jesse to his wife, or his arms to me."

Crittenden wired in return to O. M. Spencer, the Buchanan County prosecutor:

"Just informed your officers will not turn over the body of James to his wife nor deliver his arms to me. I hope you will have done both. Humanity suggests the one and a preservation of such relics for the state the other. His jewelry should be held for the present. The *Globe-Democrat* said he had on my lost watch."

The last was a bit of facetiousness by the governor. Some fifteen years before someone had stolen his "fine gold watch" and some of the Republican papers wrote with tongue in cheek that Jesse James was wearing it, and had wired Crittenden to come and get it. The entire incident, now folklore, was nothing more than a newspaper joke.

That evening, with a large mob watching silently as the soft April twilight closed in, a messenger from the prosecutor's office climbed aboard the train with orders to proceed. Before the train could start for Cameron, however, Mrs. Samuel insisted on being led back to the baggage car to view the coffin of her son to make sure it was still there and had not been stolen.

She was led back by the officers to view the five-hundred-dollar casket which had caused the *Ralls County Herald* to say that morning: "When he gets across the creek the people over there will take him for a banker."

Satisfied that the corpse of her son was safe, Mrs. Samuel joined her daughter-in-law and the train set out for Cameron.

As the train left St. Jo's station, the *Kansas City Times* reported: "A man pulled a pistol on Mrs. Samuel but was promptly thrown out the door to land in the street. He was shot at but not hit."

The scene at the station must have been a weird one with the Clay County officers leaning out the windows blasting away at the mysterious stranger while the mob ducked for cover and, in the coach, the grief-stricken wife of the outlaw hugging her two small children and wondering what more could happen to her in this world of guns and violence.

The same reporter described the huge crowds lining the roads and fighting and brawling at each stop to catch a glimpse of the casket or the outlaw's wife and mother.

In Kearney, a *Kansas City Journal* reporter joined Dr. Reuben Samuel as the farmer-physician sadly paced the streets. He was in his late fifties, the reporter declared, about five feet eight inches in height, with gray hair and beard and dark eyes. He wore an old black felt hat, woolen shirt, dark coat, and reddish overalls tucked in heavy boots. He seemed "very much affected" by the outlaw's death and "spoke severely of the manner of his death." He showed the newspaperman two telegrams. One was from Timberlake which read: "Will bring the remains by special train today." The other was from Mrs. Samuel. It said: "Will be in Kearney at 2 P.M. How is John?" John, Jesse's half-brother who had been shot at a neighborhood party, was still very low. Young Samuel, who recovered, was a quiet and mannerly young man "but decidedly wild when under the influence of liquor," the *Journal* declared.

A son-in-law, William Nicholson, waiting for the train, said that the family "was not surprised" by Jesse's sudden death. "It was looked for and expected," he added. Jesse, he said, had been warned many times about "giving his confidence to supposed friends." In Kentucky, Hite, the crippled storekeeper, echoed the same doubts:

"I could hardly believe he would trust a boy like Ford and let him know where he lived."

The following day the coffin was set up on chairs in the lobby of the Kearney House, the local hotel, and the lid removed. Large crowds filed past. Many were residents of Kearney who knew of Jesse only as some fabulous legendary character. More than one was heard to gasp and whisper: "Is that him? Why, I used to see him riding down the street!"

Jesse must have laughed in the shades. Even in death he was only a name without a face.

Funeral services were held at the Kearney Baptist Church where a passage from the Book of Job was read—

"Man that is born of woman is of few days and full of trouble."

Before the funeral cortege set out for the Samuel farmhouse the pastor requested that because John Samuel, the wounded boy, "was very low" and the grave was close to the house, only relatives attend the interment.

In the quiet of the dying afternoon the coffin was lowered into the deep grave at the foot of a coffee-bean tree, in a corner of the yard of the Samuel place. After the mound had been patted down with shovels, Mrs. Samuel and Jesse's widow planted flowers. Later a white marble shaft was erected above the grave, with this inscription:

Jesse W. James
Died April 3, 1882
Aged 34 years, 6 months, 28 days.
Murdered by a traitor and a coward whose name is not worthy to appear here.

Jesse James had come home.

18

HE "CAME IN"

WHILE the curious were filing past the five-hundred-dollar coffin of the most notorious outlaw in America's history, Missouri's Republicans were making political hay out of "this act of legalized murder." Party organs fanned the temper of the public to a white heat. The incident was used to discredit Crittenden and his administration and to split the Democratic party of Missouri "by aligning union sympathizers against the ex-confederates and to gain credit for themselves."

Twice Republican members of the legislature tried to ram through resolutions condemning Crittenden for the assassination of Jesse James. It was an astute political move. Once the resolution had been passed, G.O.P. leaders could denounce the Democratic party for publicly endorsing "this act of legalized murder." If it failed, the same leaders could hail the defeat and construe it as a rebuff to Crittenden and his administration by the people's representatives.

Both resolutions were declared out of order. On a vote to take an appeal from the chair's decision, the house divided along straight party lines.

The turmoil hissed and bubbled, simmered and finally congealed. But it raged again a few months later when a solemn-faced man quietly walked into the office of Governor Crittenden and slowly unbuckled his broad leather holster from which hung a revolver and cartridges. . . .

It was just five thirty on the afternoon of October 5, 1882, when a reporter for the Sedalia, Missouri, *Dispatch*, softly closed the door of the anteroom of Governor Thomas T. Crittenden's office in Jefferson City, Missouri. The reporter nodded to several men who were huddled in a group and speaking in low and ex-

cited tones. His eyes rested thoughtfully on a slender, slightly bald
man in his late thirties, with a drooping, fair mustache who was
sitting in a chair off to one side of the room. Dressed in somber
broadcloth, he could have been a clergyman awaiting an audience
with the state's chief executive. The newspaperman crossed the
room and drew up a chair.

"Are you the noted Frank James?"

Jesse's brother smiled. He was lacking several teeth. "I am
Frank James. It does not become me to say whether I am noted
or not."

"Why did you surrender? No one knew where you were in
hiding, nor could anyone find out."

"What of that? I was tired of an outlaw's life. I have been
hunted for twenty-one years. I have literally lived in the saddle.
I have never known a day of perfect peace. It was one long,
anxious, inexorable, eternal vigil. When I slept it was literally
in the midst of an arsenal. If I heard dogs bark more fiercely than
usual, or the feet of horses in a greater volume of sound than
usual, I stood to my arms. Have you any idea of what a man must
endure who leads such a life? No, you cannot. No one can unless
he lives it for himself."

"What do you expect?"

"A fair trial. In coming as I have directly to Governor Crittenden I have acted in perfect accord with my summing up of the
man. I have always declared and do now declare that he alone
of all who engaged in the hunt for the outlaws was the one single
man actuated by a principle. The balance hunted for gain or
fame. Governor Crittenden hunted to vindicate the law and ex-
tirpate train and bank robbery from the state."

"Has Governor Crittenden made you any promises?"

"None. You have read his letter in reply to mine, and except
what that contains, he has never said another word. I do not want
him to make me any promises. Wait until the courts decide
whether I am guilty or not guilty. I do not deny that I want one
single chance to prove that my surrender is in good faith, and
that I can become once more a good citizen. Governor Crittenden
can afford to give me that chance. He has already done what has
never been done before in this state, he has made highway robbery impossible."

"Will you tell me something of your past life?"

"No, not now. I have nothing to tell you. The present is mine and the future. Let the past go, but this I can say truthfully and without boasting, that I am not nearly so bad as I have been repre- sented to be, and that there is not a drop of blood on my hands except that shed in open and honorable war. I was a guerrilla. I fought the best I knew how with Quantrill, Anderson, and Todd; but I never in all my life slew an unarmed man or a prisoner. Ask any of my comrades in Clay, Jackson, Lafayette, Howard, or Randolph counties if this is not so. You may think that I tell you this to soften my fate, and strengthen my case before the people, but I do not. I tell it to you because it is the truth, and because I have been described in some newspapers as a monster of cruelty who delighted in bloodshed and murder."

"Where do you go from here?"

"Directly to Independence, in Jackson County, where I shall remain until this whole affair is settled. I have come in volun- tarily and surrendered, and of course there can be no doubt as to my intentions. I am fully resolved to abide the result, what- ever that may be, and face the issue like a man."

"Have you been hunted much lately?"

"Yes, if the newspapers tell the truth, perhaps I have been. Within the past six months I have seen and talked to not less than eight well-known detectives and have talked with them freely about myself at that. Suspected me? No, of course not. If I had even revealed my identity they would have laughed at me for being an impostor."

"How do you account for this immunity from recognition?"

"In quite a simple manner. In the first place I have never had a picture taken of myself since 1863. That portrait of mine in Edwards' *Noted Guerrillas* was taken from that picture. If you ever have seen it you will admit, I think, that I have changed greatly since then. Again, I have been very little in Missouri for the past ten years. Those who knew me in Clay and Jackson counties knew me as a beardless soldier. You will be astonished when I tell you that I have lived in Texas, California, Arkansas, Louisiana, Mississippi, Tennessee, Virginia, Maryland, and New York. I lived four years on one farm in Tennessee and worked as hard as any man ever worked. I would have been there today but for events in Missouri over which I had no control, and which brought men to my house, whose presence would have destroyed me. I was forced to move on in self-defense, and look out for another hiding place."

"People in Missouri think that you do the most of your hiding in the brush. It is there that the authorities look for you. How about it all?"

"The best hiding place in the world for a man with money is some big city. Most people look alike there. If he will use ordinary precaution there he is comparatively safe. He must lie close, go out but little, make no acquaintances, having nothing peculiar in dress or manner, and above everything else, never talk. Ninety-nine times out of a hundred it is the talking men who get caught."

"Have you secured any lawyers yet to defend you?"

"No, I have not. My friends will attend to that for me. They will endeavor, I understand, to obtain the services of Colonel John F. Philips and the Honorable Charles P. Johnson. I am a poor man, and have but very little money. I must do the best I can."

"If you have no objection, will you tell me something about the Fords?"

"I have nothing to tell you about them. I prefer not to talk of myself in any manner, or of anyone connected with myself. I am to be tried, you know, and then you can see what will be developed."

"Have you perfect confidence in the good faith of Governor Crittenden?"

The outlaw smiled. "If I had not," he replied wryly, "would I be here in his private office? Yes, I do trust-him fully."

The incredible interview ended at this point when "quite a number of people pressed forward to shake the hand of the out-law and subject him to a multitude of questions on a number of subjects."

All of Missouri had been patiently waiting for Frank James to surrender, but the quiet unceremonious way in which he "came in" took the state by surprise. The populace was disappointed and felt somewhat cheated. After all these years and the millions of words ground out by the pulp writers, they had more or less expected him to charge into Jefferson City mounted on a big bay and bristling with guns while a gang of yipping bravos thundered past in final salute.

But this tired, weary man of thirty-eight was done with all of that. Only too well did he know that the glamor and melodramatic romance of outlawry belonged to the blood-and-thunder fiction writers; to him his career as a bandit represented only bitter, wasted years filled with murder, dark violence, twisted hates, and loneliness.

"I want to live like other men," he later said, wistfully, "you know, with a home, a wife, and children ... where you don't have to worry about receiving a ball in the back when you go out for firewood."

It was a yearning they all had for peace and security; only a few would find it.

That Frank James had surrendered was important news throughout the nation. In New York it was on page one in Dana's *Sun* and Pulitzer's *World*. The Missouri *Republican's* bold and black classic headline read: "HE CAME IN!"

The surrender was a result of a long period of negotiations. At various times, it is said, Mrs. Samuel, Mrs. Frank James, leaders in the Democratic party of Missouri, and attorneys had attempted to hold conferences but had failed. At last, on October 1, 1882, somewhere in St. Louis, Missouri, the outlaw sat down and wrote a long and verbose letter to Crittenden offering to surrender.

The letter contains many flowing phrases and bears the unmistakable fine hand of Major Edwards, the Missouri newspaperman. In it, James points out rather candidly that even during the writing of the letter, he was prompted to abandon it for fear of not receiving a fair trial, "having for twenty years proved my ability to evade capture."

He closed with:

> I submit that it is not an improper question for your consideration whether it would be better to have Frank James a hunter of fugitives than a fugitive. Whether Frank James humbled, repentant, reformed before all the world will not be an example more fraught with good to the rising generation than Frank James a mysterious stranger or the occupant of a felon's cell or grave ...
>
> I am prouder of the nerve which has enabled me to take this step in behalf of my better nature, than any courageous act of my past life.

As he wrote, or dictated, his lines the ghost over his shoulder had a strangely familiar smile; it was thin-lipped—and contemptuous.

Governor Crittenden replied the morning after he received James' letter. He wrote:

State of Missouri, Executive Dep't
City of Jefferson, Missouri, Oct. 2, 1882.

Frank James: Sir—Your letter dated St. Louis, Oct. 1, 1882, has been received in which you apply to me for amnesty or a pardon. Under the constitution of the state I cannot grant a pardon, even if agreed to, before conviction of some crime. Whether you can be convicted of any violation of the law it is not for me to say; that the courts of the state will determine in the proper way when you are before them.

I think it was wise in you to abandon the life you are charged with leading, and in surrendering to the legal authorities of the state or county in which you are located. If innocent of these charges, then you will have an opportunity to prove it to the world; if guilty, the law decrees the punishment. If you surrender, you, as any other man charged with crime, shall and will have a fair and impartial trial. The intelligence and character of the courts of this state are ample guarantees of such a trial without any prejudice or sympathy of the people but under the judicial form of justice and well established laws. As determined as I am to see the laws enforced against all grades of crime, I am none the less convinced of the importance to society of having every man within the grasp of the law protected in his rights, however lawless he may have been, when he yields voluntarily and submissively to that law and appeals to that and me for justice and mercy.

You may be innocent or you may be guilty of all the heinous crimes charged to you. That, the court will determine, as before said, and after the voice of the court is heard, then if it becomes necessary, I will decide what my action will be.

Yours truly,

Thomas T. Crittenden

James, undoubtedly in the vicinity of Jackson County, entered Jefferson City on the fourth, "coming in from the west on Conductor Hooten's train."

Frank's "friend," probably Major Edwards, that perennial defender of the gang, told the trainman who this quiet stranger was. "Notwithstanding that he had an immense train—12 cars filled to capacity—he [Hooten] found an isolated seat for James in the rear of the car, where, completely in the shadows, he would be free from all recognition."

It is an amusing scene of the flustered conductor rushing up and down the crowded aisle seeking out a quiet corner for his famous rider. One wonders what excuse he gave to oust the grumbling passenger who had that seat "in the shadows." There was probably many a night that the Hooten grandchildren heard the thrilling tale.

When the train arrived at Jefferson City, Frank did not get off at the depot but the square above, and walked to the old McCarthy House where he registered as "B. F. Winfrey, Marshall, Missouri." He was accompanied by Major Edwards.

The next morning the outlaw discussed the crops, weather, politics, and a variety of other subjects with the hotel's proprietor, Colonel Burr McCarthy, who probably thought this garrulous guest was an amiable drummer. In Heinrich's barbershop James continued his discussion as he was lathered and shaved. That afternoon he walked about Jefferson City, visited the capitol, the Supreme Court building, and the adjutant general's office where he shook hands with a number of unsuspecting high state officials.

It was as always; a name without a face.

Back at the McCarthy House, Frank was joined by Major Edwards. After lunch they bought the evening papers which the outlaw read while the newspaperman dozed. At five they left the hotel and walked slowly in the direction of Governor Crittenden's office. At five thirty they were ushered into his anteroom. Finis C. Farr, Crittenden's private secretary, was summoned and the governor's letter was handed to him. He glanced at it briefly.

"Just a moment, gentlemen," he said and went into the private office.

Frank quietly took a chair near the window where the Sedalia reporter found him.

The grapevine, meanwhile, hummed furiously. Capitol employees, political bigwigs, and state officials began drifting into the anteroom on various pretenses to catch a glimpse of the famous outlaw. Many of them shook their heads incredulously. This—this slender, almost bald man with the sad eyes, drooping mustache, and weary face; this man who looks like the picture

of Uncle Jeb in the family album—is he the famous bandit, the
brother of Jesse James...?

They stared and they wondered. It was as always. Too often we
fail to realize that the heroes and the villains who played their
roles in the past were flesh and blood. That a man of consummate
evil usually looked the part of a merchant or a bootmaker.

Farr at last returned and nodded to Edwards and James. The
bandit rose, hat in hand, and followed them into the office of the
governor of Missouri. Several openly curious state officials watched
as they entered. Crittenden had invited them, but he had refused
to disclose the reason.

After shaking hands with Governor Crittenden, Edwards, who
had a flair for the dramatic, said in a loud voice:

"Governor Crittenden, please allow me to introduce to you my
old friend, Frank James."

Governor Crittenden offered his hand. "I am glad to meet you,
Mr. James."

The outlaw smiled and shook the outstretched hand. "I am
too, sir," he said.

There was a murmur of surprise from the onlookers. They were
swept off their feet. A legend had walked into the room.

As they watched wide-eyed the fabulous bandit slowly unbuckled a thick leather belt weighted down with a holster and
cartridges. The revolver was a businesslike .44 caliber. The
bronze buckle of the belt had the stamp in the center—"U.S."
James handed the gun—butt first—to the state executive, saying
in a low calm voice:

"Governor Crittenden, I want to hand over to you that which
no other living man except myself has been permitted to touch
since 1861 and I say that I am your prisoner. I have taken all the
loads out of the weapon and you can handle it with safety." The
freebooter pointed to the buckle. "The cartridge belt has been
mine for eighteen years. I got it in Centralia, 1861."

Crittenden replied:

"You shall have every protection afforded by the laws of your
country, and as fair a trial as though you were the son of a
president."

The bandit was ordered to be taken to Independence and
jailed there to await trial.

The train trip was, as one reporter wrote who followed the

entourage of state officials, marshals, and curiosity seekers, "the most remarkable trip ever witnessed, with large crowds gathering to see the famous outlaw at every stopping place."

When the train stopped at Lee's Summit, the *Sedalia Dispatch* reporter wrote, one of his ex-guerrilla friends shouted to Frank "we are all friends up here," and the bandit responded to tell Frank Maddox to "come and see me if I am alive."

At Pleasant Hill a crowd of nearly a thousand had gathered, also at Lamonte, Warrensburg, and Holden, and "not a single harsh word was spoken of the prisoner."

It was a dramatic ending at Independence. While a huge mob watched, his one-armed mother rushed forward and threw herself into his arms sobbing, "Buck, Buck," her favorite nickname for her oldest son. Next came his wife and then his small son Robert.

"As Frank James took the handsome little boy into his arms and the child began to prattle and pat his father's cheeks the crowd broke down and stout men and sympathetic women wept."

It was a great play and the crowd loved every tear it shed.

But to many of the law-abiding citizens of the community it must have been a bewildering sight.

Prosecutor Wallace, who stood the state on its ear in 1880 when he campaigned on a platform that the James boys were thieves and murderers and he would break them up if elected, asked that the outlaw be tried for the murder of Pinkerton Detective Lull who had been killed and left for the wild hogs on the road just outside of Independence.

The evidence was so flimsy, however, that it was decided to try the Bible- and Shakespeare-quoting thief in Daviess County for the murder of Frank McMillan, the stonemason, during the train holdup near Winston on July 5, 1881.

The trial opened on August 21, 1883, and so great were the crowds who fought to get in that it was held in the opera house at Gallatin, Missouri, instead of the courthouse. The St. Louis *Post Dispatch* declared that the trial of Charles J. Guiteau for the murder of James A. Garfield "was no more carefully watched than the James trial by the people of the United States."

Poring over the records of the trial, the author of this narrative is struck with the carnival-like similarity between the trial of the famous bandit and another "trial of the century" when Bruno Richard Hauptmann was tried in the Flemington, New Jersey, courthouse for the murder-kidnaping of the Lindbergh baby. At both trials tickets had to be issued. While the politically connected no doubt got the best seats in Gallatin, at least there were no perfumed chorus girls in mink coats fighting to attend, nor were there small children shrilly selling visitors grisly replicas of the "kidnap ladder."

The trial lasted eight days. Wallace presented most of the evidence along with the prosecutor, W. P. Hamilton, of Daviess County. Frank James' legal battery was the most brilliant the state had seen for many years. It included Colonel John F. Philips of Kansas City, a federal officer in the Civil War and later a federal judge; former Lieutenant Governor Charles P. Johnson of St. Louis, one of the most brilliant criminal lawyers in the country; the Honorable John M. Glover of St. Louis who served in Congress; Colonel C. T. Garner of Rochamon; William H. Rush of Gallatin; and Joshua W. Alexander, who served in Congress, and later, for a time, as secretary of commerce in President Wilson's cabinet.

Wallace insisted that Frank James, Jesse James, and Wood Hite were the three men who had entered the coaches and fired the shots which killed the stonemason and conductor. Dick Liddell and Clarence Hite, he declared, had crawled over the roofs of the cars and guarded the engineer.

The defense stoutly declared that the fifth man was Jim Cummins and not Frank James.

Liddell, the state's star witness, took the stand and put the finger on Frank.

Yes, he said, the fifth man was Frank James and not Jim Cummins.

A number of alibi witnesses refuted him. They included Mrs. Bolton, at whose house Wood Hite was killed, and several of the Fords. All testified that James had been at their house in Texas at the time of the robbery. The married sister of the outlaw swore that he was "reading and resting" in their home about the time the crime had been committed. On the other hand a rural clergyman created a sensation when he dramatically identified Frank James and Clarence Hite as the men who had stopped at his house located near Winston on the day preceding the robbery and double murder.

Wallace brought out in his direct examination of the clergyman that James had discussed Ingersoll and Shakespeare and at one point "declaimed a piece and remarked, 'that's grand.'"

Another state's witness, Ezra Soule, also identified James as one of the two men he came upon in the woods at sundown. The scene was a short distance from the spot where the robbery took place.

During the trial Wallace notified the railroad to produce certain witnesses. The railroad kept delaying, and finally on the grounds that they might suffer recriminations, this large business corporation refused to allow one of their employees to testify. Outraged, Wallace threatened to subpoena everyone in the railroad from the president down, and under these threats the trainman was produced. But when he arrived the man was so petrified with fear that Wallace was forced to send him on his way.

"He went scooting down the street to the depot and that's the last we saw of him," the prosecutor later said.

Wherever he was Jesse must have surely grinned at such a sight.

About the third day of the trial one of the most colorful men of his day, General Jo Shelby, arrived in town to testify for his friend and former comrade in arms. Shelby was an impressive figure with his flowing shoulder-length hair and broad-brimmed stetson. He was the picture of old-fashioned southern chivalry that had gone with the wind of the Civil War. During his examination he clashed with Wallace and, as the story goes, invited the prosecutor out on the field to settle their differences. Wallace, probably bored with the general's many volunteered recommendations of the shining character of the outlaw, ignored it. Later when the day's session was over he received a note. Tradition has it that he was challenged by Shelby. No matter what it was, he tore it up and left the courthouse with a bundle of law books bound for a conference with his assistants in his office. At one point in the street a plank bridged a morass of mud and water. He was about to step over the makeshift bridge when he looked and saw Shelby also about to cross.

Both men stared at each other, the famous Confederate officer erect and glaring, Wallace cool but slightly lopsided from the cumbersome law books, and perhaps wondering if the general was seeking him with pistols at twenty paces.

Suddenly after a long, tense moment, Shelby bowed and backed off the plank. With a wave of one hand he invited Wallace to cross first. The prosecutor nodded and clumped past. Onlookers gave a sigh of relief.

The days dragged on, hot and sticky. Both sides summed up brilliantly. The jury was out three and one half hours and returned a not guilty verdict. There was "a burst of applause from the spectators who rushed up to Frank James and tried to shake his hand."

The finding of the jury was bitterly criticized. The Jefferson *Daily Tribune* announced that all the jurors were Democrats and the verdict "was nothing more than could be expected." The paper also pointed out that Colonel Philips, one of the James lawyers, "was a prominent Democrat and a power in the party."

As before, the politicians fumed and fretted; the Democrats accused the Republicans; the Republicans, the Democrats.

Wallace ordered the outlaw returned to Independence to stand trial for participation in the Blue Cut robbery. The state's highest court meanwhile handed down a decision that a person who has been convicted for a crime was not a competent witness. Liddell was a convicted horsethief and had served time in state's prison. Wallace immediately petitioned the governor for a pardon for his witness. It was refused, and the prosecutor dismissed the indictment against James.

A year later Frank was taken to Huntsville, Alabama, to stand trial for participation in the Muscle Shoals robbery of the United States postmaster in March, 1881. The evidence was weak and he was acquitted.

But before he could leave town James was startled to find himself quietly arrested by a Sheriff John F. Rogers who had secretly entered the town and registered under a false name at the hôtel. The Republican papers cried "fraud" and declared the "arrest" was nothing more than a "hoax" to prevent the outlaw from standing trial in the hostile state of Minnesota for the Northfield robbery.

On February 21, 1885, the case against Frank was mysteriously dismissed. The St. Louis *Globe-Democrat* indignantly called it a "burlesque," pointing out that the main prosecution witness was dead and adding:

"He would have been dead in a short time if he had appeared against the Democrat's pet."

Although it has been denied, there is little doubt that the

careers of Governor Crittenden and Prosecutor William Wallace
were ruined because of the fight they waged against the Clay
County outlaws. Wallace was turned down for the Congressional
nomination and Governor Crittenden "was refused by his party"
the gubernatorial chair for the second time.

In August, following the Frank James acquittal, John Sapping-
ton Marmaduke, with whom the guerrillas had fought during
Price's last raid, defeated Crittenden for the gubernatorial nomination at the Democratic convention.

The Republican Greenback and Labor parties formed a coali-
tion "to defeat the Democratic party for its alliance and protection of notorious confessed bandits whose presence in Missouri
has driven immigrants from its borders and capital from its industries."

The Republican convention met at Moberly, Missouri, but a
few days before it was to open huge posters, scattered about the
community, announced the appearance of Frank James at the
annual county fair on the day the convention was to open.

In a hastily called meeting, the Republican state committee-
men voted ten to seven to move the convention to Jefferson City.
The Democratic papers crowed lustily.

The election was bitterly fought. Old scars were rubbed raw;
forgotten hates and feuds of the Civil War were revived. When
the votes were counted, Marmaduke was Missouri's next governor.

But the ghost of the James-Younger gang could not be stilled.
Rumors swept the state following the election that the Minnesota
authorities were dusting off the old Northfield indictments and
preparing to ask Missouri to extradite their famous and now retired outlaw. The Democratic party seethed beneath the surface.
The ex-Union soldiers, officers, and sympathizers urged Marmaduke to throw Frank James to the hounds if the occasion should
arise, while the ex-Confederates in the party solemnly informed
the newly elected chief executive that his honor and the honor
of his state was at stake. After all, Jesse and Frank had ridden at
his side against the blue bellies in '64....

The issue died. Minnesota never asked for James. The indictments gathered dust in the pigeonholes. Missouri politicians soon
found more serious domestic problems to fight over and Frank
rapidly slipped into obscurity.

The James-Younger gang was resurrected by the politicians just one more time. During the Teddy Roosevelt presidential campaign Frank James endorsed the fighting roughrider. Republican papers throughout Missouri "made much of it." But in a few days it was forgotten. Old-fashioned outlawry, with its train and bank robbers, attracted only little attention from the cynical citizens of the new-born twentieth century.

19.

COLE AND JIM COME HOME

ON July 10, 1901, the Minnesota Parole Board signed paroles for Coleman and James Younger after they had served nearly twenty-five years of their life sentences. The third brother, Bob, had died of tuberculosis on September 16, 1889, slightly under thirty-three years of age.

The fight for paroles for the Youngers had been going on for years. Influential men of both Missouri and Minnesota sent out thousands of pamphlets, printed at their own expense, and inundated the parole board and the governor's office with mail.

Just as fierce in his determination that the outlaws should not be paroled was William Pinkerton and his now world-famous detective agency. The public might have forgotten, but to this man, who had such a burning respect for law and order, the Youngers had killed and looted and they must pay in full for their crimes. If the Youngers were to go free, he argued, what of the smaller criminals, the unknowns who must pay for their deeds behind bars until the last minute of their sentences? It was not justice, William Pinkerton insisted as he informed the Minnesota parole board and the governor that he would fight such applications with every faculty at his command. He did, and it was not until the turn of the twentieth century that the Youngers were finally released. The parole, however, was limited and confined them within the borders of the state of Minnesota.

Former Governor William R. Marshall was one of the many high state officials who fought for parole of the outlaws. In 1886 Coleman Younger, writing him in gratitude for his efforts, said in part:

"As for the war. I have said that I was engaged in the bloody warfare on the border of Missouri and Kansas. As you truthfully said in your letter to the *Pioneer Press,* it was little better than murder on both sides. That is the original cause of my being in prison today."

One wonders what would have been Cole's answer to the question: "Cole, what about the other men who fought at your side with Quantrill and who returned from the war to become law-abiding citizens—even leaders of your state?"

In his letter Cole also took the occasion to deny the tale that, to test a Winchester rifle, he had killed fifteen Federal prisoners captured by the guerrillas.

"The whole thing," he wrote, "was so absurd that I never supposed any sensible man to believe it. I have always supposed the story was gotten up by some reporter as a burlesque on sensational newspapers."

One wonders why he never requested that it be cut out of the original manuscript of the Appler biography, the material of which the author declared had been supplied by the outlaws themselves and members of the family.

The names of the men who wrote letters on behalf of the prisoners are indeed impressive. Among them were General Jo Shelby; Senator George G. Vest, who wrote the memorable tribute to a dog; William J. Stone, governor and senator; Thomas T. Crittenden of Missouri, who ironically enough planned for so many years to smash the James-Younger gang; the Honorable V. Stephens, governor; William W. Warren, senator; Edwin M. Stephens of Columbia, famous newspaper writer and publisher of renowned legal works, who acted at one time as moderator of the Baptist Church in America; Shepard Barclay, justice of the Supreme Court of Missouri; N. E. Benton, congressman and nephew of the great Thomas Hart Benton; and ironically, William H. Wallace who, as the prosecutor of Jackson County, had endeavored to send Frank James behind bars or to the gallows.

For years the fight was waged. From time to time Captain Warren Carter Bronaugh, former Confederate army officer, who spearheaded the campaign, traveled to Minnesota staggering under the weight of petitions signed by persons from every walk in life who wanted to see the Youngers freed. One of the most faithful workers in this campaign was Mrs. Retta Younger, sister of the outlaws. From the day she stood at the side of the bandits in the Minnesota courtroom where they received their sentence for the Northfield robbery, her faith had never wavered. On September 16, 1889, in the prison hospital, she held the hand of her brother Robert as he died and bent over to catch his last whispered words:

"Don't weep for me."

On July 11, 1901, the paroles were finally granted. The first man to break the news to Cole Younger was Captain Bronaugh. Immediately after the Board of Pardons had adjourned that afternoon, the Confederate army officer rushed to the penitentiary. A reporter for the Kansas City *Times* was on hand and recorded this scene.

> "I'd said I would be the first Missourian to shake hands with you Cole," said Captain Bronaugh who was having difficulty in restraining his emotions.
>
> "You sure are," said Cole and they shook hands again. "Well I reckon (Cole Younger habitually says, I reckon) you'll keep your promise to walk down the prison steps with us?"
>
> "You bet I will and I would have waited twenty-five years more to do it."
>
> "Reckon they know it in Jackson?"
>
> "Yes, you bet."
>
> Cole chuckled, his grin broadening until it almost reached his ears.
>
> "Bronaugh, did you send any telegrams to Missouri?"
>
> "Lots of 'em and not one to anybody that is not your friend."
>
> "I sent one myself," said Cole.
>
> "Lizzie Daniels down at Harrisonville. You know I knew her when she was a little child—so high. She's a noble girl too," and then he added with a chuckle, "a good Methodist, too."

Bronaugh was a good Methodist, as Cole knew. Jim Younger came in and there was handshaking all around. The next day, Sunday, about 10 A.M., the Youngers were released.

Before they left, both bandits were given a suit of clothes and a "telescope grip." After dinner at the prison office, the brothers, Warden Wolfer, and others "enjoyed a naphtha launch excursion on Lake St. Croix."

Everybody, it seemed, was now trying to get into the act.

When Cole and Jim were released on parole they became drummers for the N. P. Peterson Granite Company, of St. Paul and Stillwater. Each received $60 a month and expenses. Ironically enough they were put to selling tombstones.

Jim Younger turned to insurance after an accident but gave it up when he was informed that because he was an ex-criminal every policy he wrote was invalid. In 1902 he fell in love with a young newspaper reporter who worked in St. Paul. But the romance was broken up and Jim became moody and disconsolate. In the summer of 1902 he committed suicide in a room of the Reardon Hotel. More irony. A short time later the Youngers were granted a full pardon.

The body of the outlaw was brought back to Lee's Summit and buried in the family plot.

Cole Younger, meanwhile, returned to Missouri. Some time later he and Frank James joined a wild west show but quit after a while. Frank James took a job as shoe clerk in Nevada, Missouri, and in Dallas, Texas. Later he became a doorman at the roughest burlesque in St. Louis, owned by Colonel Edward Butler, the Democratic boss of the city. From time to time the outlaw served as assistant starter at the fair-ground race track in St. Louis and other cities.

Jesse's brother died on February 18, 1915, in his old bedroom at the Samuel farm. Following his last request his remains were cremated in the Missouri Crematory in St. Louis.

A year later, on March 21, 1916, Cole Younger passed away at the Lee's Summit, Missouri, home he had bought for his faithful niece, Miss Nora Hall. For a year he had suffered from heart disease and "dyspepsia." Since his return to Missouri he had lived quietly and peacefully. Nearly every child in the community knew him as "Uncle Cole."

When he died Cole still had seventeen bullets embedded in his big body. Although he had been wounded twenty-six times in his lifetime, he had lived to the ripe old age of seventy-two years.

The last of these famous American outlaws was buried in the

family plot between his mother and his brother Jim. A monument was placed at the head of the grave with this inscription:

Cole Younger
1844-1916
Rest in Peace
Our Dear Beloved

Not only a man but an era had been laid to rest.

BOOK TWO

20.

THE WEST

THE death of Jesse James brought an end to the sixteen-year reign of terror throughout the Middle Border. But far to the West a new and greater band of riders had appeared on the outlaw trail. They were a breed of men far different from the sullen Missourians. They were gay and carefree, loved song and story, had a wealth of vitality, and lived a reckless, exuberant life. They were ready to sing, to ride, or to shoot at the slightest provocation. They were lean and sinewy with faces burned by the sun to the color of old leather. Like Jesse and his men, they were expert horsemen. Tradition paints the Jameses and Youngers as expert revolver shots, but they were no match for these western riders, some of whom were incredible marksmen. Their language was characterized by the fact that they lived close to realities and primal elements. When they spoke, their words were pungent and direct. Their dress, too, was different. They wore flannel shirts with loose handkerchiefs about their necks, broad hats, jingling spurs, leather chaps, or their trousers tucked into their boots.

This new outlaw band rode under the name of the Wild Bunch. Curiously, although their deeds were more colorful and daring than those of the Jesse James gang, they are not as well known. But in the late '80's and at the turn of the century their names were familiar to every western ranch and bunkhouse. Before their leaders fell in the last crackle of gunfire, they were recognized as story-book Robin Hoods by the natives in countless villages and Indian towns of South America.

Unlike Missouri's Clay County bandits, the members of the Wild Bunch were not born of a war but of a depression in the cattle country and a changing social period. Among the factors which produced them were: the great drought through the range from Texas to the Canadian border in the spring of 1883; the crash of the beef market in 1885; and the disastrous winter a few years later. All three caused widespread unemployment and subsequent rustling among cowpunchers. The booming industries in the eastern and Pacific cities, meanwhile, led hordes of land-hungry Americans deeper and deeper into the cattle country, thus narrowing the traditional free range. The Homestead Act of 1862 and the invention of barbed wire gave great impetus to the advancing frontier by making it possible for the pioneer to fence in his land at a reasonably small expense. Because of this, great cattle kingdoms crumbled and became mere provinces of the eastern cities, adding to the increasing unemployment among the cowhands. Finally there was the sparsely populated land itself which allowed for the abuse of the law and its power.

The Wild Bunch riders were all plainsmen and working cowpunchers, expert with the lariat and the branding iron. To understand them and their beginning, it is important to examine the time in which they lived—America's fabulous longhorn era.

It was shortly after Appomattox that the expansion of the cattle kingdoms began. In the thriving northern cities and on the Indian reservations where the Redmen had been driven, beef and more beef was needed. In Texas, steers accumulated during the Civil War were virtually standing horn to horn on the lush ranges. Cattle could be bought in the Lone Star State for about five dollars a head; in the north the same animal could be sold for forty to fifty dollars. The cattle kings looked north, figures and dollar signs tumbling about in their heads. Railroads—between raids by the Jameses and Youngers—had nosed out along the prairies. The Missouri Pacific reached Sedalia. From there cattle could be shipped to the golden markets of the East.

The first cattle drive began in 1866. In that one year more than 260,000 head splashed across the Red River bound for the railheads. It is one of the most thrilling chapters in American history; the grunting, tough steers with their magnificent spread of horns, the pillar of dust rising to the sky; the cowhands on their cattle-wise horses, whooping and shouting as they rode the fringes of the slow-moving herd; the grueling days and the soft nights with the lonely night guard calming the restless steers with soothing lyrics. Thus were born our Western ballads of lonely men in a lonely land.

Then the stampede, the dread of every cowhand. There was

47. Vigilante identification button. *(Courtesy Wells Fargo Bank History Room)*

48. Express car blown up by the Wild Bunch at Wilcox, Wyoming, on June 2, 1899. This explosion was one of Cassidy's ways of showing the incited vigilantes that he wasn't intimidated. *(Courtesy Union Pacific Railroad)*

49. A retouched photograph of "Blackjack" Tom Ketchum, who, with his brother Sam, was one of the members of the Wild Bunch. (*Courtesy Pinkerton's National Detective Agency, Inc.*)

50. The amateurish hanging of Blackjack Ketchum. Captured after a single-handed robbery of the Southern Pacific on July 11, 1899. He was hung by an amateur who made the sandbags too heavy and so decapitated him. (*Courtesy Pinkerton's National Detective Agency, Inc.*)

51. The Body of Tom Ketchum. (*Courtesy Pinkerton's National Detective Agency, Inc.*)

52. The posse that trailed the Wild Bunch after the robbery of the Union Pacific at Tipton in 1900: [1.] George Hiatt, [2.] T. T. Kelliher, [3.] Joe Lefores, [4.] H. Davis, [5.] Si Funk, [6.] Jeff Carr. (*Courtesy Pinkerton's National Detective Agency, Inc.*)

Great Northern Express Co.

ST. PAUL, MINN., JULY 4, 1901.

$5000 Reward

53. Great Northern Express Co. reward notice. (*Courtesy Pinkerton's National Detective Agency, Inc.*)

The Great Northern Railway "Overland" West-bound Train No. 3 was held up about three miles east of Wagner, Mont., Wednesday afternoon, July 3, 1901, and the Great Northern Express Company's through safe blown open with dynamite and the contents taken.

There were three men connected with the hold-up, described as follows :

One was, height 5 feet and 9 inches, weight about 175 pounds, blue eyes, had a projecting brow and about two weeks growth of sandy beard on chin, wore new tan shoes, black coat, corduroy trousers, and carried a silver plated, gold mounted Colt's revolver with a pearl handle.

Second man, height 6 feet, weight about 175 pounds, sandy complexion, blue eyes, not very large with slight cast in left eye; wore workingman's shoes, blue overalls over black suit of clothes, had a boot leg for cartridge pouch suspended from his neck.

Third man resembled a half breed very strongly, had large dark eyes, smoothly shaven face, and a very prominent nose; features clear cut, weight about 180 pounds, slightly stooped in shoulders, but very square across the shoulders, and wore a light slouch hat.

All three men used very marked Texas cowboy dialect, and two of them carried Winchester rifles, one of which was new. One had a carbine, same pattern as the Winchesters. They rode away on black, white, and buckskin horses respectively.

The Great Northern Express Company will give $5000 reward for the capture and identification of the three men, or a proportionate amount for one or two and $500 additional for each conviction.

D. S. ELLIOTT,
Auditor.

Approved:

D. MILLER,
President.

54. The posse aboard train in pursuit of the Wild Bunch. (*Courtesy Pinkerton's National Detective Agency, Inc.*)

no foretelling what would cause it: the sudden bark of a coyote, a rumble of thunder or flash of lightning, the crash of a pan, the snort of a horse or the scream of a panther, or it might be for no apparent reason—a resurgence of some half-wild but dormant instinct of flight. The frightened animals would rise in the night to thunder across the dark plains with the speed of an express train and the destructive power of an army of modern steam rollers. None could tell what direction the herd would take. It might lead into canyons and break over bluffs, into the river, or into the open plains. The task of the punchers was to gain control of the herd and gradually turn the frightened animals until they were moving in a circle. To accomplish this gigantic task, man and horse became one.

The first drive of '66 was a bitter one for the Texans. When their herds reached southeastern Kansas, south Missouri, and north Arkansas, outlaw bands with watchers on the hills swooped down, stole the cattle, either killing the drivers or demanding protection money. In the northern part of the state at the time, Jesse was summoning his guerrillas for the first strike at the Liberty, Missouri, bank.

After that first season of '66 cattlemen avoided that bandit-infested district. It was a period of experimentation, and the drivers turned east, moving along the Missouri-Arkansas border in the Indian Territory heading for a railhead east of Sedalia. It was a rough stretch of land and the herds were thin. The western drive took the cattle along the south border of Kansas and into the grassy plains and shipping points from St. Jo, Missouri, and to Chicago. Other ranchers moved their longhorns as far as Iowa and Illinois.

It was a bad first year or two. But the trial and error, the fighting off of robbers who rode out of the hills, the terrible physical strain of moving armies of animals across more than twelve hundred miles of wild territory, had linked the beef-hungry North and the beef-stocked Texas.

The first man to establish permanent contact between the ranchmen of the South and the northern buyers was J. G. McCoy, one of the unsung heroes of the West. McCoy established the first cow town—Abilene, Kansas—signed contracts with the Hannibal and St. Jo Railroad, and almost singlehandedly swung the booming cattle business from St. Louis to Chicago where it remains today.

Abilene, McCoy declared, was selected because "it was entirely unsettled, well watered, and had excellent grass."

But McCoy did more than establish this roaring, bustling frontier town whose part in American history is so significant. He sent Indian-wise plainsmen to scour the prairies and seek out the straggling drovers from Texas searching for a safe haven for their beef. They were to tell them about Abilene and what was being done. Men were incredulous as they listened to the plainsmen in buckskin and moccasins. "It was almost too good to be true; could it be possible that someone was about to afford a Texan drover any other reception than outrage and robbery . . . ?"

When the first drovers came into Abilene, a thunderous celebration was held. The town blossomed overnight and its name became as well known to the ranchers as Baxter Springs, Missouri, where the outlaw gangs had their hideout.

Despite the fact that the season was late when Abilene opened for business in 1867, more than thirty-five thousand head were shipped out of the cow town.

The cattle kingdoms spread rapidly out of Texas. It was like an ever widening blot of ink on the western map. The United States Census of 1880 showed that in fifteen years, from 1866 to 1880, a total of 4,223,397 head of cattle moved out of Sam Houston's Lone Star State.

As the railroads moved west, the cattle business followed, but it was Abilene that was the jumping-off place, the goal of every Texas rancher, drover, and cowboy. It was a rough and ready town with gunfire and violence commonplace.

After the establishment of the Abilene Trail, there was a succession of other trails and cattle paths; some were named, many were not. For some reason the Chisholm Trail has displaced all others in the popular mind. Who first laid out the trail and where was its exact location are academic questions which are still argued whenever two or more Texas cattlemen meet.

West of the Chisholm Trail was the Panhandle Trail, leading into Kansas and Colorado, and the Pecos Trail, up the Pecos River Valley into New Mexico and on to Colorado and Wyoming. Cattle going to railheads to market took the more westerly trails.

The winter of 1881-1882 was mild and at its end the herds were in excellent condition. The price of beef soared and range cattle were sold from $30 to $35 a head. Ranchers were realizing a profit of 300 per cent on what they had purchased three years earlier. In the midsummer of 1882 the booming beef market had reached its peak.

By 1883 the reckoning came. A drought swept across the overstocked ranges from Texas to the Canadian border. In 1884 beef prices weakened. The next year the crash came. Cattle which had sold from $30 to $35 a head in the summer of 1882 now sold for $8 to $10—if they could be sold at all. Cattle were flung on the market at any price and disaster struck the West. Fortunes vanished overnight, small ranches were abandoned by their owners, and unemployment among cowhands was widespread.

With only their horses, blanket rolls, and six-shooters, these drifting, homeless men roamed the plains that summer of 1885, seeking shelter and food. Many times, in the tradition of the West, the horse was fed before the man.

During the winter of 1886-1887 some of these jobless cowboys drifted into a barren, empty valley located in the northern section of Wyoming. It was, and still is, called Hole in the Wall and for years had been used by horsethieves and renegade Redmen. It is approximately fifty miles south of Buffalo, Wyoming, and about one hard day's ride to Casper in the north. East of the Hole were the excellent cattle ranges of the Powder River country.

It was a desolate place which evidently had been a prehistoric lake. In the course of centuries the waters ate their way by a narrow stream through one end and formed an outlet. As age after age went by the outlet became a deep gorge. The waters of the lake sank lower and lower until in the late '80's there was a chain of little lakes and swift streams that in the spring became raging torrents. In receding the waters of the huge lake left a basin hemmed in by rugged mountains and a sheer thousand-foot red wall in the north which runs in an east and west direction for more than thirty miles. There are numerous crevices and caverns that have subterranean passages from one to the other, so that anyone familiar with the place could hide for days with his pursuers less than a hundred yards away.

The valley itself is sloping and grassy, and fed by mountain streams. Unlike the plains, there is no high moaning wind, only an eerie stillness. In the summer there is the smell of hot rock and sweet grass, and in the strong sunlight the tule grass gleams like polished brass. In the winter there is nothing but white silence. The only entrance and the only exit to this mountain stronghold is the narrow gorge—Hole in the Wall.

When the spring of 1887 arrived, Hole in the Wall was fast becoming a sizable community. Word soon seeped out to the lonely campfires beyond the red wall that here was food, warmth, and companionship. More horsemen passed through the narrow passage and crunched their way across the lonely valley.

The growth of Hole in the Wall was rapid. Soon there was a community of evil, its citizens an army of more than a hundred rustlers, horsethieves, outlaws, homeless and jobless cowhands, fugitives from abortive robberies in the Middle Border country, and a few dance-hall girls. The fortress in the hills was more impregnable than the castle of any robber baron of medieval times.

From this valley an outlaw trail ran south, a trail as marked as the Wilderness Road, the Natchez Trace, or the Santa Fe. It wound through canyons, across deserts, over mountains, and beyond the plains to Mexico, with "stations" like the Underground on the way.

The second principal "station" was Brown's Hole, later the headquarters for the Wild Bunch and the outlaw command in the West. Geographically, Brown's Hole surrounds the point where the eastern boundary of Utah and the western boundary of Colorado join the southern boundary of Wyoming. Parts of it lie in all three states. Green River enters the lush and fertile valley from the west through a deep and rugged canyon and follows the base of the Diamond Mountains. After thirty miles it roars through the Lodore canyon, a narrow slit in the sandstone walls. The valley extends from east to west for thirty miles with an average width of five miles. Steep and precarious trails lead down into the hole from the north and south rims.

Tax collectors never appeared. The only link to the outside world was a small store and post office in the Utah end of the Hole. One of the early leaders of the community built a schoolhouse and hired a teacher from Vernal, not too many miles distant. To say that the teacher had a difficult time with his wild young charges would be a gross understatement. A room of wildcats would have been preferable.

Robber's Roost, the most southerly of the outlaw stations, is located in the extreme end of Wayne County in southeastern Utah. It is about three hundred highway miles south of Brown's Hole.

There are only three entrances into Robber's Roost; one from Green River, one from Hanksville, and one from Dandy Crossing, all in Utah.

It is an ugly and desolate spot. Except for three or four springs the place is arid. Unlike Hole in the Wall and Brown's Hole it is not a gigantic scoop in the earth but an elevated plateau on the summit of the San Rafael Swell. It is bounded on its eastern side by the Green River. To the south are the five black peaks of the Henry Mountains towering in the distance.

Charles Kelly, who apparently knows the land as intimately as he knows the back of his hand, describes the only approaches to this forbidden spot in his *Outlaw Trail.*

There are three trails into the Roost; one from Green River, one from Hanksville, and one from Dandy Crossing. The Green River trail runs almost due south 20 miles to the San Rafael, a tributary of the Green, and then forty-five miles up to a gradual sandy ascent to the summit of the swell known as Sam's Mesa. In those last forty-five miles—over the original trail—water was found only at one place called the Tanks, a crevice in the sandstone rocks impossible to find unless one knew where to look. After crossing the San Rafael, the guided landmarks were two flat-topped buttes on the summit of the mesa northwest of the Roost.

The trail from Hanksville was only forty miles long but more difficult. The Dirty Devil River, which irrigates a few fertile fields at the settlement, passes into a deep canyon bisecting the desert between Hanksville and the river. It can be crossed in only one place over an extremely difficult trail. Dry lateral canyons leading into Dirty Devil make the journey from Hanksville to the Roost rough and dangerous.

The trail leading from the Roost into Colorado was as picturesque as it was difficult. It led south toward the Henry Mountains across Dirty Devil canyon and forty miles of dry, sandy desert, then down the bottom of Trachyte Canyon for another thirty miles to Dandy Crossing and Colorado. Opposite the mouth of the Trachyte, White Canyon comes in from the east, the junction of the two streams forming a ford in the Colorado passable at low water. Passing upward and eastward through White Canyon, the trail enters what is now Natural Bridges National Monument, in the Abajo Mountains, runs down the eastern slope to Monticello and then directly east to Mancos, Colorado.

There were hundreds of riders who knew this outlaw trail and the "stations": Black Jack Ketchum, Bill Carver, Elza Lay, the Logan brothers, Lonny, Johnny, and Harvey; George Curry, Flat-Nose George; Bob Lee, Camilla Hanks, Deaf Charley; Ben Kilpatrick, the Tall Texan; Harry Longbaugh, the Sundance Kid; Harry Tracy and David Lant; and George Leroy Parker, to be known as Butch Cassidy, grandson of a Mormon elder and perhaps America's greatest outlaw.

There were women too: Laura Bullion, gum-chewing nineteenth-century gun moll. In contrast there was Etta Place, a beautiful woman with lustrous brown hair, soft brown eyes, a quiet smile, and a gleaming gold Tiffany watch on her bosom. She is tantalizingly mysterious; the illegitimate offspring of an English lord, who owned vast acres of ranch land; a schoolteacher who deserted her young charges for the business of banditry after falling in love with Longbaugh...

And this we do know about her: she could ride like a Sioux wind spirit, was an excellent shot with a six-shooter or carbine; dressed as a man, she participated in a number of bank robberies in South America. She is the female star of our cast of robbers, outlaws, rustlers, and cold-blooded killers.

There were hundreds of other riders whose names run through the Pinkerton historical archives. It is impossible to name them all or to describe the humorous or tragic incidents in which they starred. They are only supporting players to Cassidy and his riders.

21.

KING OF THE RUSTLERS

HE was six feet and weighed about a hundred and ninety pounds. He had a jutting forehead and a large nose which gave him a curious, horselike look. His eyes were fierce and black and he walked with a peculiar slouch. His name was Nathan Champion, and in the Hole in the Wall country he was known as King of the Rustlers.

His riders were expert and colorful, and to distinguish them from the horsemen of the smaller rustling bands which had sprung up in that wild section, they wore a bright-red sash about their middle. They soon earned the name of the Red Sash gang with Champion as their leader. His lieutenant and close friend was Nick Rae, about whom little is known.

Among Champion's followers were the Missouri Logans, Harvey, Johnny, and Lonny; Flat-Nose George Curry, an expert horsethief and cattle rustler; Walter Putney, Wat the Watcher, so called because of his frequent use as a lookout in bank robberies; and Tom O'Day, sometimes called Peep O'Day.

The Logans were powerful men with the legacy of their Cherokee grandfather showing in their swarthy complexions and high cheekbones. They were sullen and vicious and would have found themselves at home with Jesse and his murderous guerrillas. Harvey, with a wolverine's cunning and shrewdness, was their leader.

They were born in Kentucky in the 1870's and were orphans at an early age. An aunt in Dodson, Missouri, to the west of the Jesse James country reared them. When they were in their late teens, the brothers—there were four with Henry, the only one to become a respectable citizen and the only one to die a natural death—left Missouri and drifted west. They were accompanied by a cousin, Bob Lee, later a minor figure in the Bunch. In Wyoming they met Curry, whom the Denver Pinkerton criminal file describes as "one of the biggest rustlers in Wyoming." Curry's swagger and braggadocio won the admiration of the three boys and under Curry's eye they became rustlers on a small scale. About 1890 they left Wyoming, driving a herd to Montana, and there turned honest ranchers, buying a small ranch five miles from the thriving mining town of Landusky, Montana, named after its first citizen, a scar-faced, powerful old prospector.

The old miner had four stepdaughters. One, Elfie, according to the Denver Pinkerton files, "was a well built woman, good looking with long, black hair, fair skin and brown eyes." A romance between Elfie and Lonny Logan developed and the black-haired girl was soon pregnant. Landusky, when he learned of his daughter's condition, took up the traditional shotgun and set out for the Logan ranch. But the three brothers had set out for Wyoming and Hole in the Wall. The miner returned home swearing vengeance. It was soon to come his way—but with tragic results.

By the time the Logans had returned to Wyoming their horse-faced leader, Nathan Champion, had bought the K. C. Ranch in Powder Springs—after which Kaycee, Wyoming is named—and made it the headquarters for his rustling operations. The ranch was thirty miles east of Hole in the Wall. Champion's band soon controlled the northern section of Wyoming.

The Red Sash gang became so powerful that they defied the Wyoming Live Stock Commissioners by fixing their own roundup date—a month earlier than the legitimate date—and rustled all the unbranded mavericks.

Disaster had struck the range country a second time during the winter of 1886-1887. Heavy snowfalls and subzero temperatures destroyed large herds. When spring arrived many ranches had been wiped out. Others had been able to save only 10 per cent of their stock. Rustling became widespread and the population of Hole in the Wall was doubled that year.

By 1892 Champion and his men controlled all of Johnson, Natrona, and Converse counties of Wyoming. His riders included not only outlaws and rustlers but also law-enforcement officers. The most prominent was W. G. (Red) Angus, the sheriff of Johnson County. The attorney for the outlaw gang was Charles W. Burnitt, mayor of Buffalo.

In his *Outlaw Trail* Kelly declared that a search of the Johnson

County records of that time showed that out of 180 arrests for rustling there was only one conviction.

Between the unpredictable weather and the rustling of the Red Sash gang, the herds of the cattle kings began to thin rapidly. Many of the large ranches were now owned by syndicates, and as the profits dwindled, the stockholders began to ask embarrassing questions. Homesteaders, too, were troublesome. They had established that the traditional "range rights" were fictitious and their fences were snaking across the free grass and boxing in the watering places. Their barbed wire tore both cattle and horses and infuriated the ranchers. The stockmen soon regarded the homesteaders as little better than rustlers. In return the pioneering farmers and the rustlers united against the common enemy.

Faced with the prospect of dwindling herds and declining profits, and unable to seek redress in the courts of the counties controlled by Champion's riders of the Red Sash, the cattle barons decided to take the law into their own hands.

The first rumbling of the approaching storm was heard when several men rode into Sweetwater, Carbon County, Wyoming, and hanged a homesteader and a woman known as Cattle Kate, who had settled in a rich valley in the heart of a huge cattle ranch and had refused to get off.

The case was given to the Carbon County Grand Jury. There were two witnesses, one an invalid boy, to the brutal murders. Both disappeared. The Grand Jury returned no bill and the case against the lynchers was dismissed.

What followed is summed up by A. S. Mercer, in his *Invasion of Powder Springs.* "Avoiding punishment encouraged the stockgrowers and they determined to keep up the good work."

Hired assassins began to drift into Cheyenne and other Wyoming towns and bushwacking became prevalent. Stories of dead men found in gullies "with their arms tied behind their backs" were commonplace. But Hole in the Wall still remained impregnable. Posses refused to go near that barren valley, with its watchers on the rims silhouetted against the sky. Hole in the Wall carried the same dread note as did Clay, Jackson, and Ray counties in Missouri when the name of Jesse James was "whispered in back rooms."

The Red Sash gang openly defied the syndicates. By 1892 they had become so brazen that they plastered posters about the community announcing roundup dates always weeks before those dates were set by the Wyoming Board of Live Stock Commissioners. That spring the flow of cattle with new or changed brands into the Hole was endless. The "running irons" were constantly hot and the branding fires burned day and night behind the red walls.

Beset on every side by rapidly dwindling profits, clamoring stockholders, homesteaders settling on the ranges, wire fences, windmills, and the open defiance of Champion's riders of the Red Sash, the rulers of the cattle kingdoms decided to act. Secret messages were sent out, and in the winter of 1892 stockmen from Wyoming, Utah, and Colorado met in a hotel in Cheyenne. An immediate invasion of Hole in the Wall was agreed upon. An "Extermination Fund"—estimated anywhere from $50,000 to $100,000—was pledged to hire an army of mercenaries. Some of the cattlemen, realizing the futility of fighting the inevitable advance of a new age, wanted to adopt more peaceful methods, but pressure was put on "and they were forced into line."

Cheyenne was the headquarters of the "Exterminating Committee" and during the winter members of the Wyoming Board of Live Stock Commissioners, state senators, nearly all of them stockmen, and the ex-governor, who was in charge of the state militia, "met in his office to consult over private business."

A nationwide campaign was begun to enlist public sympathy, and newspapers in New York, Washington, Philadelphia, Chicago, and Omaha ran daily stories, nearly all echoing the stockman's charge that "a reign of terror exists that can only be overcome by the use of arms."

The powerful forces of the syndicates began to work behind the scenes in Washington. Later it was charged that President Harrison, "ignorant of the true condition," had given his official approval for the ranchers' invasion. This is undoubtedly true. He never officially condemned it, and with the nation's newspapers filled with accounts of the gathering forces and with Wyoming's governor, ex-governor, senators, and state militia involved, he certainly must have known about it.

The stockmen's recruiting parties, meanwhile, began to travel through the West and Middle West hiring anyone who could use a gun. There were no questions asked of pedigree. Guns began to arrive in crates in Douglas and were transshipped to Cheyenne. Stockmen in the Pan Handle and in other states promised reinforcements.

Then, on March 23, 1892, the state militia was ordered to join the invaders in their war against the citizens of Hole in the Wall and Johnson County. General Order No. 4 was ordered by Colonel De Forest Richards, commander of the First Regiment of Wyoming's National Guards, to "instruct his company commanders that they shall obey only such orders to assemble their commands as may be received from these headquarters to assist the civil authorities in the preservation or enforcement of the laws of the State of Wyoming."

The order was issued by Frank Stilzer, the state's adjutant general. The general order was a move to protect the invaders and to tie the hands of any local sheriff. It was in direct violation of the laws of the state which said that, "when in any county there is a tumult, violence, etc., the sheriff, judge and mayor in absence of the Governor may issue the call to the commanding officer of any regiment, battalion, company, or troop to order his command."

According to the subsequent confession of Dunning, a member of the invading army, which the newspapers could not print because of the terrific pressure exerted by the syndicates—the document was called "immoral and unfit to be sent through the mails," although an examination fails to reveal anything "immoral"—the hired gunfighters were paid "five dollars a day, fifty dollars for each scalp, all expenses paid, a mount of horses, pistols and rifles."

The "recruiting agents" roamed through the Southwest and Idaho offering their terms. But recruiting was not too brisk, Dunning confessed, "when their duties were explained to them."

On April 1, 1892, "a sufficient number had been hired" and were summoned to Denver, Colorado. Here they were met "by a committee after the annual meeting of stockgrowers."

Earlier, the following resolution was offered and passed unanimously. It read:

> WHEREAS, the cattle interests of the state have been seriously jeopardized by the thieves and outlaws:
> WHEREAS, many herds are leaving the state to seek protection, elsewhere; be it

RESOLVED, that the Wyoming Stockgrowers Association appreciates and endorses the able and fearless manner in which the Board of Livestock Commissioners have attempted to guard the interests of honest cattlemen in the state, acting as they are without compensation or reward and solely for the general good and property of the state...

The stock interests had now put on the record that they were a law unto themselves.

At Cheyenne guns, ammunition, and blanket rolls were made ready and the supply wagons piled high.

Assassination was a part of the plan and Sheriff Red Angus, who rode with the outlaws, was marked for death. The thriving community of Buffalo, Angus' headquarters, was to be captured and controlled by the invaders. From there they would push on against the fortress in the hills. The invaders were given a list of men charged with rustling, and murder was the order of the day. Spies had been sent into the outlaw land and the names sent back. Champion and the Logans headed the list.

The special train carrying the invaders highballed out of Denver bound for Casper, Wyoming, with the commander of the group telling the engineer, "put us at Casper and we will do the rest."

It was clear track, and the two-hundred-mile run to the northwest was made in good time. The train ground to a stop outside the town. The wagons loaded, the horsemen mounted and the local sympathizers emerged from the shadows to take their places at the head of the column. The wires were cut and the little town was completely isolated. Seven miles out a halt was made for breakfast. The mercenaries sat about the fires in the crisp morning air, gulping bacon and coffee and spinning their revolver cylinders for a last check. As they were about to start a foreman for a large beef syndicate rode into camp and told the leaders that some rustlers were "holed up" at Champion's K. C. Ranch, on the north fork of the Powder River.

April 8, a Friday, was spent waiting for the supply wagons. The next morning they hit the ranch at daybreak, with sappers moving through the brush with dynamite. The daylight broke too fast and that idea was abandoned. The lines were drawn and the ranch completely surrounded.

"Await orders to fire," was whispered from man to man.

Two men came out for water and were quietly captured. They were identified as trappers and held for a later release. The next man to come out of the cabin was Champion's partner, Nick Rae. He was shot and fell before he left the porch. The wounded outlaw cried out for help and the horse-faced Champion rushed out, six-shooters blazing, and dragged his dying partner back into the house.

The war had begun.

The shooting lasted most of the day. Hundreds of rounds of ammunition were fired. By noon a thick cloud of acrid gunpowder smoke hung over the scene. During a lull in the afternoon a neighboring rancher came riding up the road in a buckboard with his stepson. The posse fired on them but they escaped without injury.

"There was no time to lose now," Dunning said in his confession, "a wagon was fired and driven into the house."

The invaders rose out of the bushes and from behind the trees to watch the crackling flames. The tinder-dry sides of the house caught fire and the dwelling became a roaring torch. It seemed impossible that anything could remain alive for very long in that inferno. Then, almost unbelievably, Champion leaped through the wall of flames, a Winchester across his shoulders and two revolvers working. One posseman whirled around and fell; the others leaped for cover. His clothes charred rags, the king of the rustlers ran leaping for cover. The circle of rifles opened fire. Champion fell but rose again. Spurts of dust dogged the outlaw's steps. Not all the hired gunmen were poor shots. Champion fell a second and last time. The firing continued. There weren't any spurts of dust. It's hard to miss a stationary, six-foot target.

The blood-stained body was stripped, the twenty-eight bullet holes counted, and a crude card hung across the big chest.

"Rustlers beware."

In a pocket of the blue denim shirt they found a blood-stained and bullet-punctured sheet of paper. It was Champion's last testament scrawled with a stub of a pencil as he ran from window to window pumping lead and administering to his dying friend, Nick Rae.

It is a moving little document and curiously enough, although it is addressed to his "boys"—the rustlers and the outlaws who rode with him—there is no order to them to seek vengeance. Between the lines one can sense the indifference to death they all had; the philosophical acceptance of death by the gun as the fruit of having lived by the gun.

April 9th—Me and Nick was getting breakfast when the attack took place. Two men here with us: Bill Jones and a man named Walker (Trappers). The old man went after water and did not come back. Nick started out and I told him to look out that I thought there was someone at the stable and would not let him come back. Nick is shot but not dead yet. He is awful sick. I must go and wait on him.

It is now two hours since the first shot. Nick is still alive. They are shooting and all around the house. Boys, there is bullets coming in like hail. Them fellows is in such shape I can't get at them. They are shooting from the stable and river and back of the house. Nick is dead; he died at 9 o'clock. I see a smoke down at the stable. I think they have fired it. I don't think they intend to let me get away this time.

Noon. There is someone at the stable yet. They are throwing a rope at the door and drawing it back. I guess it is to draw me out. I wish that duck would get out further so I could get a shot at him. Boys, I don't know what they have done with them two fellows that staid here last night. Boys, I feel pretty lonesome right now. I wish there was someone here with me so we could watch all sides at once. They may fool around until I get a good shot before they leave. It's about three o'clock now. There was a man in the buckboard and one on horseback just passed [the Flaggs]. They fired on them as they went by. I don't know if they killed them or not. I seen lots of men come out on horses on the other side of the river and take after them. I shot at them men in the stable just now; I don't know if I got any or not. I must go and look out again. It doesn't look as if there is much show of my getting away. I see twelve or fifteen men. One looks like [here a name is scratched out]. I don't know whether it is or not. I hope they did not catch them fellows who run over the bridge toward Smith's. They are now shooting at the house. If I had a pair of glasses I believe I could know some of those men. They are now coming. I've got to look out.

Well they have got through shelling the house like hail. I hear them splitting wood. I guess they are going to fire the house tonight. I think I will make a break tonight, if still alive.

Shooting again. I think they will fire the house this time. It's not night yet. The house is now all fired. Goodbye boys, if I never see you again.

Signed

Nathan D. Champion.

The document was passed from hand to hand. It finally came to rest with the army who turned it over to civil authorities.

With the night breeze clearing away the gun smoke the wagons of the invaders, like any army chowwagons, came up from the rear and "the cooks served a heavy meal to the hungry men."

But there were some desertions that night. Some of "the best citizens" found the dead man, rustler or not, stiffening in the night chill, too much to take. They feigned sickness and left. After the evening meal the mercenaries set out to "capture" Buffalo, Wyoming, six miles away.

It was a march "against the doomed city of the plains," the leaders dramatically told their men.

But Champion's neighbor had brought the warning. Riders raced out of Buffalo for Hole in the Wall and distant ranches and homesteads. The hardest riding herald was the storekeeper of Buffalo whose best customers were the rustlers. At the outlaw stations and in Hole in the Wall, he cried as he sawed at the reins to control his plunging mount:

"They've come to invade us and they're all over the countryside. Champion's dead and they're going to do the same for the rest of us. We've got to fight them or lose our homes. If you got a gun, fall in line."

There was a long column of "more than a hundred" grim-faced horsemen—outlaws and homesteaders—who swung into line behind him before an hour had passed. As the invading army approached Buffalo and the alarm spread throughout the countryside, "the forces of the defenders mounted by the hour."

Sheriff Angus who was marked for assassination, it is recorded, rode 120 miles in fourteen hours.

"Monday night pits were dug; Tuesday, recruits came from

Sheridan and parts of Johnson County and from Hole in the Wall."

The battle started at daybreak. "There was no break in the firing, it was constant," Mercer says in his *Powder Springs Invasion*. The outlaw forces "built breastworks from wagons six feet high with five portholes which could protect forty men."

By afternoon the outlaw army began a foot-by-foot advance against the "whitecaps," as the cattlemen were called. The battle lasted two days and nights. On the twilight of the second day the outlaws and homesteaders were within 100 yards of the stockmen's forces when the sweet notes of the Cavalry "assembly" echoed in the evening air. Four troops of United States Cavalry rode up to the front lines, the stars and stripes stiff in the wind and the outlaws rose "and cheered the sight."

But the motley army of outlaws and homesteaders was still in charge. At a conference they told the army to demand a surrender or accept responsibility for the consequences. The colonel agreed and, with his staff and the aide-de-camp to the governor of Wyoming, rode up to the ranch house under a truce flag. Sheriff Angus who was now on the scene accompanied them.

After a short parley under the white flag, the stockmen's forces surrendered and were arrested for murder and insurrection at the insistence of the rustlers! The world had certainly turned upside down that day; lawless law against lawlessness suppressed by the law.

Two hours later the stockmen's mercenaries who had been hired to suppress the "state of terror" marched past the column of blues as prisoners, bound for Fort McKinney. They had to pass the rustlers and thieves they had come out to destroy and who had defeated them.

From Fort McKinney the prisoners and their leaders were escorted fifty miles to Cheyenne. Sheriff Angus pompously requested the governor to return forty-four of the hired gunmen. The state executive, who knew what the verdict of any jury in the outlaw country would be, answered with a terse, one-word telegram: "No."

At Cheyenne the governor immediately paroled the prisoners and many journeyed through Montana and Omaha to "get their friends to help."

"The paroles were easy to get," Mercer says succinctly.

But Cheyenne was far different from Johnson County. There the power of the beef men was still strong. Lengthy legal proceedings followed the invasion and the decisions handed down were the most important for many years to the growing communities of the West.

Willis Vandevanter, later a United States Supreme Court justice, defended them. Finally the charges of insurrection and murder were dismissed, and the cattlemen were released, declaring that they would return a second time to Johnson County "and clean out the rascals."

22.

BUTCH CASSIDY

AT about the time Nathan Champion was pumping lead through the windows of his K. C. Ranch at the Wyoming invaders, a square-jawed youth of about twenty, with a "cheery and affable manner," as the Pinkerton wanted posters later described him, was working in a butcher shop in Rock Springs, Sweetwater County, Wyoming. He was broad shouldered and stocky with light complexion and flaxen hair. His name was George Leroy Parker and he was a grandson of a Mormon bishop and saint.

He was born in Circle Valley, Utah, in 1867, the oldest of a family of seven children. He spent most of his boyhood on his father's ranch, twelve miles south of Circleville. Horsethieves and cattle rustlers are said to have used the ranch because it was within easy reach of the wild and desolate section now known as Bryce National Park.

One of the cowhands who stayed to work the ranch after it was purchased by Maximilian Parker, young George's father, was Mike Cassidy, a well-known horse and cattle thief. The boy became his eager protégé. Shooting and riding were included in

Cassidy's curriculum and young Parker soon became the best rider and shot in the valley.

Cassidy, meanwhile, continued to collect his stolen cattle. He hid them in the breaks of Bryce Canyon until the herd got too big, then moved them to another hideout in the Henry Mountains near the Colorado Mountains. Young Parker helped him and they drove the steers into Robber's Roost. Mike knew every foot of the barren, dangerous land and showed his young rider the hidden trails and few waterholes.

The rustlers were well organized in the Roost country and had a unique arrangement for disposing of stolen cattle. When spring arrived Cassidy sent out word to the representatives of the rustlers that he was ready to move his herd. Hard-eyed punchers began arriving at the Roost. Each selected a few cattle and began heading for the rendezvous. The second day the stolen stock would be left on some small isolated ranch. The owner would pick up "the strays" left on his land, add a few head, and drive them to another rustler's ranch or station. Every member of the ring had a perfect alibi: he was gone only a day from his ranch; he had not stolen any cattle, only moved "a few strays" off his land.

Cassidy's herd of stolen cattle was finally assembled in one of the Roost's isolated canyons and sold either at Greenriver or to some dealer in Colorado. They returned to Circle Valley, with Young Parker now familiar with every trick of stealing horses and rustling cattle.

That summer, to show his admiration for his instructor George Leroy Parker changed his name to Cassidy. He was soon known to the thieves and rustlers as George (Butch) Cassidy. Mike "got into some difficulty with the law" and left in a hurry for Mexico. Young Parker—or Cassidy—left the valley soon after him.

Butch Cassidy next appears in Colorado where he worked for a time in the booming mining district of Telluride, Colorado, packing high-grade ore down a mountainside on muleback. There he met and joined the McCarty gang and as a minor rider participated in his first train robbery.

Like the Jameses and Youngers, the McCartys—Bill, Tom, and George—were a blood brotherhood. Bill is said to have ridden under Jesse James, but his name does not appear in the Pinkerton archives, criminals' indictments, confessions, or memoirs of any of the gang. Tom McCarty married a sister of Willard

Christiansen, another son of a Mormon bishop, and was to become known throughout the West as Matt Warner, a bank and train robber. Warner, who died in 1937, eventually became a courageous law officer and a justice of the peace, after serving a long term in jail.

Butch Cassidy's first train robbery with the McCartys was on the Denver and Rio Grande tracks, five miles east of Grand Junction, Colorado, on the evening of November 3, 1887. It was not expert. An express company messenger with a pistol at his temple refused to open the safe. The five robbers then held a vote, in the best democratic fashion on robbing the passengers. The nays had it, and they removed the piled ties, bade the engineer and messenger a cheery good night, and rode off.

But on March 30, 1889, Tom McCarty and another member of the gang, probably Cassidy, robbed the First National Bank of Denver with McCarty coolly informing the president that he had overheard a plot to rob the institution.

"My God! How did you happen to know of the plot?" the bank president gasped.

"Because I'm the man who planned it," answered the grinning bandit.

Producing a small bottle, McCarty then told the bank official that it contained nitroglycerin and he would blow the bank sky high unless "I get a signed check for twenty-one thousand dollars." Escorted by McCarty carelessly juggling the bottle, the bank president ordered the check cashed. McCarty dashed outside, slipped the money to a member of the gang, and returned to the hotel where he tossed the bottle into a wastepaper basket. Nothing happened. Water, of course, does not explode.

The McCarty gang, including Cassidy, fled to Star Valley, a desolate stretch of land which lies partly in Wyoming and partly in Idaho. There the gang bought a ranch. Like Hole in the Wall, Star Valley was another community of evil, populated with rustlers, holdup men, killers, and horsethieves. Matt Warner opened a saloon in the valley and it was easily one of the most weird drinking places in the West.

The wall in back of the bar was papered with greenbacks of every denomination. In the center was a $10,000 bill, said to have been part of the Denver robbery, which the outlaws knew they could never change because the bank had a record of its number.

It was a standing rule of the house that drinks were "free to friends." The outlaws, their pockets bulging with greenbacks, soon became the most popular men in the valley. The golden-walled saloon did a roaring business but made little profit. Every customer, it appeared, was "a friend."

For three months the McCarty gang hid out in Star Valley drinking at Warner's saloon under the wallpaper of dollar signs. Then, on June 24, 1889, they rode out to rob the San Miguel Valley Bank at Telluride, Colorado. Butch Cassidy, who knew the territory and the town, undoubtedly planned the crime. About a month before the holdup he drifted into town riding a fine Kentucky horse.

For days, while the townspeople stood about and guffawed, he trained his mount to stand motionless while he vaulted into the saddle and then galloped at top speed for a mile or two before stopping.

The robbery went without a hitch. Cassidy, Warner, and Tom McCarty were the holdup men. The bookkeeper was covered, $10,500 dropped into a sack, and they were off. They soon lost the posses and returned to the golden-walled saloon in Star Valley. Butch spent the winter with the gang, but when spring arrived and the McCartys set out for Oregon, he stayed on in the valley.

From 1890 to 1892 Cassidy worked on various ranches throughout Wyoming as a cowhand. He was an expert with the branding iron, a skillful rider, and, unlike the outlaws of the Middle Border, was a sharpshooter. It was said he could ride at full speed past an ace of spades nailed to a tree and plant three or four slugs in the center of the card. Such stories are told about every one of our western outlaws and are undoubtedly exaggerated. But despite the endless tales about his skill with the gun, Butch Cassidy was a deadshot.

In 1892 he rode into Rock Springs where he donned the butcher's apron. It is curious to consider that as an experienced cowhand he should accept such an incongruous job. The townspeople were attracted by his easy smile and good humor and soon were calling him Butch. The nickname stuck.

Cassidy's stay in Rock Springs was short. He was accused of rolling a drunk and jailed. The Mormon cowboy was outraged at the charge. A glance at his record seemingly justified his rage. He was a horsethief, rustler, bank and train robber, but he had never stooped to such petty thievery. He was arraigned and quickly acquitted. Swearing revenge he left the town.

He returned to the hills and began selling a form of the modern protection racket to the ranchers. He was known as an expert rustler and it was a case of the cattlemen either putting him on their pay rolls or losing some of their valuable steers. After a short period of this employment Cassidy and another Mormon cowboy, Al Rainer, purchased a small ranch near where Dubois, Wyoming, stands today. Corrals were built and they did a brisk business in horses. The truth was, Butch Cassidy was rapidly taking Dingus James' place in the sun as the "finest horsethief in the West."

That winter a flu epidemic struck the nearby community of Wind River and Butch played a hero's role. He was in the saddle day and night, once riding fifty miles through drifts and howling gales with medicine to the home of a Mrs. Simpson, the only white woman in that wild and desolate territory.

The Simpson family took a liking to the young horsethief and Butch became a frequent visitor. It was said that he "told many tall tales to Mrs. Simpson which she believed." Butch, it seems, not only had a ready six-shooter, but also a ready tongue.

In the spring of 1894 Cassidy and his friend, Al Rainer, returned to Star Valley with thirty stolen horses. Sheriff John Ward of Uintah County, Wyoming, traced them to the valley hideout by following the daughter of a local rancher when she came to the nearby town of Afton, Wyoming, to pick up the outlaw's mail. Ward and his deputy questioned the girl, who told them that Rainer was working at a small sawmill a short distance away and Cassidy was resting in his cabin.

Rainer was taken into custody after a fight and tied to a tree while the two law enforcement officers continued on to the young Mormon's cabin. They took him by surprise. Cassidy made a lunge toward his guns hanging over a chair. He managed to yank one of the revolvers from the holster, but the bullet went wild. Ward's deputy fired and the slug plowed a superficial furrow along the horsethief's scalp. Handcuffs were slipped on his wrists as he lay stunned. It was the last time the law was to take him into custody.

In Lander, where he was well known and well liked, Cassidy's trial on charges of stealing horses attracted a great deal of attention. It was said that Bill Simpson, the son of Mrs. Simpson who had listened during those long winter nights to the young cowboy's "tall tales," was prosecuting attorney. Before the trial came up some of Cassidy's friends forged a bill of sale for the horses, but the man whose name they had forged showed up in court and the spurious document was never introduced as evidence.

Cassidy was found guilty and sentenced to the penitentiary for two years. Rainer was acquitted. The night before he was to leave for Laramie City, Butch asked permission to leave the jail. He gave his word that he would return the next morning. It is difficult today to visualize a convicted criminal leaving his cell the night before he is to go to the penitentiary, but in the West of 1894, a man's word was his bond—outlaw or cattleman. To break one's word was equal to the crime of poisoning a desert waterhole.

Cassidy appeared the next morning and turned in his guns. Where he went, whom he saw, or what he discussed was never known.

He entered the pen as No. 187 on July 15, 1894. He was twenty-seven.

Meanwhile, back at Landusky, the Logans were riding high. With their Hole in the Wall outlaw friends they bossed the town. The Christmas of 1894 was a bang-up celebration. The streets were decorated and a dance was held. Lonny Logan fiddled and Johnny called the turns. Liquor flowed like rain water and the whooping cowhands and rustlers made it a dangerous business for a sober man to walk down Main Street. The celebration lasted for three days. Harvey Logan, whom the Pinkerton criminal file describes rather morally as "an outlaw who drinks heavily and has bad habits," and old Pike Landusky went on a roaring drunk. On the afternoon of the twenty-seventh, Pike was leaning on the bar of the clothing store–saloon, run by a one-legged merchant.

Harvey and Lonny Logan and another Hole in the Wall rustler, Jim Thornhill, entered.

As he passed, Harvey smashed Pike in the face. The miner went down but came back raging. While Lonny and Thornhill held the crowd back with six-shooters, Logan went to work on the tough fifty-year-old miner. It was a brutal brawl with no holds barred. Landusky was hampered by a heavy coat, and Logan soon had the old man's face battered into an unrecognizable pulp. Through broken teeth Pike begged for mercy. But Logan was in the grip of a homicidal rage which was to flare up many times in his dark future. He kept beating the old man's head against the floor. With a last burst of strength, Landusky managed to open his heavy coat and yank out a six-shooter. But it had a new mechanism, and while he fumbled with it, Logan calmly blew out his brains.

Holding the townspeople at bay, Lonny stole a buckboard and the three outlaws made their escape. Back at the ranch they summoned Johnny Logan and hit the trail for the safety of Hole in the Wall.

In the Hole, Curry, who had taken the command when Champion fell, welcomed them with open arms. They were appointed as his lieutenants and the gang entered new fields of outlawry, holding up banks, trains, cattle camps, post offices, and stores.

But a bitter hate kept gnawing at the mind of Harvey Logan. Winters, the stockman, was still alive. So in January of 1896 Harvey led his brother back to Montana "to take care of him." But they had boasted too long and too loud about the campfires. Word had reached Winters and he was ready to receive them. A shotgun blast of glass and scrap iron almost tore off Johnny Logan's head and Harvey and Lonny fled back to Hole in the Wall. There Harvey swore a blood oath.

"I'll get him if I have to ride to hell after him," he vowed.

About the time Logan was swearing his oath Butch Cassidy was sitting in the office of Governor William A. Richards, a former president of the Wyoming Stock Growers Association, arguing for a pardon.

"Will you give me your word that you'll go straight?" the state executive asked.

Butch grinned and shook his head. "Can't do that, Governor," he said, "because I'll only have to break it and that I won't do. But I'll promise this: if you'll pardon me I'll promise never to molest the state of Wyoming again."

Richards sighed. "Pardon granted," he said.

Years later Richards told the story to the governor of Utah, who said dryly:

"I certainly wish you had gotten him to extend his amnesty to the state of Utah."

On the afternoon of January 19, 1896, Butch Cassidy stood on the steps of the Laramie City penitentiary for a moment after the gates had clanged behind him. His face was gaunt and stamped with prison pallor. He filled his lungs with the free air and then, with his head bent against the icy wind, hurried down the street. A few hours later he headed out of town bound for a new rendezvous, Brown's Hole, second only to Hole in the Wall as the headquarters of the outlaw high command.

Butch was given a warm welcome by the outlaw community when he arrived at the Hole. Unlike Jesse James, he was a cheery fellow with many admirers. Although he was never a heavy drinker, he was always ready for a roughhouse and was a favorite with the camp followers of the outlaws.

Before long he was back in the saddle with the raw winds burning away the sickly prison pallor. Rustling was his game and he returned to it with a relish.

In the spring of that year a slender, soft-spoken rider appeared. He wore broadcloth, with trousers tucked into his boot tops, and a black string tie.

He was Elza Lay and about seventeen.

His file in the Pinkerton archives describes him: "He is a gentlemanly sort of a man, apparently equipped with a better education than the others." Lay had a rustling record in New Mexico and was head of a band at Robber's Roost, another outlaw station, to the north. Little is known about his early background or how or where he received his "education," if he really had one. Many times he used the alias of William McGuinness.

Lay and Butch met and a firm friendship grew. Cassidy liked the quiet-spoken rustler and Lay was attracted by the Mormon's grin and easy ways. Bob Meeks, another outlaw, came in that same spring and was accepted by Cassidy. Several other young thieves joined up and Butch started his own band. A hideout high on the Diamond mountain and protected on three sides by cliffs was built. Today it is known as Cassidy Point.

More riders drifted in, but a special greeting was given Matt Warner when he arrived. Whisky flowed in the smoky cabins while Cassidy and the owner of the saloon in Star Valley talked over the old days. It was from Warner that Cassidy probably heard of his friends, the McCartys. Their careers had finished in a burst of gunfire in Delta, Colorado, in a scene similar to the breakup of the James-Younger band at Northfield and the Daltons at Coffeeville, Kansas. The Merchant's Bank was their target. Tom McCarty killed the cashier in cold blood and the gang fled. But again like Northfield, a young hardware merchant heard the shouts. W. Ray Simpson, the junior partner of W. G. Simpson and Son, grabbed a repeating Sharps rifle and a handful of shells. He caught the gang as they rounded a corner. Bill McCarty fell, with the top of his head blown off. His son, Fred, swung his horse about and returned to kneel beside his father's body. A shot split his heart. Tom McCarty's horse was next, but Tom escaped to join Matt Warner, the horse holder on that occasion. Tom returned later to Delta, sending word to Simpson that he planned to kill him. Young Simpson handed the outlaw's emissary a small piece of black cardboard. There were ten holes in a half dollar circle.

"At 225 feet" the hardware junior partner quietly told the emissary.

Tom McCarty left the same day.

After rustling during the day and listening to the tall tales at night, Butch and his outlaws would ride into the nearby towns of Vernal and Rock Springs on a Saturday night and take over the community. They would return to the hills on a Monday morning, nursing hangovers, and the battered, bullet-marked town would shake itself and the bartenders would begin their count of the rustlers' gold in their tills. From their boisterous antics Cassidy and his followers soon came to be known as "the Wild Bunch." The tag name stuck. The frontier newspapers picked up the nickname and the outlaws adopted it with a reckless sort of pride.

Back in Hole in the Wall, the Logans and Curry were attending to their flourishing rustling business, from headquarters at Champion's old ranch where the king of the rustlers died in the dust four years before. On April 13, 1897, a newly elected deputy sheriff, William Deane, decided to seek some glory and rode out to take the Logans and Curry into custody singlehanded. The brave but foolhardy law officer went down under a volley and his body was quickly buried. The murder made the evil community restless and the Logans and Curry began to look for a new hideout. A week later news of an incident came to their ears which decided the course for them to take.

On April 21, 1897, Butch Cassidy and his new recruit, Elza Lay, held up the pay roll of a mining camp at Castle Gate, Utah, and took eight thousand dollars from paymaster E. L. Carpenter. It was a daring holdup quietly executed in broad daylight.

The paymaster's office was located over a store and was jammed with men at the time of the stickup. Butch and Lay grabbed Carpenter on the stairs and the money was passed without an outcry. As they were vaulting in their saddles, Lay dropped a bag of silver. He started to turn and retrieve it but obeyed orders when Cassidy cried, "Leave it, leave it."

A short time before the robbery Cassidy rode up on a beautiful bay to a ranch just outside of Price, county seat of Carbon County, Utah. The ranch owner's name was Neibauer, and he was said to have been a member of the staff of Crown Prince Rudolph of Austria. After the tragedy at Mayerling, he fled to America. He drifted about the West and worked for a short time at the mines near Bingham Canyon, Utah, then purchased the ranch. In time he became acquainted with the passing outlaws.

"Keep my horse for me," Cassidy asked when he rode up. "I'll get him in about a week." Neibauer agreed. A week later Cassidy collected his sleek getaway mount and rode into Castle Gate with Lay.

There is also another story connected with the robbery which may or may not be true. Previous to the stickup Cassidy visited the town and was cleaned in a poker game. He beckoned to the proprietor and said:

"There are two of us camping outside the town and we're going out with some cattle in the morning. I sure hate to go back without the three bottles of Old Crow the boys asked me to get."

The bartender gave Cassidy three bottles "on credit."

"I'll be around shortly with it," the outlaw leader said with a slow smile.

"Anytime you're riding back," replied the strangely philanthropic barroom owner.

After the pay-roll holdup, a package was delivered to the saloon containing ten dollars and a note from Cassidy saying: "This is to pay for the bottles of Old Crow."

Back in Brown's Hole the gang celebrated the success of the stick-up. The camp followers flocked to the rough saloon and the whisky flowed for days.

These were no sullen-faced riders of Jesse James' Middle Border command. They were of a different breed. They lived by the gun and they expected to die by the gun, but in the meantime there seemed little sense in brooding about it; that, apparently, was their philosophy. It was another aspect of that western "isolated body of men."

The news of the Castle Gate robbery passed from band to band along the outlaw stations and soon reached the ears of the Logans and Flat-Nose George Curry. They all agreed it was an inspired piece of banditry and one worthy of equaling. The map was produced, and dirt-rimmed fingernails picked out the victims. The Butte County Bank at Belle Fourche, North Dakota, was selected.

At 9 A.M., June 26, 1897, Longbaugh, Harvey and Lonny Logan, Putney, and O'Day rode into Belle Fourche and reined in at the hitching post outside the county bank. They entered and drew guns on the cashier, the assistant cashier, and other bank employees on duty. The loot was a miserable hundred dollars in silver and bills. The cashier tried to peg a shot at the Logans but the gun jammed and the gang rode off. There was a wonderful comic-opera touch to the crime. O'Day, a dark-skinned man whose file in the Pinkerton archives describes him as "quarrelsome and a heavy drinker," had a jittery mount which shied when he tried a getaway. He kept cursing and swearing at the horse but failed to get aboard. Meanwhile, according to a Deadwood, Dakota, paper, "every man who had a gun took after them" and the street in front of the bank was jammed. O'Day let his horse go and ran over to a mule tied to a hitching post. A clergyman who was in the bank and who owned the mule recognized O'Day, who was grabbed. A posse pounded out of town and found the outlaws holed up in a ranch twelve miles from Belle Fourche. Wagons loaded with possemen surrounded the ranch and a heavy fire started.

"No one was hurt," the Deadwood paper remarked, "but Mr. Day, the hardware merchant, caught a stray bullet which took off part of his ear and Mr. Miller who was in front of the pursuers had his horse killed by the people in the rear."

Putney, the Logans, and Curry were captured and lodged in the Deadwood jail "as the Butte jail burned down last week."

Jesse James, that inimitable robber of banks, must have shuddered in the shades. The cashier of the bank echoed his sentiments. "The members of the gang were amateurs at the business," he said.

Logan and Curry were in jail only a few days. They broke out without any trouble and stole some horses and headed for Hole in the Wall. Tom O'Day, that "quarrelsome man," was acquitted and the outraged bank officials refused to prosecute Putney. The Pinkertons, who constantly kept check on their outlaws, noted in Denver File # 1728 in 1900, "Putney has settled down in Lost Cabin and seems to have reformed."

Back at Hole in the Wall conditions were changing. The stockmen were again gathering. A posse of twenty men prepared to search the outlaw land for stolen cattle and gave the outlaws fair notice. They printed their intentions in a newspaper!

The outlaws replied with their own press release, saying: "We have enuff men up here to kill you and we are going to get you or lose 12 more men." It went on to warn the leader of the stockmen not to "stick that damned old gray head of yours in this country again if you don't want it shot off."

The ranchers ignored this threat and set out for Hole in the Wall. The rustlers came out to meet them and a dramatic scene followed. Both sides rode past each other down the narrow canyon, rifles rigid, eyes glaring. After he had ridden a short distance, one of the outlaws dismounted. A posseman interpreted that as a hostile move. He swung out of his saddle, aimed, and fired. Outlaws and peace officers scattered, leaping for cover. Rifles barked and the air in the gorge was soon thick with dust and gun smoke and the whine of ricocheting bullets. The rifle duel lasted almost an hour. During a lull one of the rustlers came out from behind a boulder with his hands held high. The leader of the posse and one of his deputies were found to have been wounded. One outlaw had a bullet through a lung and died a few hours later.

The rustler who surrendered was brought into Casper, Wyoming, and then transferred to Buffalo. There was no trial. He was released a few days later with the sheriff of Johnson county shrugging his shoulders and saying:

55. One of the most famous pictures in Western lore is this one of the Wild Bunch. The original print in possession of the author shows that it was taken by John Swartz, 705 Main Street, Fort Worth, Texas. A Pinkerton agent who found the print identified the sedate-looking outlaws as: *Left to Right*, standing, William "Bill" Carver and Harvey Logan, alias "Kid Curry;" *Left to Right* sitting, Harry Longbaugh, the "Sundance Kid," Ben Kilpatrick, the "Tall Texan" and George Leroy Parker and Butch Cassidy. (*Courtesy Pinkerton's National Detective Agency, Inc.*)

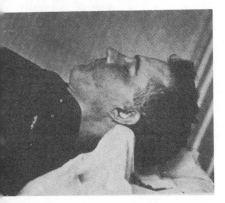

56. Lonny Logan in death. After a long run from the law he was shot down outside his Aunt Lee's home. (*Courtesy Pinkerton's National Detective Agency, Inc.*)

HARVEY LOGAN,
Retrato tomado en 1900.

Harvey Logan (*a*) Harvey Curry, (*a*) "Kid" Curry, (*a*) Tom Jones, (a) Bob Jones, se escapó el 27 de Junio de 1903 de la cárcel del Condado de Knox, Knoxville, Tenn., E. U. de A., donde estaba esperando á ser trasladado al presidio de Columbus, Ohio, para cumplir la sentencia de 20 años que se le impuso por circular billetes de bancos alterados, robados del carro del "Great Northern Express" en el ferrocarril "Great Northern," el 3 de Julio de 1901, por asaltadores de caminos de los que Logan era el jefe, y los cuales asaltaron dicho tren, contuvieron con armas de fuego á los empleados del tren, saltaron con dinamita la caja de hierro y sacaron de la misma $45,000 en billetes de banco sin firmar, que se llevaron.

SEÑAS PERSONALES.

NOMBRE...Harvey Logan

ALIAS......Harvey Curry, "Kid" Curry, Bob Jones, Tom Jones, Bob Nevilles, Robt. Nelson, R. T. Whelan.

RESIDENCIA......Se huyó de la cárcel del Condado, Knoxville, Tenn., el sábado 27 de Junio de 1903.

LUGAR DONDE NACIÓ........Dodson, Mo...COLOR...... ....blanco

OCUPACIÓN..Vaquero, tratante

OCUPACIÓN CRIMINAL...........Asaltador de bancos y trenes, ladrón de caballos y ganado asaltador de caminos y asesino.

EDAD......... ....38 años [en 1903.]

OJOS OSCUROS...Estatura, 5 piés 7½ pulgadas

PESO......de 145 á 150 libras, ...CONSTITUCIÓN...................Regular

TEZ......trigueña, atezada........................NARIZ......Prominente, larga, grande y recta

COLOR DEL PELO..Negro

BARBA..........afeitada cuando se escapó, pero puede dejarse crecer una barba espesa y bigote de color algo mas claro que el pelo.

ADVERTENCIAS.—Tiene una herida de bala en el brazo derecho, entre la muñeca y el codo; habla despacio; es un poco estevado y de carácter reservado Padece bronquitis aguda, jadea mucho; su estado físico no es del mejor; tiene dos cicatrices en la espalda que parecen proceder de una descarga con perdigones; tiene el hombro izquierdo mucho más bajo que el derecho, á causa de la herida; tiene los brazos más largos que la generalidad de las personas de su estatura; tiene los dedos bastante largos. HARVEY LOGAN también asesinó á Pike Landusky, en Landusky, Montana, el 25 de Diciembre de 1894, y tomó parte en gran número de asaltos y robos, entre ellos el robo del tren del Ferrocarril Unión del Pacífico, en Wilcox, Wyoming, el 2 de Junio de 1899, despues de lo cual la fuerza civil alcanzó á Logan y su banda cerca de Casper, Wyoming, y al tratar de prender á los ladrones, el alguacil mayor, Joseph Hazen, del Condado de Converse, Wyoming fué asesinado.

GEORGE PARKER.
Primer retrato tomado el 15 de Julio de 1894.

NOMBRE.......................George Parker

ALIAS........"Butch" Cassidy [*a*] George Cassidy; [*a*] Ingerfield.

NACIONALIDAD ....Americano

OCUPACIÓN..............Vaquero, tratante

OCUPACIÓN CRIMINAL......Ladrón de bancos y asaltador de caminos, ladrón de ganado y caballos.

EDAD......................36 años [en 1901]

ESTATURA..................5 piés 9 pulgadas

PESO.............................. 165

CONSTITUCIÓN..........................Regular

TEZ..Clara

COLOR DEL PELO......................Blondo

OJOS.. Azules

BIGOTE..........................Leonado, si lo usa

OBSERVACIONES.—Tiene dos cicatrices en la nuca; cicatriz pequeña debajo del ojo izquierdo, pequeño lunar en la pantorrilla. "Butch" Cassidy es conocido como un criminal principalmente en Wyoming, Utah, Idaho, Colorado y Nevada, y ha cumplido sentencia en el presidio del Estado de Wyoming en Laramie por robo, pero fué perdonado el 19 de Enero de 1896.

GEORGE PARKER.
Último retrato tomado el 21 de Noviembre de 1900.

LOS RETRATOS, SEÑAS PERSONALES Y LA HISTORIA CRIMINAL DE CADA UNO DE LOS INDIVIDUOS SOSPECHOSOS, SE DAN Á CONTINUACIÓN.

HARRY LONGBAUGH.
Retrato tomado el 21 de Noviembre de 1900.

NOMBRE......Harry Longbaugh, (*a*) "Kid" Longbaugh, (*a*) Harry Alonzo, (*a*) Frank Jones, (*a*) Frank Body, (*a*) el "Sundance Kid."

NACIONALIDAD......sueco-americano...........PROFESION...........Vaquero; tratante

OCUPACIÓN CRIMINAL......Salteador de caminos, ladrón de bancos, de ganado y de caballos.

EDAD.........35 años.............. ....ESTATURA............5 pies 10 pulgadas

PESO.........de 165 á 175 libras.....................CONSTITUCION.....................Buena

OJOS.........Azules ó pardos...... ....COLOR ....Trigueño claro

BIGOTE Ó BARBA......[si tiene] castaño natural con matiz rojizo.

FACCIONES.........tipo griego........................NARIZ.......................Más bien larga

COLOR DEL PELO.. ......castaño, puede habérselo teñido; se peina pompadour.

ES ESTEVADO Y TIENE LOS PIES MUY SEPARADOS.

OBSERVACIONES. ....Harry Longbaugh estuvo 18 meses cumpliendo sentencia en la cárcel de Sundance, Condado de Cook, Wyoming, cuando era muchacho, por robo de caballos. En Diciembre de 1892, Harry Longbaugh, Bill Madden y Henry Bass asaltaron un tren del Ferrocarril "Great Northern" en Malta, Montana. Bass y Madden fueron juzgados por este crimen y sentenciados á 10 y 14 años de presidio, respectivamente; Lonbaugh se escapó y desde entonces es un prófugo. En 28 de Junio de 1897 y bajo el nombre de Frank Jones, Longbaugh en compañía de Harvy Logan [*a*] Curry, Tom Day y Walter Putney, tomó parte en el robo de un banco en Belle Fourche, South Dakota. Todos cayeron en manos de la policía, pero Longbaugh y Harvey Logan lograron escaparse de la cárcel de Deadwood, en 31 de Octubre del mismo año. Desde entonces Longbaugh no ha vuelto á estar preso.

LA ESPOSA DE HARRY LONGBAUGH.

NOMBRE......... .... Sra. de Harry Longbaugh

ALIAS...... ....Sra. de Harry A. Place ; Sra. Ethel Place

NACIONALIDAD ....Americana

OCUPACIÓN, ... desconocida

OCUPACIÓN CRIMINAL..

EDAD.........de 27 á 28 años [en 1906]...........ESTATURA.........5 pies 5 ó 5 pulgadas

PESO.........de 110 á 115 libras.....................CONSTITUCION........................Regular

COLOR.........Trigueña..................................COLOR DEL PELO......Castaño oscuro

OBSERVACIONES.........Usa peinado alto formado por un moño enroscado desde la frente.

AL IR Á PRENDER Á CUALQUIERA DE LOS INDIVIDUOS DE ESTA BANDA DE LADRONES, SE RECOMIENDA Á LOS POLICIAS QUE LO INTENTEN QUE ESTEN BIEN REFORZADOS, PERFECTAMENTE ARMADOS, QUE NO SE ARRIESGUEN, PUES DICHOS CRIMINALES RESISTEN TEMERARIAMENTE ANTES DE RENDIRSE, Y NO TITUBEAN EN MATAR SI ES NECESARIO PARA SALVARSE. SON BUENOS TIRADORES, EXPERTOS GINETES, ACOSTUMBRAN Á VIVIR EN LAS LLANURAS Y SON HÁBILES EN LA CRÍA DE GANADO.

58. Annie Rogers and Harvey Logan, who met in Fannie Porter's Sporting House. The photograph was taken just before Cassidy broke up the Wild Bunch. (*Courtesy Pinkerton's National Detective Agency, Inc.*)

59. Harry Longbaugh, the "Sundance Kid," and the mysterious Ette Place just before their flight to Buenos Aires where they were to meet Butch Cassidy. This photograph was taken by De Young, a well-known New York society photographer, at 826 Broadway. Note Tiffany's gold watch pinned to Miss Place's breast. (*Courtesy Pinkerton's National Detective Agency, Inc.*)

RY LONGBAUGH IDENTIFIED AS "THE LONE TEXAN

60. [ABOVE] In St. Louis in 1901 Ben Kilpatrick was caught by the police through the stolen bank notes he passed. Laura Bullion, also captured, fooled the police, as this newspaper page from the The Butte *Inter Mountain* (November 15, 1901) indicates, by claiming Kilpatrick was Harry Longbaugh. (*Courtesy Pinkerton's National Detective Agency, Inc.*) 61. [RIGHT] Laura Bullion, long-time camp follower of the Wild Bunch, devotedly loved the handsome, but not too bright Kilpatrick, who stayed away from the Wild Bunch's sprees to be with her. (*Courtesy Pinkerton's National Detective Agency, Inc.*)

BANDIT LOGAN WAS LAST SEEN
FIVE MILES FROM CITY SATURDA

He Was Riding Leisurely Along a Byroad
Having Left the Pike---Spoke to
No One He Met

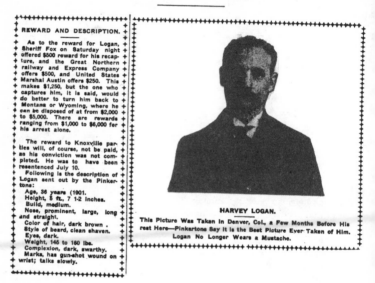

REWARD AND DESCRIPTION.

As to the reward for Logan, Sheriff Fox on Saturday night offered $500 reward for his recapture, and the Great Northern railway and Express Company offers $500, and United States Marshal Austin offers $250. This makes $1,250, but the one who captures him, it is said, would do better to turn him back to Montana or Wyoming, where he can be disposed of at from $2,000 to $5,000. There are rewards ranging from $1,000 to $6,000 for his arrest alone.

The reward to Knoxville parties will, of course, not be paid, as his conviction was not completed. He was to have been resentenced July 10.

Following is the description of Logan sent out by the Pinkertons:

Age, 36 years (1901).
Height, 5 ft., 7 1-2 inches.
Build, medium.
Nose, prominent, large, long and straight.
Color of hair, dark brown.
Style of beard, clean shaven.
Eyes, dark.
Weight, 145 to 160 lbs.
Complexion, dark, swarthy.
Marks, has gun-shot wound on wrist; talks slowly.

HARVEY LOGAN.

This Picture Was Taken In Denver, Col., a Few Months Before His rest Here—Pinkertons Say It Is the Best Picture Ever Taken of Him. Logan No Longer Wears a Mustache.

62. Newspaper account of Harvey Logan's escape from prison. *The Knoxville Sentinel,* June 27, 1903. *(Courtesy Pinkerton's National Detective Agency, Inc.)*

"What's the use of trying him here. He'll never be convicted."

For two weeks there was no news of the gun battle in the Buffalo *Bulletin*. Finally the story was told and ended on this delightful note:

"Finally, we beg it as a favor, do not believe that the *Bulletin* is 'adjusted' to any situation, except the obligation laid on every newspaper to tell the truth."

The editor of the newspaper was in a precarious situation. When the Hole in the Wall riders wanted supplies they bought them in Buffalo. The town's merchants depended on this trade. Had the *Bulletin* openly defied the outlaw gang, the merchants would have undoubtedly pulled out their advertising. Thus, it would have been impossible for the newspaper to survive. Then, too, there was the gang itself. It would have been an easy job for them to shoot up the newspaper office—and perhaps the editor— along with the wooden signs, street lamps, and store windows they shattered every time they came to Buffalo to celebrate.

Later that same month, sheriffs from Wyoming, Utah, and Colorado, along with a posse from South Dakota who were trailing the Belle Fourche bank robbers, embarked on another wide-scale invasion of Hole in the Wall. This time the entire outlaw command was waiting.

As the sheriffs and their deputies entered the valley they found large posters warning them to "keep out," but these they ignored. They could see the watchers on the hills and groups of horsemen in the distance. No shots were fired, and the stolen herds were driven out of the Hole. It was then that a curious scene took place. One of the sheriffs encountered some members of the gang but let them go "after he had given them a good talking to." We can imagine that law-enforcement officer lecturing to the grim-faced badmen on the evils of their ways as the lowing steers moved past them to beyond the red wall.

About this time some Wyoming newspapers denounced the law-enforcement officers for their failure to break up the Hole in the Wall gang. One, the Douglas *News*, declared:

> The attitude of a number of the Johnson county persons in upholding the Hole in the Wall thieves, is not likely to increase the number of advocates favoring a state appropriation of money to pay for the Invasion trial expenses. A county that

persistently tolerates a gang of outlaws in its midst; that even refuses or neglects to protect property owners, will receive no support from the lawabiding citizens of the rest of their state.

If the Hole in the Wall gang had been in any other county in the state the whole outfit would have been in the penitentiary years ago for the full limit of the law.

The *Basin City Herald* went further and charged that there were "moneyed scoundrels" who were aiding the gang by selling the stolen stock and sharing in the profits. There were rumors at the time that a well-known and seemingly respectable Wyoming banker was a behind-the-scene member of the Hole in the Wall gang and financed the stolen shipments. Another banker in the state was said to have worked with the thieves in this fashion.

A public announcement would be made of a shipment of gold going by stage. The departure time would be posted. Riders would thunder out from behind the red-walled fortress and hold up the stage. The express box—filled with either dirt or rocks—would be tossed down to the masked highwaymen. The banker would then collect from the stage or express company for the shipment of gold, which had, of course, never been sent.

Then there is the story which Charles Kelly found in the *Wyoming Derrick*. A short time after the invasion of Hole in the Wall by the posses the gang rode down "in a body" to engage the sheepmen "in a shooting match."

"Refreshments were served and a good time was had by all."

The uninvited sheriffs, probably irked because they were not invited, boycotted the party.

But between social engagements the outlaws had work to do. The posse from South Dakota had caught up with the Logans and Curry, who had fled to Montana and back again after the bank robbery at Belle Fourche. The sheriffs leading the men from Dakota were no lecturers, but they might well have been for all the good their guns did them. They invaded the Hole, fought a pitched battle for hours with the outlaws in cabins, and finally left in disgust after they saw what little damage their bullets did to the log walls.

Curry and the Logans then decided to leave the Hole and enlist under Butch Cassidy, who was becoming the most talked about outlaw in the West. On August 18, 1897, with nearly a hundred riders, the Logans and Curry left for Cassidy's headquarters on Powder Springs, a few miles north of Brown's Hole. They rode out of the slit in the rock and crossed the Lander, Wyoming, stage road at Lost Soldier's Pass. They made the journey a prosperous one; there was scarcely a sheep camp on their route that they didn't rob.

23.

THE TRAIN ROBBER'S
SYNDICATE

ESPAIR and frustration are well known to the historian who attempts a biography on the life and times of our Western outlaws. The documents in their case are meager, incomplete, or greatly distorted. There are no "Outlaw Papers" in which one could examine the hopes, dreams, disappointments, and philosophy of life in old diaries, family papers, orderly journals.

The outlaws of the West held the center spotlight of the stage for years. The newspapers wrote columns about them, legislatures denounced them, political parties shook to their foundations because of them, and hostilities on a wartime scale took place with the approval of the president of the United States and the state's chief executive. They stopped immigration and capital, controlled sections of three of the largest states in the Union, and for generations their deeds have been sung in ballad and song; but, for all of this, their lives are hopelessly hidden.

Nowhere can we find a glimpse into the inner man; what was Jesse James thinking when he stood on the porch and looked into the distance—peace, security, despair; or big Cole Younger, who bluntly told a lecture audience that any man who becomes an outlaw is either a fool or a madman but forgot to tell the audience which he was; or Butch Cassidy, who wanted to quit but couldn't; or the quiet-spoken Harry Longbaugh, who one day said, smiling, "I'll never be taken alive"; or Harry Tracy, that ingenious and fearless outlaw, who spoke of his family to a frightened farm woman while posses, in the nation's biggest manhunt, swarmed about the Northwest. Then there was Etta Place, who joined the gang just before they left the United States. From her pictures she appears to be a woman of refinement, yet she was as fearless a bank robber as Butch Cassidy or Dingus James. Where did she come from, why did she join this band of freebooters and killers?

This lack of material that would supply an insight into our bandits is demonstrated in the documents covering the period of 1897 when Curry and the Logans rode into Powder Springs to enlist in the ranks of Cassidy's gang.

The young Mormon leader must have experienced the intoxicating feeling of too much power, because a short time later he turned his back on horse stealing and rustling—"tin horns" he later called them contemptuously—and made outlawry his business.

Butch established the Train Robber's Syndicate.

This syndicate represented no idle boasting of a band of thieving egomaniacs, but was recognized by the Pinkertons and law officers of the west and the newspapers. William Pinkerton gave it the official stamp when he wrote to J. P. McPharland, his Denver superintendent:

> The Train Robber's Syndicate is composed of outlaws and thieves headed by George LeRoy Parker, alias Butch Cassidy, a cowboy gambler and rustler, and is composed of members of the Curry and Logan gangs. From reliable information we have received they intend to make railroads and express companies their victims. We must use every facility at our command to break up this criminal organization.

Cassidy's syndicate was a large organization ruled by a hierarchy with an iron hand. Besides Cassidy there were the Logans, dark-skinned and vicious; Harry Longbaugh, the Sundance Kid, like his leader a cool and fearless hand; Bill Carver, whom the wanted posters once described as "smelling like a polecat" after he had fought a losing battle with a skunk while on the way to rob a bank; O. C. Hanks, Deaf Charley, the court jester, with his shrewd, beady eyes and head cocked to one side to favor his good ear; Harry Tracy, cold as marble; Ben Kilpatrick, the Tall Texan, a powerful man and fast on the draw; Laura Bullion, a camp follower who loved to tell how the outlaws passed her from one to another because "they felt sorry for me"; Bob Lee, cousin to the Logans, who had left Missouri with them; Flat-Nose George Curry with his grotesque face and stoop-shouldered walk.

This was the inner circle. There were many others who rode in and out of Powder Springs, but they were only hired hands receiving a small share of the loot and not taking any part in the planning.

There are no accounts of where Cassidy got the idea for such an organization, but he soon put it in operation. Riders were sent out to scout the gold shipments and to bribe railroad company employees. His plans were so elaborate and involved such large forces that through the inevitable grapevine they came to the ears of the officials of the railroads selected as victims.

The gang had made a tactical error in picking the Union Pacific Railroad, protected by Pinkerton's National Detective Agency, who began an immediate investigation. William Pinkerton hurried to Denver and a conference took place. The Pinkertons were moving into line; the battleground was to be almost every state in the West, east into New York City, then South America. The Wild Bunch would feel the same terrifying pressure that dogged James and his gang. In the end it would kill them off, send them to the gallows, make them take their own lives, or drive them out of the country.

A short time after the conference in Denver, a stranger drifted into the Powder River outlaw community. He was a slight man, almost grizzled, with pointed, handle-bar mustaches and a sun-blackened face. He had piercing gray eyes and wore his six-shooters, draw-fighter style, the holster tied with rawhide to his side. He was an expert horseman and genial at the bar. Men liked but respected him at the first meeting. His name, he said, was Charles L. Carter.

This newcomer was an experienced cowboy and he said himself "on the run" from a murder charge. This remarkable stranger succeeded in joining the ranks of the Wild Bunch and so ingratiated himself into the Train Robber's Inner Circle that he managed to learn all their secret codes and plans and then he vanished as mysteriously as he had come. He was Pinkerton Operative Charles A. Siringo, of the Agency's Denver office, and the information he obtained, together with the secret code he had learned, was soon in the hands of the gang's intended victims. The leakage of this information held up the plan of the gang for nearly a year.

This is an excerpt from the agency's file on the syndicate. Overshadowing it is the figure of one of the most famous men of the West. Siringo, who was a crack operative for the Pinkertons for years, was born in southern Texas in 1855 and was a cowboy at twelve. For more than forty years he lived a life of thrilling experiences as a cowboy-detective. "The risks he ran," says John Hays Hammond, "the deadly situations through which his extraordinary nerve took him safely, his resourcefulness, his loyalty, and above all his cold-blooded bravery, always made men remember this picturesque, modest figure of the American frontier." Siringo was known to every great western figure, from Billy the Kid to Will Rogers.

He will appear again after the Wilcox train robbery, dogging the Bunch over mountains, deserts, across raging rivers, through blizzards, from Wyoming to Arkansas "where a moonshiner put me on their trail" and back again. He was four years in the saddle chasing the Bunch and covered an estimated twenty-five thousand miles.

Shortly after Siringo, the mysterious Charlie Carter, left, the gang met other complications. Matt Warner, with two companions, Wall and Coleman, had shot and killed two prospectors named Staunton and Melton at Dry Fork, Utah. Warner and his companions were arrested for the crime and lodged in jail at Vernal, Utah.

Butch paid a visit to the jail, "leaving his decorations" behind with the sheriff.

"How are you fixed for funds, Matt?" he asked.

Warner shrugged his shoulders. "Broke."

Butch rubbed his chin reflectively. He nodded to his followers. "I'll take care of things, Matt."

Outside he collected the guns and rode back to headquarters.

He gathered his gang about him and explained the situation. Warner was in jail and without a lawyer and funds. It was the duty of the gang to go to his aid. Money was needed and fast. Rustling would take too much time. A bank stickup was the only thing. It was agreed. The map was pulled out and Butch picked the victim. It was to be the bank in Montpelier, Idaho. There were to be only three riders. Butch elected Elza Lay with Bob Meeks as the horse holder.

Cassidy had another plan. If the trial went against Warner he would lead the Bunch into Vernal, take over the town by storm, and deliver the prisoners.

From Brown's Hole Butch, Lay, and Meeks rode to Cokeville, Wyoming, just over the Idaho line, and went to work on a ranch eight miles outside of Cokeville. During their stay they made several trips into Montpelier to case the bank.

On August 13, 1896, the three outlaws rode up to the bank as cashier Gray was chatting with an acquaintance outside, a few minutes before closing time for the day. Cassidy and Lay, with guns under their coats, forced them into the bank, where, with another employee, they were lined up, facing the wall.

Cassidy then swept all the visible money into a sack and it amounted to $7,160.

The employee, Mackintosh, who was near a window, saw a man across the street holding three horses and, judging him to be one of the gang, studied him.

The bandits fled from the bank and, with Meeks, rode away with their loot. A posse was quickly organized and followed in pursuit. But Butch had arranged for relays of horses to be stationed along the trail and they made good their escape to Powder Springs.

Back at Brown's Hole, the sack was split open and the bills and silver pieces counted. The next day Douglas V. Preston, later attorney general of the state of Wyoming, and two other attorneys were retained for the Vernal trial.

At their preliminary arraignment, counsel for Warner, Wall, and Coleman asked for a change of venue because of high feeling in Vernal and the threats of lynching. The application was granted. The attorneys appearing for Warner and his companions were D. N. Straup and Judge Thurman, both of whom later became members of the state's Supreme Court. The trial was moved to Ogden, Utah, and Sheriff Pope ordered to deliver his prisoners to the authorities there.

Pope's task was difficult. Back at Brown's Hole, Cassidy had been informed of the court's decision and had sent word into Vernal that Warner and the two other defendants would never leave town. Governor Thomas, when he heard of the contemplated jail delivery, telegraphed to Pope instructing him to "deputize an army of a hundred men," while the commander of the nearby Fort Duchesne sent word he was ready to ride with his troopers as escort.

But Pope had an ace to play. At midnight one night he handcuffed his prisoners, saddled up, and left town with five deputies traveling along an old abandoned military road leading over the Uintah range, northwest of Fort Duchesne. At Ogden, Pope delivered his prisoners.

Preston appeared at Ogden and the case went to trial. On September 9, 1896, the Salt Lake *Herald* announced in glaring headlines that a "most desperate plot is unearthed." The subheads read: "There may be a battle. How Cassidy and his gang propose to liberate their pals. . . ."

The paper was only printing what everybody in town knew. The trial was going against Warner, Coleman, and Wall. Word was dispatched to Cassidy, and with his entire outlaw command he rode down on Ogden and camped in a canyon seven miles out.

The *Herald* declared:

"The robbers, it is believed, have been reinforced and all are prepared for an emergency."

The newspaper also disclosed the connection between the Montpelier bank robbery and Warner's imprisonment.

"But the members of the gang are not relying solely on this to secure the release of their partner. A bold plot to set him free at the point of pistol had been discovered. Cassidy, at the head of his gang of desperadoes, has planned to be present at Warner's trial. When the opportunity would present itself, Sheriff Wright and his deputies were to be overpowered and shot down like dogs if necessary, and the prisoners liberated. And this is not all. The outlaws have a perfect organization. They have threatened to kill anyone who has dared to take the stand against any of the three men, and sufficient evidence has come into the hands of the authorities to demonstrate the seriousness of the situation."

The article then goes on to describe Cassidy's riders as more powerful than the Jameses and Youngers "in their palmiest days."

The newspaper warned its readers that, should a posse make an attempt to run down Cassidy and his gang, "there will be a bloody fight. They are well mounted, well supplied with fire arms, and in case of a conflict it would be doubtful if any of these desperate men would be taken alive."

While the community trembled, Cassidy sent a note to Warner in jail by Coleman's partner. But the police intercepted the message which read:

Dear Matt:
The boys are here. If you say the word we'll come and take you out.

Under the eyes of Chief of Police Davenport, the message was delivered and Warner wrote back:

Dear Butch:
Don't do it. The boys here have been mighty good to me and I wouldn't want them to get hurt. Preston says they can't convict us. If they do we'll be out in a couple of years. Don't take the chance. Thanks anyway.

Butch said farewell in the last note. It read:

Dear Matt:
If they keep you more than two years we'll come and take the place apart sure as hell. Good luck.

After a short trial, in which one of the state's witnesses was charged by the prosecutor as having "diarrhea of the jawbone," Warner and Wall were convicted and sentenced to five years in the penitentiary. Coleman, curiously, was acquitted and disappeared. Warner was thirty-two when the prison gates clanged behind him.

After the last note had been sent to Warner, Cassidy led his gang back to Brown's Hole. There, as the result of the wide publicity he had received, he was welcomed by the outlaws as a conquering hero. While the law officers chased about the country declaring that the McCarty brothers were the Montpelier robbers, Butch laughed and told the story of the raid. There were several young riders who basked in his reflected glory, and after hearing the tale they organized their own gang and called it the Junior Wild Bunch. It had a short career.

There were four riders, all teen agers: George Harris, George Bain, Joe Rolls, and Young Shirley. They selected their first strike as the bank of Meeker, Colorado, just seventy-five miles east of Brown's Hole. Like the Wild Bunch, Sr., they established a horse relay, with Joe Rolls in charge of the mounts.

The boys entered Meeker on the morning of October 13, 1896, and hitched outside the small banking house. Inside they lined up the employees, one firing his six-shooter. They swept the money into sacks and ran out. The shot had attracted the citizens who surrounded the bank with six-shooters, rifles, and shotguns. A short but furious gun duel followed. When the smoke lifted, two of the boys were dead and one was dying. That afternoon the three were buried.

Beyond the town young Rolls rolled his cigarettes and walked about the horses impatiently. After some time passed he realized what had happened and, leaving the horses behind, fled to the Hole. Other riders returning to the outlaw's hideout informed Butch of what had happened. The Wild Bunch was outraged and sent word into Meeker that they were riding in. But the citizens of Meeker, like those of Northfield, had had just about enough of outlawry. The town armed itself and let word seep back into the Hole that there were plenty of rifles and shotguns in town—loaded—if they wanted to ride in and do any shooting. . . .

The gang growled and threatened but the big raid failed to come off.

For about four months Cassidy ceased operations in order to consolidate his gang. Recruits were drifting into Powder Springs from all over the West and the Bunch was growing. Brown's Hole soon became the headquarters for almost every American outlaw. It became so prominent in the nation's news that the Buffalo, Wyoming, *Bulletin* indignantly informed its readers that there was a vast difference between Powder River and Powder Springs. It admitted, however, that there were outlaws at both places but declared that the group at Powder Springs "was more desperate."

While Butch Cassidy was directing operations of his gang, William Pinkerton was organizing his operatives in a move to put an end to the Wild Bunch. Like Jesse James and his Middle Border bandits, the Bunch had made a tactical error when they had robbed the Montpelier Bank, which was a member of the American Banking Association and under the protection of the Pinkertons.

The first break for the Pinkertons came when Bob Meeks was arrested by Sheriff John Ward at Fort Bridger, near Powder Springs, as a suspect in a minor crime there. The Pinkertons learned of the arrest and rushed teller Mackintosh to Fort Bridger to identify Meeks as one of the Montpelier outlaws. Mackintosh positively identified Cassidy's rider as the horse holder he had studied outside the bank. Meeks was tried and convicted. He was sentenced to serve thirty-two years in the Idaho state prison, the maximum term for armed robbery under state law.

The outlaws were stunned when they heard the news. It was the heaviest sentence ever given for robbery. Why, even for murder, Warner had received only five years! Then more trouble arrived on the first windy day of March, 1898.

"Swede" Johnson, who was neither a Swede nor an Irishman, was a new recruit, having ridden into the Hole as a fugitive from a murder charge in Thompson Springs, Utah. He was accepted by Cassidy and became friendly with Tracy and Dave Lant, also fugitives from Utah justice. On that March day, Johnson, who was coming into the Hole, shot and killed Willy Strang, a young boy who had playfully knocked a water dipper from the bandit's hand. Johnson, with Tracy and Lant rode out of the Hole a few hours later and headed eastward toward Colorado.

Rustling, thievery, robbery, and even murder committed outside the Hole by the outlaws were tolerated, but murder of one of its own citizens could not be tolerated by the small, law-abiding group in the valley. Valentine Hoy, "a rancher who stood for law and order," gathered a posse together and rode in pursuit. The three outlaws were caught in a canyon and in the gun battle which followed Hoy was killed and Jack Bennett, a trafficker in Indian squaws and liquor for the Indians, who was bringing supplies for the three outlaws to an earlier agreed rendezvous, was taken. Meanwhile posses from the three bordering states began gathering at the Bassetts' Ranch on Green River as the body of Hoy was brought down from the mountain by his two brothers, Harry and J. S. Hoy. The corpse had been lowered down the cliffs with ropes, carried for five miles on horseback along the twisting, narrow trails, and then put in a buckboard.

The Hoys were in a murderous rage as they stretched the riddled body of their brother out on the crude bier of rough planks. They brushed aside the law officers and dragged Bassett from the room where he had been guarded. The only cottonwoods were on the shores of the Green River on the opposite side of the valley, but the Hoys couldn't wait that long. The noose was flung over the corral crosspieces, and there Bassett kicked out his life while the posses rode back to Diamond Mountain after the three fugitives.

While the Hoys were hoisting Bassett, Tracy, Lant, and Johnson had sneaked down out of the mountains and were headed for the outlaw stronghold of the Wild Bunch at Powder Springs. A sharp wind was rising as the tri-state posse split to cut off all avenues of escape. They found the outlaws' camp where a colt had been killed and chunks cut and roasted. The hide had been cut to make crude moccasins, but the bloody tracks were visible.

Late that afternoon from the top of a high ridge they saw the small black specks moving across the valley. The outlaws had covered fifty miles on foot in a day and a night. The snow was still deep this high in the mountains, and the bloody tracks were easy to follow. The killers were finally surrounded in a gully and Tracy shouted to "come and get us."

Hours passed. The wind moaned through the passes and the possemen shivered in the freezing temperature. Tracy shouted again and asked "for a trial in Wyoming," but the answer was that no promises would be made. The outlaws continued to taunt the sheriffs to come near and start shooting, but when the sun dropped and the watery light faded there was silence.

Suddenly a man rose and stumbled from behind a rock. It was Johnson, numb with the cold. Through chattering teeth he shouted his surrender and "came in." Lant followed, crying, "Don't shoot," but Tracy held back. Earlier he had warned Johnson and Lant that if they made a move to surrender he would kill them. For some reason he failed to keep his evil promise. But as the blue twilight fell over the gully Tracy finally surrendered, taunting the sheriffs and possemen for cowards.

With their prisoners bound hand and foot the posse made their way down the torturous trails. Back at Hoy's ranch that night,

Tracy, Johnson, and Lant were arraigned on the murder charges with J. S. Hoy acting as justice of the peace. It was a grim scene in the lantern light of the ranch with the weary sheriffs and their deputies crowding the small room as the sneering Tracy and his two exhausted followers were brought before the brother of the dead man, who was justice in the valley of the outlaws. Not too far away, the stiffened body of the squaw man creaked in the wind.

There was a dispute among the law officers as to what state the prisoners would be taken to, but it was finally agreed that Johnson would go to Wyoming and Tracy and Lant to Colorado. The prisoners were jailed and then the governors of the three states, like their sheriffs, began brawling in print over the custody of their prisoners. J. S. Hoy entered the discussion with a long letter to the Denver papers. Amid the hysterical demands for the state militia to come and wipe out the Wild Bunch and the interstate wrangling, the rancher's letter made sense.

It would be just as well to send a "bunch of schoolboys" as to send the militia, Hoy said. He pointed out that hunting men on the plains or in a thickly settled country is one thing, but to stalk killers "in these mountains, snow capped in sections the year round, cut by impassable canyons, unfordable rivers, gulches, gullies, and where nearly every section of land affords a hiding place, is another proposition." If these desperadoes, he said, were to be cleaned out, it would have to be done by men living in that section and acting in "concert with law-abiding citizens."

A reward of one thousand dollars apiece should be offered by each state, he added, and "that will do the work."

"One or two men on the trail of a criminal will succeed where a hundred men will fail. They must be hunted like wild animals, once on their trail, stay on it, camp on it until the scoundrels are run down, and there are men who will do it who are as brave and cunning as these outlaws themselves."

Hoy's letter produced an uproar. At Powder Springs Cassidy read the paper and there was no smile on his face when he summoned his lieutenants.

"Saddle up," he ordered. "We'll teach that bastard a lesson."

On March 14, the column of riders swung out of the outlaw headquarters to attack one of Hoy's cattle camps over the line in Colorado. They destroyed everything they could find. What horses or cattle they couldn't take with them, they wantonly killed.

Ten days later Tracy and Lant broke out of the jail at Hahn's Peak, Colorado, slugging Sheriff Neiman as he gave them breakfast. They not only robbed him of ninety dollars, but locked him in his own cell. But Neiman was a tough law officer. A deputy pried off the cell lock—the outlaws had thrown away the key—and the sheriff picked up their trail to Steamboat Springs, Colorado. Reasoning that they might head for the railroad, he took the stage at Steamboat Springs which went southwest.

Six miles out the drivers slammed on the brake and brought the swaying coach to a stop. Two passengers swung aboard. They looked weary and footsore and sighed with relief as they slumped into the hard seats and the whip cracked and the stage jerked forward. It was then the cold barrel of the shotgun reached out of the shadows and touched Tracy's temple.

"Good morning, Tracy," Sheriff Neiman said. "There's a breakfast waiting back at the jail."

The outlaw held out his hands and the manacles snapped. Lant followed.

"Who in the hell thought anybody from Hahn's Peak would be up this early," Tracy growled as the sheriff ordered the driver to swing his team about for Steamboat Springs.

After their capture Tracy and Lant were removed to Aspen, Colorado. There Tracy whittled a wooden gun, covered it with tin foil, subdued the guards, and with Lant escaped. Thirty-seven years later, John Dillinger, who took Tracy's position as America's Number One Enemy, followed the precedent at Crown Point Penitentiary, when he used "a cell-made wooden pistol to intimidate his guards, overpowered the soldier on guard in the warden's office, stole two machine guns, and then rode away in the sheriff's car."

Tracy would have sneered at this. When he broke out of jail he forced the state of Oregon to fight him on both land and sea; he stole a steam launch to cruise past a United States military prison to "see if we can knock off a couple of guards from the wall," fought off a dozen posses and militia, traveled four hundred miles on foot, and fooled some of the best manhunters in the west.

After they had broken out of the Aspen, Colorado, jail, Tracy and Lant dissolved their evil partnership. Tracy was too blood-thirsty for the young cowpuncher. Lant returned to the Bunch at Powder Springs and Tracy moved north to Oregon where he teamed up with another outlaw, David Merrill. Strangely enough they looked alike. It was as though the evil in Tracy was too much for one man and the devil had fashioned him a twin. Before long they had launched a reign of terror that rivaled anything the Northwest has since known.

They had started working their way toward Brown's Hole when they were arrested and sentenced to long terms in the Oregon state penitentiary. Their story is not ended; in a subsequent chapter their escape, chase, and capture, perhaps one of the most exciting in American criminal history, will be told.

At Rock Springs, Wyoming, Swede Johnson was tried on a murder charge. He was convicted, but two years later his convic-tion was reversed by the Wyoming State Supreme Court. He was released from prison but arrested by the sheriff of Routt County and taken to Aspen, Colorado, where he was convicted of being an accomplice in the murder of Valentine Hoy. He served two years and disappeared. He never again appeared in the outlaw country.

Back at Brown's Hole, Butch Cassidy was reorganizing his Train Robber's Syndicate, but the recent manhunt for Tracy, Lant, and Johnson, and the killing of young Strang and rancher Hoy, had focused national attention on his rendezvous. The Denver *News* called his gang "the greatest organized band of thieves and murderers in the west with a line of strongholds from Powder Springs, Wyoming, in a southwesterly direction across the entire state of Utah and down into Arizona, giving them easy access to Mexico... the number of outlaws is variously estimated at from 50 to 500. ..."

The Denver paper also made reference to the contemplated holdup of the Union Pacific by Cassidy's syndicate which was disorganized by Siringo. "The gang," the article added, "now communicate with each other by courier and cipher dispatches."

A few weeks later the *News* declared that the Wild Bunch had almost "depopulated the ranges within 200 miles of their retreat and farmers' freight wagons have been robbed so frequent as to cause little comment, while the large cattle companies have almost been driven out of business."

The storm gathered swiftly. The cattle syndicates, who had

sworn to "come back and clean the rascals out" after the '92 invasion, now met in secret to make plans "for a war of extermination." Cattle barons conferred with the governors of the three states and informed them "that a state of terror now exists, the like of which does not have a parallel in western or eastern history." Martial law was asked and troops requested to fling "an impregnable cordon around the territory, for a gradual closing in."

At last the governors of the three states acted and the telegraph began to hum....

Wyoming will co-operate ... Utah will co-operate in every way possible ... Colorado is ready ...

On March 14 the three state executives met at Denver with representatives of the cattlemen's association. There would be no repetition of the mob rule of six years before; it was to be a war of extermination but executed in a law-abiding fashion.

A plan similar to that suggested by Hoy was adopted. The invaders this time would be fifteen picked officers, five from each state. They would be paid one hundred dollars a month. Each man would be familiar with the territory.

No details of the plan were made public, but it would soon be put in motion, the governors hinted to newsmen.

Back at Brown's Hole and Powder Springs the grapevine brought the news to Cassidy. He shrugged it off and summoned his riders. There was more to be considered than a lot of damn-fool sheriffs and sprouting politicians. It was train robbery time again and plans had to be made. The Union Pacific was the victim.

But something happened which halted his grandiose plans and the tri-state war of extermination. The United States declared war on Spain. On April 25, 1898, the outlaws and governors alike stared at the bold and black headlines: the *Maine* had been sunk and the troops were marching.

The war against the Wild Bunch was forgotten and in the cabins of Powder Springs Butch Cassidy spread the word. Every rider was to enlist, and the hard-riding troop was to be called the Wild Bunch. It was a grand plan and it caught the imagination of the outlaws. Cassidy's order was relayed to the other stations and the rendezvous was set for Steamboat Springs, Colorado. What a sight it must have been when Cassidy and his men rode into that small community armed to the teeth, the young Mormon leader grinning at the townspeople, the Logans at his side, dark and wooden faced; Longbaugh and Elza Lay and Kilpatrick the Tall Texan slouched in the saddle; Deaf Charley, his head cocked for what the boys were saying; Dave Lant, who broke with Tracy; and all the rest of the less important thieves, rustlers, and badmen who had come to the Powder Springs hideout as fugitives from the society they now waited to defend.

Where they met and what was said is lost. Probably they gathered in some saloon with the piano stilled and the dance-hall girls hanging on the arms of the men whose names were now known throughout every section of the West. Butch's leadership was never questioned and he must have presided over the meeting, unless he turned the gavel—more likely a gun butt—to Elza Lay who was "educated."

If they had their way the young bucks would have ridden into Denver and enlisted en masse. But the older and more experienced of the outlaws vetoed the plan and their objections made sense. Did they think for one minute that the law would turn the other way just because they had come in to join the army? Wouldn't they be flung into jail? Rustling wasn't too bad, but what about murder and the train robberies...?

The Bunch spent a few days at Steamboat Springs and then returned to Brown's Hole. But some of the younger riders enlisted. They served their country with distinction and never returned to the outlaw land.

Kelly spoke to General J. P. O'Neil of Portland, Oregon, who tells a wonderful story about some of the Wild Bunch riders in action.

After putting five hundred mules aboard ship they were given a shore leave before sailing. That night they were escorted back to the ship by sixty policemen. The Barbary Coast, which thought it had seen everything, had called for help. The Wild Bunch riders had taken over the notorious red-light district and were systematically taking the place apart when the police arrived. More police were called, and then the riot squad.

Kelly quotes O'Neil:

The reputation followed these men to Manila. In Mindanao the pack trains could hardly get through on account of the constant forays of the fierce Moros. When these fifty packers were assigned to this, the Moros jumped them as they did the others. After the first two or three pack trains had gone over the trail, complaints began pouring into headquarters that the packers were killing large numbers of Moros and leaving their bodies on the trail. Not a single pack train of which these men were in charge failed to arrive at its destination. These packers were also responsible for many an insurgent and many a fierce ladrone arriving at the happy hunting ground of wherever dead Moros go.

24.

THE WILCOX TRAIN ROBBERY

AFTER his first flush of patriotism, Butch Cassidy again turned to his plans for robbing trains. He decided that the Union Pacific, which usually carried large gold shipments in its express cars, was to be their chief target. But Cassidy was still bound by his promise to Governor Richards not to "molest the state of Wyoming," and so, instead of riding along with the Bunch, he planned the robberies and put them into execution.

The first robbery took place at 2:30 A.M. on June 2, 1899. The first section of train Number One of the Overland Flyer was stopped at Wilcox, Wyoming. To stop the train the robbers, who were George Curry, that flat-nosed leader of Hole in the Wall rustlers who had surrendered his command to Cassidy, Harvey Logan, and Elza Lay, had adopted the technique of Jesse James by placing a red lantern on the tracks. Like Jesse's holdup at Little Blue, the train was stopped near a small wooden bridge. Two men, armed and masked, leaped into the locomotive's cab and ordered W. R. "Rhinestone" Jones to uncouple the express car and to move the train across the bridge; when Jones refused, he was beaten over the head with gun butts. His life was spared by one of the bandits who ordered the beating stopped. Then, getting behind the throttle, the outlaw drove the train across the bridge, which they blew up. A brakeman crawled away in the darkness and made his way across the gap to warn the approaching second section of the limited.

Meanwhile the outlaws went to the express car and banged on the door demanding that messenger Woodcock open it. Woodcock refused, turned out the lights in the car, took up a shotgun, and shouted that he would kill the first man to enter.

Cassidy, in his planning of the robbery, had modernized the James-train-robbery technique by supplying his men with dynamite. A stick was placed under the car and touched off. The blast blew out one side of the car and Woodcock was thrown against the iron safe and knocked unconscious. He was dumped out on the side of the tracks and the train robbers attempted to revive him to obtain the safe's combination. But it wasn't any use. Again dynamite was used. The impatient bandits placed an approximate ten pounds on the safe. The fuse was touched off and the explosion blew the safe in half and shattered the car. There was a snow storm of paper money and bonds. What the outlaws thought was a pool of blood turned out to be a small shipment of raspberries. In the brilliant moonlight the currency was swept up and thrown into the sack and the riders vanished in the night toward Medicine Bow Mountains. The loot was an estimated thirty thousand dollars. There was none of the wild whooping and revolver-firing farewells of the ex-guerrillas of the Middle Border.

The second section of the train was several minutes late and saved from disaster by the brakeman. After the wires spread the news of the holdup a special train was dispatched to the scene from Cheyenne, one hundred and twenty-five miles to the west, carrying officials of the Union Pacific, Pinkerton operatives, and a posse of men and horses. Another special train carrying seven flat cars of horses and men moved out of Laramie a few hours later. Arriving at Wilcox, they were divided into two groups, one scouring the Northwest, the other the Southwest. Pinkerton operatives, trying to obtain a description of the outlaws, questioned the groggy Woodcock and the engineer, Jones, as he rubbed the goose egg on his head.

Curry, Lay, and Logan meanwhile were trailed to the Platte River at Casper, Wyoming, which they crossed early on Sunday morning. There a posse of men from Converse County took up the chase. Thirty miles north of Casper, at Teapot Creek, the fugitives were cornered and a gun battle took place. The three outlaws retreated slowly, the gullies, canyons, and mountain passes echoing with their gunfire. After ten miles they selected a small rock formation which was a natural fortress and made a stand.

Sheriff Joseph Hazen, who was leading the attack, was killed and his outraged possemen began crawling toward the rocks determined to wipe out the gang at any cost. Curry, Logan, and Lay were so hard pressed that they left their horses and, keeping up a running fire, took up another position a mile beyond. Night quickly gathered and the three men found themselves hemmed in on all sides. While they sat and shivered in the darkness, they could see the twinkling fires of the posses on every side. They fired a few shots at moving shadows and the answering rifle bullets screamed overhead. Gradually a stillness hung over the place. There was no moon and the night was cold and black. In the hills a coyote raised his head and howled.

The three besieged men held a vote. It was decided to take a chance. The morning could only bring death. They could never hope to hold out against all of them. Like Shawnee braves slithering through the grass to cut out a horse from a rival tribe and gain a coup, the three men crawled down the hill, foot by foot, digging in with toes and elbows with the sacks of gold hanging like millstones about their necks.

Then it was over and they were past the guards. They traveled all that night and the next day, desperately trying to gain Hole in the Wall. Posses were everywhere trying to cut them off. They finally reached a ranch on the north fork of the Powder River where they obtained horses, clothing, and food. They moved from station to station along the outlaw trail and beat their way toward Lost Cabin country. The posses and the bloodhounds turned back. Somewhere in that wild land the three fugitives joined Butch and the others and the money was divided. The Bunch rode three hundred miles out of Brown's Hole to Robber's Roost.

At the Roost, the outlaw trust split with Curry and a few others running stolen horses. Cassidy and the rest of the gang continued on south into Arizona and New Mexico. This was the longest ride the Wild Bunch had ever made.

In Alma, New Mexico, the most southern station on the outlaw trail, Cassidy, Logan, and Lay got jobs as ranch hands. They took on new names; Cassidy became Jim Lowe; Logan, Tom Capehart; and Elza Lay, William McGuinness. Curiously enough all rustling stopped, new men drifted in, and before long Cassidy and his Wild Bunch riders had taken over the WS Ranch, the largest ranch in the vicinity of Alma, New Mexico.

In Denver, while Cassidy and his men branded, roped, and cared for the WS stock, Charlie Siringo, the cowboy-detective, had been summoned to the Denver Pinkerton office.

Superintendent J. P. McPharland tossed a telegram across the desk to him.

CHICAGO, JULY 1, 1899

SAYLES LEAVING HERE TODAY. CONTACT SIRINGO AND ASSIGN THEM TO WILCOX ROBBERY.

SIGNED,

WILLIAM A. PINKERTON

"I thought Sayles was in South Africa," Siringo said.

McPharland nodded. "He has just returned. He'll be here in a day or two." He pulled out a map. "Have you read about the Wilcox holdup?"

Siringo nodded. "Is it Cassidy's gang?"

McPharland replied, "From the descriptions it was probably Harvey Logan, Curry, and Lay. Cassidy rode off with them from Lost Cabin."

The Pinkerton superintendent ran his finger down the map. "Some of the gang have been seen running some horses south and it looks like they're headed for Brown's Hole. When Sayles arrives it'll be best if you go with him to Salt Lake City for your supplies and then cross the border into Colorado."

Outside of Price, Utah, the two operatives were caught in a driving downpour and almost drowned in a swollen creek. Soaked to the skin they waited all day in the rain until the stream subsided and then crossed that night in the pitch blackness. At Price they stopped at a small hotel and were immediately arrested as two of the gang. After they had established their identity well enough to the town's officers, the armed posse that had surrounded the hotel was called off.

At their arrival at Hanksville, Utah, they learned that two men acting suspiciously had been seen to cross the Colorado River at Dandy Crossing with thirteen horses ten days before, and that less than a week previously, a third man had crossed at the same place with ten horses. From the descriptions given to Siringo, there was no doubt that the last man was George Curry. Siringo took up the trail of Curry and followed it for several days but lost it and then returned to Hanksville. Then with Sayles he picked up the trail of the first two men driving the thirteen horses.

For a hundred and twenty miles through the roughest country in the West, the two Pinkerton operatives followed the track of the small herd of horses. On the way one of their pack animals died from a rattlesnake bite and they were forced to jettison some of their supplies. At Bluff City, on the San Juan River, Siringo and Sayles learned that two other Pinkerton detectives, Garman and Darkbird, had passed through having cut across from Flagstaff, Arizona, in an effort to head off the thieves.

In his biography, *Riata and Spurs*, Siringo gives a humorous picture of the two agents hearing the news that there were others ahead of them in the chase.

> Sayles and I figured we were born leaders of men; hence we didn't like the idea of being up in the rear, three days behind the other operatives. We put our jaded horses in pasture, stocked our supplies and taking our saddles boarded the Denver and Rio Grande Railroad for Durango. Here we overtook Garman and his chum. From Durango, Sayles and I led the chase by riding in trains, buggies, and on hired saddle horses. We left the two other boys far behind.

At Lumberton, New Mexico, Siringo received a report that two men driving a herd of horses were on their way south. Siringo went on to check the report while Sayles searched the country around Pagosa Springs, Colorado. At Sante Fe, the cowboy-detective received a wire from his partner saying he had picked up the trail of the men and horses and to join him at Canyon City, Colorado. There both men met, but Sayles was recalled to Denver by William Pinkerton after some of the stolen bank notes began to turn up in Montana.

Siringo continued the hunt alone, following the Arkansas River and stopping for a few days at Dodge City, the toughest town in the West. From there, by buggy, saddle horse, and train he tailed the gang to Kansas, through the Indian Territory, and then to Fort Smith, Arkansas. There he was joined by operative Darkbird. They pushed on to Pine Bluffs and then to Hot Springs, Arkansas. The trail was lost and the two detectives split up to check the surrounding country. At Nashville Darkbird fell ill with malaria and returned to Denver. Siringo went into the mountains from Hot Springs and lived for a time with a band of moonshiners. One old man, who had heard of the men and the thirteen horses, discussed it one night about the campfire. The next morning the slender little man was not to be found and the moonshiners wondered who he was and where he had gone.

Little Rock, and then through the horrible swamps. At Stuggart Siringo found that the horses had been turned over to "a long haired old man by the name of La Cutts, who lived not far from the Arkansas River."

Curry and his horsethieves, mounted on the two best bays in the herd, struck north for the White River, then down that stream to the Clarendon, then east to Helena to the Mississippi. They crossed and rode hard, twisting and turning in an effort to throw Siringo off. But the quiet little man continued to dog their tracks. They doubled back to the Mississippi and there engaged a scow to cross to the mouth of the Arkansas River. There they split, scattering in all directions. Through some means the Pinkerton sleuth discovered that they were to meet somewhere along the Mississippi.

To cover all avenues of escape Siringo visited all the larger cities and towns, notifying sheriffs and marshals of the presence of the gang and gave out descriptions of Flat-Nose George.

A telegram from Denver caught up with him and Siringo went to Helena, Montana, where he met Sayles and another Pinkerton operative. Sayles informed him that the agency had discovered Lonny Logan in Hardin, Montana, where he ran a saloon, but he had skipped before they could grab him. The agency, however, had found the Logans' hideout near Landusky, Montana, and Siringo was ordered to go there and see what information he could find about the Missourians. After indescribable hardships, including an eighty-five mile ride through a raging blizzard, Siringo reached Landusky. He adopted the name of Charlie Carter, and soon the town was whispering about that hard-eyed man riding the big white horse. It was said he had killed ten men and was an outlaw leader in New Mexico.

Siringo was soon in solid with the rustlers and thieves who had stayed there after the Logans had returned to Hole in the Wall. Before long he was a constant visitor at the house of the dead Pike Landusky, and Elfie, Lonny's sweetheart, was soon confiding in the quiet little man with the mustache.

In his memoirs, Siringo says:

> I had made myself in solid with Elfie Curry, as she was called; hence read all of her letters and was told all of her secrets. During my stay, Lonny's offspring, a bright little three-year-old boy named Harvey after the notorious outlaw, wandered into the woods and was lost for a night in the bitter cold. But he proved to be as tough as his daddy, and they found him sleeping next to his dog. The warmth from the animal's body, no doubt, had saved his life.

While Siringo was listening to Elfie's secrets, Cassidy, now top hand on the WS ranch in Alma, New Mexico, summoned the inner circle of the Train Robber's Syndicate for another strike. There were some new faces: Sam Ketchum and his brother Tom, called Black Jack, and Bill Carver, all killers and train robbers.

Black Jack apparently was a bit of a psychopath; it is said he used to beat himself over the head with a gun butt or lariat for punishment when anything went wrong and he discovered that it was his own fault. The usual story is told about his unrequited love driving him into Hole in the Wall. Cassidy knew Ketchum before their visit to Texas, and the union of the gang was probably a routine affair.

No one can say for certain whether Cassidy rode the night of July 11, 1899, when the Colorado and Southern Railroad was held up at Folsom, New Mexico, eighty miles south of Trinidad. It is definite that Elza Lay, Harvey Logan, and Sam Ketchum were there, and the use of dynamite put the Cassidy stamp on the robbery.

The stickup was in the usual Jesse James style, with two of the gang who had posed as passengers crawling over the tender and jamming a gun into the engineer's back as they reached the spot where the rest of the riders waited. The messenger held out against opening the door of the express car for a while, but when the outlaws began to splinter it with bullets he slid it back. But before he did so he opened the safe, hid the valuables, and then spun the dial. The outlaws blew the iron box in with dynamite but failed to find a bent copper. An hour had passed and there was no time to rob the train's passengers, so the outlaws rode off into the night cursing the hard-hearted railroad.

A posse gathered at Trinidad, New Mexico, when the train chugged in, bell clanging. The outlaws were trailed to Turkey Canyon, ten miles above Cimarron, New Mexico, where they were trapped by the posse. In the gun battle, Elza Lay was shot in the arm and in the back.

The siege lasted nearly all that day with the fearless Harvey Logan bringing the fight to the posse again and again. Ketchum caught a slug in the right arm and with Lay was out of the fight.

On September 12, 1899, W. H. Reno, special agent of the railroad, wrote a description of the battle in a letter to a magazine editor.

> In the fight with these robbers the sheriff and myself took a position to the left of the basin where the battle occurred; after about 20 minutes shooting with Winchesters. The two sheriffs were killed and laid out under the next tree to me about ten feet distant. One was shot three times. I had a very narrow escape, receiving three or four Winchester bullets through my clothing, one cutting two Winchester bullets in twain in my pocket. I considered myself fortunate in escaping fatal wounds.

Logan kept up the fight all day, slipping from rock to rock, his Winchester barking in the narrow canyon as the answering bullets from the posse screamed off the rocky walls. At dusk, with the gun flashes dangerous targets for the sharpshooting bandit, the posse withdrew, but they had given the Bunch its fiercest fight.

In a statement which he gave after his capture five days later, Ketchum told what happened behind the rocks in the soft purple light.

> They placed me on the horse twice but I could not sit there. I was the first one shot. When I saw I could not ride I told the kid [Kid Curry or Logan] to pull out and leave me. If you

want my gun and ammunition it is hid up in the mountains
and you can have them if you find them. When they commenced firing I threw up my hands and then I was shot. If
they had told us to throw up our hands we would have done
so.

After they left me I was wet through. I could not get kindling to build a fire and matches were all damp and I could
not light one after trying the whole box. I am a brother of
Tom Ketchum, the original Black Jack.

Described as a "muscular man over six feet with a thick mustache" Ketchum grinned as the physicians began to probe the
neglected wound.

"Guess I can stand a little thing like that," he joked.

At Soringer, New Mexico, Sam was identified by the Pinkertons
and arraigned on charges of killing two United States marshals, for
delaying the United States mails, and on a territorial charge of
murder and train robbery. He pleaded not guilty to all charges.
He was removed to the Santa Fe prison for safekeeping and there
died on July 24, of blood poisoning.

His last whispered words when he was asked to make a statement
identifying his companions were:

"The other fellows will tell the story."

On August 16, Sam's brother, Black Jack, made a foolhardy
attempt to hold up a train near Folsom singlehanded, supposedly
in revenge against the railroad for his brother's death. The conductor and the express agent wounded him in the right arm, but
like Jim Younger at Northfield, Black Jack was an ambidextrous
gunman. He swung his rifle to his left shoulder and continued
firing, wounding the two trainmen. The outlaw was losing blood
fast, and when he attempted to flee he collapsed and was taken
prisoner the next morning. He gave his name as Frank Stevens,
but Pinkerton operatives identified him and he was removed to
Santa Fe prison where his brother had died only a few weeks
before. Physicians amputated his right arm and the outlaw was
placed in the prison hospital under heavy guard to await trial.

Ten days later Elza Lay was arrested at Carlsbad, New Mexico,
"after a brief but tough fight," according to the Pinkerton archives, and was identified by operatives and agents of the railroad
although he had insisted that his name was William McGuinness.

On October 10, Cassidy's able lieutenant was found guilty of killing one of the law officers in the Turkey Canyon duel and sentenced to life imprisonment.

With Lay behind bars, and Black Jack Ketchum awaiting trial, probably swearing because the doctors had taken off his right arm and he could no longer beat himself for his mistakes, Cassidy and Harvey Logan left the WS ranch and headed north toward outlaw land.

25.

ROUGH ON CROOKS

AFTER he sold his saloon in Hardin, Montana, Lonny Logan fled back to Hole in the Wall, but the posses were entering the slit in the red wall every week or so and he quickly pulled stakes. At Brown's Hole the rustlers and thieves told him it wasn't much use staying, the cattlemen were sending in hired bushwackers, and a few of the boys had already been found dead in their cabins or in lonely gullies. Lonny rode off again, back to Montana and then down into Arkansas. At every friendly hideout he received word that strangers had been inquiring about him.

He drifted from state to state, working as a cowhand or in bars. At the time, the Pinkerton posters described him as "dark, good looking, with a tiny mole on the left cheek. He wears a flannel shirt and a soft hat pulled down on the right eye." Again back in Montana he joined a gang of horsethieves operating in the vicinity of Perry, with a hideout in the Bear Paw Mountains. But the gang was broken up after a violent two-day gun battle with a posse, in which some of the outlaws were killed.

Back in the towns the news kept following him. He heard it from drifters, rustlers, and horsethieves; the misfit cadging a drink, the cowboy returning to Wyoming. It was always the same.

Somebody was asking about Lonny Logan, Kid Curry's brother.

On New Year's Day, 1900, he returned to the only refuge left in his dark world, the farmhouse just outside Dodson, Missouri, and Mrs. Lee, his aunt, that "estimable little old lady who had no knowledge of the sort of life her nephew led" as the Kansas City *Post* was to say.

Back in Montana, operative Sayles, that mysterious questioner, was doggedly following Lonny's trail. Through mining towns, mountain hamlets, and ranches he went, stopping at saloons and buying drinks, talking to stage drivers, horse dealers, provision merchants, general store clerks, and railroad men. Following the agency's strict rule, every night he wrote out a list of the details he had uncovered and sent it in cipher to Denver. Back there Pinkerton Superintendent McPharland, the man who broke the back of the Molly Maguires, carefully put the pieces together and kept up a steady flow of communications to William Pinkerton in Chicago and with other agency heads throughout the country.

Then early in February the break came. A telegram arrived in Denver from the Kansas City, Missouri, office. It read:

WILCOX BILLS FOUND IN VICINITY OF DODSON, HOME OF LOGANS.

The wires hummed from Denver to Chicago and William Pinkerton flashed back word to send Sayles to Missouri and raid the farmhouse with a posse. The operative hurried to Kansas City. A posse was formed of Pinkerton agents and Kansas City police officers. At 8 A.M., on the morning of February 28, 1900, they rode out to the farmhouse in four buggies. The carriages were left about a mile from the house and the men pushed through the knee-deep snow. It was a bitter morning and a raw wind was rising.

The Lee house was situated on a small hill and the posse split up, one group covering the front door, the second going around the back. Lonny must have been watching from the window, for as the second group began circling the house he flung open the kitchen door and bolted.

Someone shouted, "That's our man" and a Winchester cracked. Lonny dived behind a small mound of snow. The barrel of a rifle slid over the edge of the tiny fort and a bullet plucked the hat from the head of a Kansas City police officer.

The battle lasted twenty-five minutes. During a short lull, Sayles ordered the outlaw to surrender. But there was no surrender in the dark-faced rider from Hole in the Wall. He sprang to his feet and stumbled through the snow toward the kneeling possemen, a six-shooter in each hand.

The law officers opened fire at the charging target. Almost torn in two by the hail of bullets, the bandit slowly slumped to his knees, then fell over on one side, his blood crimsoning the snow. As he stood over the dead outlaw Sayles thoughtfully fingered his torn coat. A bullet had traveled through the sleeve without scratching the skin.

Logan's body was brought back to Kansas City in one of the carriages and a public announcement was made of his death. The Kansas City *Post* later told the story in a laconic headline:

LONNY LOGAN KILLED NEAR KANSAS CITY; TOUGH HERE ON CROOKS.

The three-thousand-dollar reward money for the bandit was turned over to the Kansas City police who took part in the raid. Pinkerton operatives, under an iron-bound rule of the agency, still in effect, are forbidden to share in any reward money.

At almost the same hour that Lonny died in the snow, Bob Lee, his cousin, who had left Dodson with the Logans in '85, was arrested by a Pinkerton operative at Cripple Creek, Wyoming. He was convicted of rustling and sent away for a long term in Wyoming state prison.

A shadow continued to hover over Cassidy's riders.

Two months after Lonny had been buried, Flat-Nose George Curry, the second commander of the Hole in the Wall gang before it united with the Wild Bunch, was shot and killed at Castle Dale, Utah, in a running six-mile fight with a sheriff. After Cassidy and his men departed for Alma, New Mexico, Curry had returned to rustling under the name of Tom Dilley.

Curry was spotted, by the manager of a cattle company, changing a brand with a running iron. The sheriff of Vernal was summoned and the fight began. The rustler swam the Green River but was trapped by another posse and shot in the head. The law officer, who believed he had killed a small-time rustler, was startled to discover his victim was the notorious Hole in the Wall leader.

He later collected the three-thousand-dollar reward offered for the outlaw—dead or alive—by the Union Pacific Railroad.

About the time the sheriff of Vernal was counting the unexpected greenbacks, a deep-chested stranger almost seven feet tall with a lined face burned dark as old leather was riding into Brown's Hole. He was lean and taciturn and said his name was Tom Hix, a horse buyer. For weeks he drifted about the valley ranches, supposedly examining the horseflesh, most of it stolen.

The rustlers became uneasy. They didn't like this silent giant with the quiet who-the-hell-are-you look, but they were afraid to ask any questions. There weren't any of the Wild Bunch leaders at the old hideout; Butch Cassidy, Longbaugh, the Sundance Kid, Kilpatrick, the Tall Texan, had not yet arrived at the Hole. Harvey Logan was rustling somewhere in the North and Lonny was dead . . . it wasn't like the old days when Kid Curry's cold stare or Harry Tracy's "I'm Tracy," was enough to freeze the marrow in a man's bones. . . .

The tall stranger continued to drift from bunkhouse to bunkhouse, not doing much of anything—just looking and listening.

Then one day the news broke. Matt Rash, an old-time rustler, was dry-gulched outside his cabin on Cold Springs Mountain. He never had a chance; the killer got him on his doorstep.

A few days later the warning that hadn't been sounded in any of the outlaw stations since the invaders of '92 had tied the crude sign on Nat Champion's bullet-riddled body appeared: "Rustlers, get out."

Isam Dart, a Negro rustler and horsethief got it next. Bushwacked. More posters.

The outlaws took the hint. Faces disappeared. Legend still has Hix going to Cheyenne or Denver collecting his fee of five hundred dollars a scalp, which was ten times more than the hired gun-toters had been paid eight years before. But Hix—Tom Horn, famous Indian scout and capturer of Geronimo, the Apache chief; colonel in the Spanish American war; frontiersman; a living legend of terror in the West and a misfit in the new century— had done a good job for the cattleman. He was a one-man army.

Before he had turned bushwacker Horn wore a Pinkerton badge and captured singlehanded a former Hole in the Wall horsethief and his gang who had turned to train robbery.

"They didn't give me any trouble," Horn told Superintendent McPharland in the Denver office.

One wonders what "trouble" he would have encountered had he met up with Cassidy, Harvey Logan, or that criminal lunatic, Harry Tracy. . . .

NEW LANDS TO CONQUER

THERE was none of the brooding sullenness of the Middle Border bandits in Butch Cassidy. The young Mormon was a complete extrovert. Even the Pinkertons recognized his happy-go-lucky disposition. "He is cheerful and amiable," they described him in the wanted posters. Unlike Jesse James, Cassidy did not alienate his followers; his councils were open for discussion and when the advice was sound he accepted it. Absolute power corrupts absolutely, and Butch, although he never heard the ancient adage, followed its reasoning.

By the time he and Harvey Logan had reached Brown's Hole Cassidy had read the handwriting on the wall. Law and order was fast coming to the West; rustling and horse stealing were not only precarious but unprofitable; bank and train robberies a risky and unpredictable business. The last frontier had disappeared. Barbed-wire fences now were everywhere. Even the water was fenced in at some spots. This disturbed Cassidy. Before he was a thief, a rustler, a bank and train robber, Cassidy was a cowboy and plainsman. He belonged to the open range and the grazing herds. The only cattle countries left—where train and bank robberies could be extracurricular and profitable—were Australia and South America.

Before the turn of the century American cowpunchers had begun to make their way down to the Argentine pampas. While he was in New Mexico Butch may well have heard some stories or spoken to a newly returned cowhand, because by the time he was nearing the Utah border he was talking of taking the Wild Bunch to South America.

Longbaugh, the Sundance Kid, agreed, but some of his riders like Kilpatrick, the Tall Texan, and Harvey Logan argued against the plan. It was a big decision to make and the discussion around the campfires under the star-studded heavens, with the coyotes barking in the hills, must have lasted far into the night.

But before he left the states and burned his bridges behind him Cassidy was determined to make one last effort to regain his place in society. The last few violent months undoubtedly had made a grave impression on him; Lonny Logan, Flat-Nose George Curry, and Sam Ketchum were dead; Black Jack Ketchum was ready to swing; Elza Lay was awaiting a possible life term; and the Pinkertons were everywhere.

According to Kelly, Cassidy walked into the office of one of Utah's biggest attorneys and asked what were his chances of getting a pardon if he surrendered. The attorney, also a judge, bluntly told him the odds were slim; he would first have to be convicted before he could be pardoned, and if he were pardoned every cattleman in the state would be filing charges against him. Then, there was the Telluride Bank robbery and the Wilcox train stickup. . . .

Butch sighed and wished the attorney a good morning.

The governor pardoned two other young outlaws and Butch tried again. This time he met the sheriff who had interceded for the other two men. The bandit and the law enforcement officer met in the office of Governor Wells of Utah to plead their case. The state executive was impressed and said it might be arranged if Cassidy was not guilty of murder. They were to return within a few days.

At the second meeting Governor Wells informed them that a search by the attorney general of Wyoming had uncovered a murder charge pending against the Mormon outlaw, and therefore he could not be granted amnesty. The sheriff and Butch protested, but in vain. That afternoon, bitterly disappointed, Butch rode back to Powder Springs.

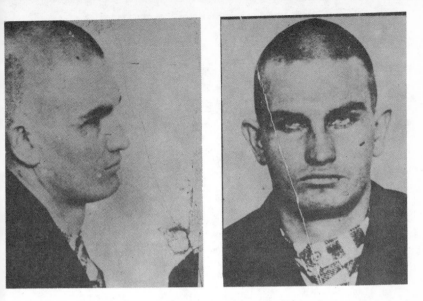

63. Harry Tracy's mug picture taken at the Oregon State Penitentiary.

64. Tracy's "Honeymoon cottage" at 207 Market Street, Portland. *(Courtesy James D. Horan Western Americana Collection.)*

65. Artist s sketch of Tracy and Merrill breaking out of the Oregon Penitentiary. *(Courtesy James D. Horan Western Americana Collection)*

66. The launch which Tracy commandeered to make his flight across Puget Sound. *(Courtesy James D. Horan Western Americana Collection.)*

67. House where Tracy watched the posse ride past. *(Courtesy James D. Horan Western Americana Collection.)*

68. Posse resting during the long manhunt for Harry Tracy after he had narrowed down their target by shooting Merrill. (*Courtesy James D. Horan Western Americana Collection*)

69. Eugene Eddy.

70. Lucius Eddy (*Courtesy Robert E. Eddy*)

71. Harry Tracy was helping Eugene Eddy fix the roof of the barn at left when he spotted the posse and they began firing. *(Courtesy Robert E. Eddy)*

72. The route taken by Tracy from the barn to his final resting place is marked in white line. *(Courtesy Chelan County Historical Society, Cashmere, Washington)*

73. Tracy's body as it lay in the field. After he had been wounded he crawled there. Toward morning as the posse started to move in for the kill Tracy killed himself. *(Courtesy Robert E. Eddy)*

The attorney general was mistaken. There was no murder charge against Cassidy. This is confirmed by the files of the Pinkerton National Detective Agency. When Butch boasted, "I have never killed a man," he told the truth. He was a bandit, thief, and rustler, but unlike Jesse James, the leader of the Wild Bunch was not a cold-blooded murderer.

Later, however, according to Kelly, the attorney whom Cassidy had first visited was impressed with the bandit's sincerity and contacted the officials of the Union Pacific and told them:

"Here is my proposition: If the railroad will agree to forget all past offenses I will try to see Cassidy again and with your permission will offer him a permanent job as an express guard on your trains, at a good salary. If he was in your employ I believe he would perform his duties faithfully. If the other outlaws knew he was riding the trains, they would never attempt to rob them. Cassidy's salary would be a sort of robbery insurance and cheap at half the price. What do you say?"

After a long discussion the railroad officials agreed. Word was sent to Douglas A. Preston, Cassidy's old attorney, and he rode into Brown's Hole and put the proposition before the Wild Bunch's leader. Butch agreed and a rendezvous was made. "Meet me in ten days from today," he told Preston, "at Lost Soldier Pass and bring the U.P.'s chief detective and some official with power to make an agreement. I'll be there alone; tell 'em not to pull any funny stuff. This is on the level. If they promise not to prosecute I'll take the job."

Preston delivered Cassidy's message. Ten days later the officials of the railroad and Preston started out for Lost Soldier's Pass in a buckboard.

By a strange twist of fate they were delayed by an unexpected storm. Cassidy, who feared it might be a trap, returned to Powder Springs. He left a note under a stone at the lonely pass which damned Preston for doublecrossing him and to "tell the U.P. to go to hell and you with them."

The state tried once more a short time later. Matt Warner, the owner of the saloon papered with dollar signs back in Star Valley when Butch was a minor rider with the McCartys, was released from the pen and offered to take the offer to Butch at the outlaw hideout. He was given $175 in expense money and left by train at Rock Springs bound for Powder Springs. At Fort

Bridger, east of Evanston, the conductor handed him an urgent telegram. It read:

ALL AGREEMENTS OFF. CASSIDY JUST HELD UP TRAIN AT TIPTON.

Butch was only trying for steamship fare to South America for himself and his riders.

The holdup at Tipton was in the best train robber's tradition. It took place at 8:30 P.M. on August 29, 1900, at a point two and a half miles west of Tipton, Sweetwater County, Wyoming, and like the two previous robberies, dynamite was used to blow the safe.

Train Number Three of the Union Pacific Railroad was crawling up a rather sharp grade when a masked man crept over the top of the tender and at gun point forced the engineer and fireman to stop the train where a small fire was blazing at the side of the tracks. Three other men moved on the train from out of the darkness as the train halted. Conductor Kerrigan swung off his platform and came forward on the run to see what the trouble was. One of the bandits grabbed him and growled an order to cut loose the express and mail car. The plucky trainman pushed the robber aside and began mounting the steps of the first coach.

"Goddammit, cut loose the cars."

Kerrigan turned and answered calmly:

"This train is on a grade and before anything is done the brakes must be set or there will be a bad accident."

The bandit hesitated, then waved him into the car. The brakes were set, Kerrigan was herded into the locomotive, and at the command of the robbers the locomotive pulled the shortened train down the track about a mile distant from the scene of the holdup. There the highwaymen, leaving one of their followers guarding the train crew, turned their attention to the express car.

The express messenger, by a strange coincidence, was Woodcock, whom the gang had to blow out of the car with dynamite at Wilcox. Again the messenger bolted the door and shouted that anyone who tried to force it back would be fired upon.

Conductor Kerrigan was produced and he joined the thieves in pleading with Woodcock. Several sticks of dynamite were being readied when Kerrigan at last persuaded the messenger to open the door.

It is said that Butch Cassidy, who led the riders that night, ordered Woodcock to throw down his weapons before he left the door.

The shotgun fell at the gang leader's feet.

"Come out with your hands up."

Woodcock protested, but Cassidy said grimly: "Anybody that has to be blown out of a car would have enough courage to try and shoot one of us." He gave a grunt of triumph when he searched the messenger. A six-shooter was hidden under an arm-pit. Woodcock was shoved forward under guard and the sticks of dynamite placed beneath the heavy iron safe. It cracked in two and eager fingers tore apart the sacks. Cassidy cursed long and loud. The total loot was only $50.40. Somehow he had gotten wind of a $100,000 shipment in gold being shipped to the Bank of the Philippines on this train. Unaccountably it was delayed for a few hours. The next train carried the king's ransom.

Rewards of a thousand dollars for each bandit were offered by the railroad, and posses from Rawlins and Rock Springs covered the countryside. But the gang led by Cassidy escaped to the hide-out at Powder Springs. His riders that night were Harry Long-baugh, the Sundance Kid, and Harvey Logan. The identity of the other two was not disclosed. It could have been Deaf Charley, Hanks, Kilpatrick, or any of the Wild Bunch who were returning to the outlaw command now that the riders were bringing word that Butch had returned.

The loot of the Tipton robbery was enough to summon the boys to belly up to the bar and order a finger of Old Crow, but that was about all. South America was still over the horizon, so Cassidy planned a second strike less than three weeks later. The victim this time was the First National Bank of Winnemucca, Nevada. Trains were too undependable; banks always had money.

Cassidy's riders were the Sundance Kid, and Bill Carver, a dark-skinned young outlaw who was one of Black Jack Ketchum's men. The holdup was fast and furious with delightful overtones.

In the Pinkerton archives there is a wonderful account of the robbery given to one of the Pinkerton operatives by "Informant # 85."

The informant uses Cassidy's favorite alias of Jim Lowe. It reads:

Informant # 85 reports:

Jim Lowe, Harry Longbaugh, and Bill Carver, started for British possession to look for something on the road. They met a man they knew who informed them about the Winnemucca Bank being a dead easy one. This man worked for a time for old Senator Nixton and I think he was in a position to know something about bank affairs. So Jim Lowe, Longbaugh, and Carver came and stayed at a ranch near the river close to town and watched things.

The morning they came into town to rob the bank they came across a field and cut the wire of a place their friend told them about so they could pass through. Carver had a couple of blankets rolled up and tied with a strap. He had on hob-nailed shoes and certainly looked like a tramp. Inside this roll of blankets he had a 30-40 carbine. After cutting the fence they separated. Jim Lowe and Longbaugh came into town first. Carver stopped on the way to kill a skunk but got the worse of the battle. After killing the skunk he came into town and tied his horse and stood near the bank (I think at a public watering place). Anyway he was there waiting for a signal that the coast was clear. During the time Carver was standing there an old lady and an old man came by to stop to talk to him and roasted the town for being so "slow." They said it should be dead and buried. Carver told them that if they waited around for a while things would be pretty lively.

The old man looked at Carver and said: "Say, stranger, what's going to happen, earthquake or something?"

Just then Carver got the signal from Jim Lowe and Longbaugh that the coast was clear and the boys started in. The Sundance Kid and Jim Lowe went in first. Carver came last with the roll of blankets and sat them on end between his knees and began fumbling around in his pockets while the other two covered the outfit and went to work. Jim Lowe climbed over the railing and gathered in all the "dough." As they comes out of the bank the old party before mentioned see them and yells "robbers" so Longbaugh "drops a couple" under the old gent's heels. The old man and the old lady began tearing up the street with the old lady yelling for them not "to shoot pa as he won't hurt you-uns."

Carver later said the old gent's coattails were sticking out

straight behind. The boys said the clerks in the bank kept
sniffing when Carver came in and Carver said he could hardly
stand it himself. This was on account of his battle with the
skunk. They dropped one sack of money on the street and
Jim Lowe turned back to get it. When the people saw him
coming they all broke for cover as though they thought he was
coming back to kill them so they got out of his way.

The boys rode all that day and cached their money and
changed their clothes and separated, each going his direction
to meet later. Carver's clothes stunk like hell.

Reported to H.

San Francisco, 4-5-09

According to the *Anaconda Standard,* which reported in detail
nearly all of the robberies in that section of the West, the outlaw
who dropped the gold had a balky horse, and after he retrieved the
sack of gold and tried to remount, the bank employees opened
fire. Apparently the aim was not very effective because the *Standard* declared:

"Two men were so excited they blew out the windows of a
nearby saloon."

The posse left Winnemucca on a train and it is said that for
a time they kept up a running fire at the bandits who were traveling the road which paralleled the tracks. The train was so
crowded that possemen hung from the sides of the cars, and when
one fell off the engineer had to jam on his brakes and wait for
his companions to drag him back on board.

Before the posse left Winnemucca the sheriff sent a warning
over the telegraph to Golconda, seventeen miles east, to try
and head the gang off. But they were left behind in the dust. When
the Winnemucca men arrived, both posses banded together and
started to sweep the countryside.

Cassidy used his relay system in planning the Winnemucca robbery and had hidden four fresh horses at a small ranch three
miles beyond Lost Soldier's Pass, the spot where a strange fate
had refused to allow him to become an honest man again. From
there he and his men rode for Squaw Valley, twenty miles to the
north, where they divided the money and threw away the canvas
sacks, which the posse later found. The Pinkerton posters describe
the loot as being $31,000 in twenty-dollar gold coins, $1,200 in

five- and ten-dollar gold coins, and the balance in currency including one fifty-dollar bill. The outlaws separated, but Fort Worth, Texas, was the agreed rendezvous.

The Winnemucca bank was a member of the American Banking Association and the Pinkerton operatives began to comb the Southwest. In large black type on the posters they distributed, one of the bank robbers is described as "very determined in face and smelling like a polecat."

After the Winnemucca bank robbery the outlaws rode south to Fort Worth, Texas. Along with Cassidy in Fort Worth were Longbaugh, Kilpatrick, Carver, and Harvey Logan. With bulging pockets they strolled down the main street. A clothing store display caught their eye and they went inside. When they came out the change was startling. The inner circle of the Bank Robber's Syndicate looked like five pillars of Fort Worth's society. Instead of their rough jeans, sombreros, spurs, and high-heeled boots, they wore conservative broadcloth, derbies, patent leather shoes, and stickpins.

Passing a photographer's studio they agreed that it was a good idea to have a group picture taken as a memento of the occasion. The portrait of these solemn-faced men is hard on the popular illusion of what our western outlaws looked like. The portrait could have found its place in any American family album. Harvey Logan, the Kid Curry of the West, with a flower in his buttonhole, might well be Uncle John, deacon of the church and the town's postman for forty-five years; Kilpatrick, the Tall Texan, father's cousin who became a fireman; Carver, the relative who worked for the express company and loved his horses; and Harry Longbaugh, the Sundance Kid, the cashier in the town's bank whose mother said he never swore or "let liquor pass his lips." There was a hint of deviltry about Cassidy. Wearing a slight grin and with his derby rakishly perched on his head, he could be Uncle Joe who played cards down at the corner saloon and who, it was said, went to the city and had an affair with a dancing girl. . . .

The innocent picture was the gang's ruination. A Well's Fargo detective posing as a gambler in the red-light district spotted the Bunch as they emerged from the studio and obtained a copy of the portrait. Before the day had ended copies were on their way to the Pinkertons, railroads, sheriffs, and marshals. The wanted posters soon appeared.

The Bunch heard about the posters and disappeared into the red-light district of San Antonio, Texas, where they hid out at "Fanny Porter's Sporting House." Carver adopted the name of Bill Casey; Logan, Bob Nevilles; and Cassidy, Jim Lowe. At Fanny's, Logan fell for Lillie, one of Fanny's best. They stayed at the bordello for three months. The bicycle craze was sweeping the country at the time and Butch became an expert rider. It must have been a wonderful scene with Cassidy, his derby perched off to one side of his head, cycling up the street of the red-light district as Fanny and her girls shrilled encouragement.

But the Pinkertons appeared again and Cassidy gathered his men and headed back for the Powder Springs outlaw headquarters. He was ready for South America, but Harvey Logan was still firm in his refusal to go. Butch, who knew the value of this fearless killer, put off the trip temporarily while he tried to change the Missourian's mind.

At Landusky, Logan managed to persuade Cassidy to agree to one last raid in the United States. The Great Northern Railroad was selected; the robbery was to be pulled at Wagner, Montana, one hundred and ninety miles east of Great Falls. Deaf Charley Hanks, whom Butch probably met in Texas, was in charge of the horses.

It is said that Laura Bullion, who was the camp follower for Black Jack Ketchum and his men, participated in the Wagner holdup. Laura, a black-haired woman of about twenty-five, with Indian or Spanish blood showing in her swarthy face and high cheekbones, had been Bill Carver's girl. After Carver had been killed that year in Sonora, Texas, she hid out at her uncle's place in Arizona. She was brought back to Texas by one of Carver's friends "who sort of felt sorry for me" and was introduced to Kilpatrick as "a fellow who could take care of me." However, to this writer, it is improbable that Cassidy would allow a woman to be included among his riders. The Pinkerton agency agrees with this conclusion.

At 2 P.M. on July 3, 1901, Logan climbed aboard the blind end of the baggage car and the Sundance Kid boarded one of the coaches as a paying passenger when the train stopped at Malta, Montana.

Near Wagner, Logan, armed with two six-shooters, crawled over the tender into the locomotive and ordered the engineer to halt the train. Longbaugh slid out of his seat and ran up and down the coaches firing a few shots to emphasize his order to "keep your heads in. . . ." At Logan's command the express car was uncoupled and pulled across the bridge, where Cassidy and Hanks, who had been hiding at a ranch seven miles away, were waiting with the horses and the dynamite. Cassidy forced the fireman to carry his canvas bag of explosives and place a charge against the safe. The fuse was touched and the car shattered. Two more sticks cracked the big iron safe. The haul was forty thousand dollars of incomplete bank notes of the National Bank of Montana at Helena, Montana, en route from the United States Treasury, and five hundred dollars in incomplete bank notes of the American National Bank, also from the United States Treasury. The denominations of the stolen bills were ten dollars and twenty dollars. All the notes lacked the signature of both the president and cashier of the banks to which they were consigned.

The loot was tossed into a canvas bag and the gang rode off. When the train finally reached Wagner, the news of the holdup was telegraphed back to Malta and a hundred-man posse pounded out of the town. But Cassidy and his men had vanished in the hills. The investigation was taken over by Pinkerton's National Detective Agency, which, in addition to being the agent of the victimized railroad and the Great Northern Express Company, was also the investigating force of the American Bankers Association. Agents sped to Wagner and questioned the engineer and the fireman and several of the passengers. From the description his men furnished, William A. Pinkerton announced that the holdup was the work of the Wild Bunch. Logan, Hanks, and Longbaugh were positively identified.

Circulars furnishing a full description and photographs of Logan, Longbaugh, and Hanks, along with a list of the serial numbers of the stolen bills, were distributed to all police stations, sheriffs, marshals, banks, express companies, railroad stations, general stores, and livery stables through the United States. Rewards totaling $6,500 were offered for the capture of the bandits.

The confession of Lillie, the young Texas prostitute, discloses that Logan and some of the gang fled to Idaho after the robbery "with," she said, "six or seven sacks filled with gold. They had the sacks in a trunk," she said, "and also a big bundle of paper money. The gold was in twenty-dollar gold pieces. They had a satchel stolen from them on this trip which contained a big gun and they did considerable complaining and grieving over the loss of the satchel."

When William Pinkerton showed Lillie the group picture the Wild Bunch had taken in Texas she "positively recognized Cassidy, Longbaugh, Logan, Carver, and Kilpatrick. "Jim Lowe [Cassidy]," she said, "was an expert bicycle rider and an athletic looking fellow. He was quiet and apparently had little money."

The outlaws apparently became bored with the two young prostitutes because, Lillie said, "Harvey Logan sent me home to Texas with $167 all in gold coin with the exception of two dollars. I received seventy dollars in paper and that is all the money I got. I have not received one word since March, 1901. Bob Nevilles [Logan] later told me that Bill was in California, but Fanny Porter, when drunk, said Bill was dead. I remained in Palestine, Texas, until April 2, then went to San Antonio and to Fanny's sporting house."

Logan paid a flying visit to Texas and, as Lillie said, "we took in all the hook shops [sporting houses] and had a good time, getting home about 3 A.M. Bob slept in Fanny Porter's bed."

While Logan and his prostitute made the round of San Antonio's "hook shops," the Pinkertons discovered that some of the stolen bank notes were being passed in the district. Soon operatives were everywhere asking endless questions and showing copies of the wanted posters. Cassidy met Logan and probably warned him.

"The last time I saw Bob [Logan] and Jim Lowe [Cassidy] they were dressed in cowboy suits and they said they had to leave," Lillie sadly declared.

"If I had known who they were I would have taken them for all they had," she added as an afterthought.

TRAIL'S END

WHERE Butch Cassidy hid out after leaving Texas is not known. He was ready for South America and probably tried for the last time to change Logan's mind. Failing, he said good-by to his faithful follower and rode off to join Longbaugh. Logan and he never met again.

"After the Wagner train robbery," the Pinkerton Denver file of 1901 reported, "Logan visited Kansas City and Dodson, Missouri. In July of 1901 he traveled 200 miles to shoot and kill James Winters who had some time previous taken an interest in the capture of Kid Curry and his brothers and had given the law officers information in regard to him. Logan killed him in cold blood for revenge.

"After killing Winters, Logan visited Fort Worth, San Antonio, Texas, Mena, Arkansas, and several other points. His associates were chiefly prostitutes."

Logan was apparently cheating on Lillie because the Pinkerton file reports:

"On September 18, 1901, he was located in Mena, Arkansas, by a Pinkerton operative living with Annie Rogers, a young prostitute whom he had met in Fanny Porter's sporting house in Texas. They went to Shreveport, Louisiana, and from there traveled in the direction of Tennessee."

The loot from the Wagner robbery was notes unsigned by the president and treasurer of the bank to whom they were consigned. The gang's crude forgeries were easy to spot and the Pinkerton operatives trailed them from Montana to Texas and north again.

The first break in the investigation came on the afternoon of October 26, 1901, when a man who gave his name as Ferguson attempted to pass one of the bills in a Nashville, Tennessee, clothing store. The clerk became suspicious and sent word by another customer to the police. Two Nashville officers hurried to the store and tried to take the stranger in custody. He drew two six-shooters and knocked them down. He jumped aboard a passing ice wagon, booted the Negro driver out of the seat, and raced down the street. One of the horses stumbled and broke its leg after several blocks. The fugitive commandeered a passing buggy, ousted its driver, and continued on toward the Cumberland River. He stole another horse a few hours later, reached the river, and at gun point forced two Negro fishermen in a boat to row him across. He disappeared in the cane brakes on the other side. From the description given by the clerk and the police officers, Pinkerton operatives identified the fugitive as Deaf Charley Hanks.

The Denver file of the agency of 1901 says: "We have every reason to believe that the man who made this fight and escape was O. C. Hanks. Hanks, under the name of Sullivan, was in Memphis just before this occurrence. It is to be assumed that Hanks will be in communication with his mother in Abilene, Texas, and possibly with a step brother who is a cattle man at Las Cruces, New Mexico."

On November 5 several of the unsigned bank notes were found in circulation in the vicinity of St. Louis, Missouri, and Robert Pinkerton ordered J. P. McPharland, superintendent of the Denver Pinkerton office, to send several crack operatives to St. Louis to aid the police in combing the city. On November 7, Victor Jacquemin, a sharp-eyed teller of the Merchant's Bank of St. Louis, then located on the southeast corner of Fourth and Pine streets, spotted four twenty-dollar notes from the Wagner robbery as they were given to him by a local jeweler for a deposit.

"These are stolen bank notes," he told the startled merchant.

The bank notified the United States Secret Service, the Pinkertons, and the local police. A Pinkerton wanted poster was produced and the jeweler identified Mr. Arnold, who had given him the notes, as Ben Kilpatrick, the Tall Texan. Every available detective, Pinkerton operative, and secret-service man joined in the search for the "tall and rather handsome man with violet blue eyes and a ruddy complexion." A cordon was thrown around the Union Station on the theory that the train robber might try to leave the city.

On November 8, a Knoxville detective spotted a carriage

racing down Twentieth and Chestnut streets. He caught a glimpse of the passenger through the window. It looked to be Kilpatrick. The officer hired another carriage and followed. Kilpatrick stopped off at "Manley's saloon on Chestnut Street where he had a few." The detective followed and stood at the end of the bar where he could get a full view of the man he was following. There was no doubt that it was the famous western outlaw. When Kilpatrick left the saloon the officer tailed him to 2005 Chestnut Street. The detective later told how he arrested Kilpatrick:

> I followed the carriage and saw it stop in front of 2005 Chestnut Street. The man entered. Just at the time some other detectives came along and I related what had occurred. We then planned his capture. We all entered the house. We located our man in the middle parlor. Myself and another detective feigned intoxication and we staggered into the room. I entered, shouting: "I'm drunk, but I'm a good fellow." Our man was taken in by this and we were on him in a second.
>
> Before he had a chance to do anything I jerked his right hand and yanked his revolver from his hip pocket. The other detective did the same thing on the other side. We threw the muzzles of our own guns into his face and by this time the others were upon him. He had no chance to resist and we had him before he knew it.

In one of Kilpatrick's pockets the detectives found a hotel key. There was no name on the key and after Kilpatrick, who insisted he was J. D. Rose, a gambler of Memphis, Tennessee, who had won the several stolen bank notes found in his wallet "in a game," had been thrown into the lockup, several police officers and Pinkerton operatives began to canvass the city hotels and rooming houses. They struck paydirt at the Laclede Hotel. The room number on the key had been torn off and the detectives were obliged to wait all night while the desk clerks made an inventory. Just before dawn it was found that the key had been issued for room 100 to a couple who had signed the hotel register as Mr. and Mrs. J. D. Rose.

There was no one in the room, but a chambermaid told the detectives that Mrs. Rose was on her way out of the hotel "with a big valise." The detectives surrounded the building and found

Mrs. Rose in a writing room holding the "big valise" and talking to two expressmen about removing her trunks to the Union Station.

"She protested gently that she was innocent," the St. Louis *Times* reported, "but at the same time was on the lookout for a chance to escape, but saw none." She was described by the *Times* reporter as a "slender, well-dressed woman with a graceful figure and neatly dressed in a gray, tailor made suit. Her features are strong. She has gray eyes which are expressionless, except in times of high excitement. She can control herself admirably. Only at intervals while she was being questioned did she display any interest."

"After three hours of sweating," the St. Louis *Dispatch* announced the next day, November 8, "Della Rose broke down and admitted that she was Laura Bullion and that the $7,000 in bank notes which were stuffed in the valise were part of the Wagner train robbery."

Chief of Detectives Desmond of St. Louis, one of the finest police officers in the West, who had charge of the investigation, announced later that same day, after spending several hours with Kilpatrick's girl, who had been brought to St. Louis with Kilpatrick, "It is not improbable that Laura Bullion disguised as a boy took part in the Great Northern Train robbery at Wagner, Montana.

"I wouldn't think helping to hold up a train was too much for her," Desmond said. "She is cool, absolutely fearless, and in male attire, would readily pass for a boy. She has a masculine face, and that would give her assurance in disguise. I know some instances where young boys were used as accomplices, and I think it is not improbable there was a girl in this case."

Laura, Desmond revealed, broke down and admitted her identity after she had been identified by an Illinois merchant brought to St. Louis by the Pinkertons. The merchant had once hired her as a housecleaner. A St. Louis *Globe-Democrat* reporter who sat in on the "sweating period" printed Laura's remarks verbatim as she sat in Chief Desmond's office "chewing gum."

Of course I'll talk. Look at the fix this fellow got me into. I knew he had the money and I saw him sign some of the notes right here in St. Louis with a fountain pen he bought after I met him. He gave it to me later. Did I sign any notes? No. I just told the chief here that story because I was mad clean through. He played me dirt, a-going off and a-leaving me but when I heard they had him roped I was just lighting out for Kansas City with the stuff when the detectives corralled me. I knew he was crooked but he was no train robber. I've only known him a short time. I was Bill Carver's girl and after he got plugged Bill's friends sort of felt sorry for me. So when they got away and went north they kept looking for somebody to take care of me. One of the boys introduced me to this one at Fort Worth, Texas. Then him and me came here. No, I never have been in Montana and I don't know any train robbers and if this is one I don't know it and never did. I am 35. Mother was a German. I don't know who my father was. Some say I have injun blood in me and some say greaser but that's a lie. My man and me never had a fight. He never swore or got drunk.

I like to read the papers about the murders and excitement. Don't you think they are exciting? I hate a city. This is the only one I was ever in. Give me a ranch and the cowboys. I don't care if they do get drunk. They won't hurt me. No, I can't shoot much but I have once or twice. I ain't done a thing but just been traveling around with this man. What names did we go by? Oh, any kind, Cunningham, Rose, Smith or Jones. Any one that came to our minds. I never asked him any questions. No, I don't know any more about him. He's Mr. Rose, that's all and I ain't done nothing.

The St. Louis *Globe-Democrat* reporter who was listening in on the interview reported it to be "a continual line of chatter, with here and there a steely gleam of fox-like shrewdness. There is nothing bold or masculine about this woman."

The following day's headlines announced that "the notorious Butch Cassidy is in St. Louis." Chief Desmond and the Pinkertons called the story untrue, with Desmond saying:

This gang is not made up of fools. Of course Butch Cassidy is not here but elsewhere in the country "shoving" stolen notes.

The work in this line in St. Louis was for these two and they fell down on it. Cassidy will be caught before long but he is not in St. Louis and as far as we know has never been here. So far of the two we have been breaking down there is nothing in what they say yet. The man is as dumb as a post and the woman is lying as cheerfully as ever. She is one of the most expert I have ever seen. She did not faint nor weaken in any way, today as far as confessing went, although three hours of sweating would make any woman physically tired.

The man is surly and non-communicative. It took him ten minutes to order his breakfast.

The next day Desmond announced that Laura Bullion "had made admissions which amounted to a confession."

The *Post Dispatch* printed it in full. In part Laura Bullion said:

It was in Fort Worth, Texas, that I met the prisoner. We have lived in various cities under many names.

Before I met him I was with Bill Carver. Carver was a train robber and when the authorities were too hot for him we would be separated. Carver was a member of a gang which operated in Texas. Last March the officers got after them. The gang was in hiding and Carver and another member of the gang went to Sonora, Texas, where they were recognized. The sheriff got a posse together and gave chase. Carver was killed. That was on April 2nd of this year.

A member of the gang knew I was stopping at my uncle's in Douglas, Arizona, and after Bill Carver was killed he came and told me all about it and told me he had another sweetheart for me. He told me that this new man was in Fort Worth, Texas, and would take care of me and he gave me money to go there. There I was introduced to the prisoner.

We went by many names in many different cities. We always changed names wherever we went. He had plenty of money and I never asked him where he got it. He gave me the money that was in my possession when I was arrested. I don't know where he got it. I never asked him and he never told me. I don't know anything about the Wagner train robbery.

A few days later Desmond mistakenly identified the prisoner in his custody as Harry Longbaugh, the Sundance Kid. The Pinkertons, however, dispatched a copy of the group picture of the Wild Bunch to St. Louis from Denver and Kilpatrick was identified.

But the Wild Bunch rider was still "dumb as a post." Even though he was confronted by the picture he refused to admit his identity.

"You're good at guessing," he told Chief Desmond, "why don't you keep on guessing?"

"What were you doing the night of July 3, last?" Desmond asked.

Kilpatrick answered grimly: "Don't remember."

"How long were you in Montana?"

"Don't remember."

"You have a poor memory, Kilpatrick, haven't you?"

"It seems that way, doesn't it," the outlaw replied coolly.

"You may as well tell us all about yourself. We'll learn the details just as we found out you are Kilpatrick and not Longbaugh."

"There's nothing to tell."

"Well, Kilpatrick, you're still obstinate today, I see."

"Kilpatrick is not my name. Call me Rose, or Arnold, or something like that and you'll be nearer to it."

For ten days and nights the questioning continued in the office of the St. Louis police chief. Desmond, who had been a police officer for twenty-five years, knew all the tricks. He was soft-spoken but relentless in his questioning. Once he kept Kilpatrick in his office twenty-four hours asking him the same questions over and over.

"The sweating continued," the St. Louis *Post Dispatch* reported on November 24. "Kilpatrick looked Desmond in the eye at every interview; he was determined not to talk and all the king's horses and all the king's men could not get him to open his mouth and pull out one little admission."

Desmond began to interrupt his questioning with sudden, barked commands: "Take off your hat; uncross your legs; throw away that cigar; wake up," and soon the weary outlaw was obeying automatically.

On the tenth evening Kilpatrick was brought into Desmond's office and offered a cigar. Kilpatrick bit off an end and leaned forward to accept a light.

"By the way, Kilpatrick," Desmond said quietly, "I have talked to you now for ten days. The police commissioner has promised me ten more days. I think I can promise you that this will go on until you are ready to talk all right."

The tall Texan blinked but said nothing. The questioning continued. Kilpatrick was returned to his cell. That evening he sent for Desmond and said to him wearily:

"Chief, I'm tired tonight and worn out. I don't feel well. If you excuse me tonight I'll answer any question you want in the morning."

Desmond nodded. "Just one question tonight then. What is your real name?"

The train robber threw up his hands helplessly. "Ben Kilpatrick."

Desmond gave the bandit a cigar and they shook hands. The next day Kilpatrick confessed. On December 12, 1901, he pleaded guilty to the last count in the twelve-count indictment that he had in his possession national bank notes "to defraud." He was sentenced to fifteen years in the federal penitentiary at Atlanta. Death was mandatory in Montana for train robbery, and the tall Texan hurriedly pleaded guilty when he heard that Montana authorities were in St. Louis seeking his release.

The following day Laura Bullion, dressed in somber gray, was sentenced in the same court to serve five years in the Jefferson City, Tennessee, penitentiary, after pleading guilty to a similar charge.

Two days after Laura was led from the federal court in St. Louis to begin her term, Harvey Logan walked into a saloon in the downtown section of Knoxville, Tennessee. Since early November he had been hiding out in the city, "patronizing drinking places and sporting houses," according to the Pinkerton files. The swarthy outlaw was invited to take part in a pool game and accepted. He took off his coat, selected a cue from the rack, and began playing. The game lasted almost an hour. The stakes became larger, and after he missed a few he became quarrelsome. He accused one of the other players of cheating and a fight started. The outlaw yanked a six-shooter from his hip pocket and began to gun-whip one of the players. Someone called the police and two officers hurried to the scene.

Logan severely wounded both patrolmen but he himself was shot. Clutching his side he ran out a back door only to leap more than thirty feet into space. The exit opened into a railroad culvert. But Harvey Logan, like Jim Younger, "was a rough man used to rough ways." Cut, and bruised, and bleeding badly, he ran down the culvert and managed to find a carriage. He rode for an hour telling the cab driver to "keep going until I tell you to stop." Approximately ten miles outside of Knoxville he paid off the driver. When the carriage disappeared he stumbled through the woods to the railroad tracks and began walking in the freezing cold, unarmed and without a coat.

He walked all night. Early in the morning he reached the outskirts of Jefferson City, a small town thirty miles east of Knoxville. He gathered a few twigs and branches and built a small fire. He crouched over the tiny blaze all day groaning from the pains of his wound.

As the James and Youngers had done twenty-five years before him in the dripping woods of Minnesota, Logan spent that Sunday listening to the measured summons of the church bells in the distance. It is not hard to visualize him hugging the small fire, his teeth chattering, and pressing the blood-soaked handkerchief against the bullet hole in his side.

The following morning the delirious outlaw staggered down the main street of Jefferson City. He was spotted at once and a telephone call was put through to Knoxville. A posse boarded a special train and soon arrived in Jefferson City.

Logan saw the crowds gathering and fled back to the woods. Stumbling, falling, then crawling, he made his way through the underbrush, his blood leaving a crimson trail in the snow. A dragnet was thrown about the countryside and the possemen advanced, rifles cocked and safeties off. Logan saw them coming and surrendered.

At 6:30 P.M., on December 15, the desperado was returned to Knoxville and the posse had to fight their way through a mob of more than five thousand curious spectators milling about the depot. The police forced Logan into a carriage and, escorted on both sides by a heavily armed guard, he was delivered to the Central Police Station.

A few days later a tall, athletic-looking man walked into the jail and stared intently through the bars at Logan. The outlaw looked up and said calmly:

"Hello Spence."

Lowell Spence, a famous Pinkerton detective and assistant superintendent of the Chicago Pinkerton office, nodded and turned to the local police and federal officers who crowded behind him.

"This is Harvey Logan," he said.

Logan stared back at him, his dark face expressionless. After Spence had left, the outlaw told one of the guards:

"Someday I'll have to kill that man. He's very troublesome."

That same week a battered black valise stuffed with ten thousand dollars in currency was discovered in the check room of the Southern Railway Depot in Nashville and Logan was identified as its owner. There wasn't a single bank note. Unlike Kilpatrick, he had successfully exchanged all of his share of the loot.

"We have Harvey Logan and we intend to keep him," one Knoxville police official declared triumphantly.

That, as it developed, was one man's opinion.

THE BIG CITY

WHERE Harry Longbaugh, the Sundance Kid, met Etta Place is not known. There is almost nothing about her in the Pinkerton archives. Her file, the smallest in the five huge volumes, has only this to say:

"She is about twenty-seven years old, five feet four inches in height, weighing about 110 pounds, medium complexion and wears her brown hair on the top of her head in a roll from forehead. She appears to be a refined type. Her nationality is not known."

There is no doubt that Etta was not one of Fanny Porter's girls. The Pinkerton operatives, who filed away details about a fugitive down to the last mole and birthmark, would have known about it. But they were stumped by this young female outlaw. She was—and still is—a mystery.

Cassidy was introduced to Etta Place by Longbaugh when he joined the Sundance Kid to leave for South America. Where their rendezvous was is not known, but Butch must have been surprised and disturbed when Longbaugh announced that she was to go along. William Pinkerton later described Etta as a "clever rider and expert shot with both revolver and rifle." And Cassidy, to whom the South American venture meant so much, may well have insisted on seeing her qualifications to be a Wild Bunch rider. She proved satisfactory, as later events showed.

While the law officers of almost every state in the West and the Pinkertons were combing the country for them, Cassidy and Longbaugh arrived in New York City with Etta Place on the morning of February 1, 1901. That afternoon, according to a report filed by William Pinkerton, several months later, they climbed the steps of a brownstone at 234 West Twelfth Street and rang the bell. A Mrs. Taylor, who operated a fashionable boardinghouse at the address, answered the ring. Cassidy introduced himself as Jim Ryan, Longbaugh as Harry D. Place, and Etta as Mrs. Place. Butch paid a week in advance.

The first thing Cassidy and Longbaugh did while in the city was to visit Tiffany's and buy Etta Place a gold lapel watch. It is a wonderful scene to visualize the two outlaws—with six-shooters on their hip—examining the tray of expensive timepieces and discussing in low tones the qualities of each one as the studiously attentive clerk stifles a yawn. Over their shoulder the ghost of Jesse James, that expert collector of gold "supers," must have smacked his lips.

To the two train robbers who had known little more than the empty life of the frontier saloons and the terrifying loneliness of the desolate outlaw station, New York City must have been a world of incredible wonders. The first subway was being built, automobiles were chugging down the street, distracting, as one of the newspapers put it, "attention from Lillian Russell's great six white horses and many carriages"; and there was the Flatiron Building, and the glittering lights of Broadway. Strangely enough, only a few blocks away from Mrs. Taylor's boardinghouse, was the northern boundary of the territory of Monk Eastman and his band of Hudson Dusters.

The Wild Bunch outlaws loved to have their pictures taken, and a few days after their arrival in Manhattan, Longbaugh and

Etta Place visited De Young's Photographic Studio at 826 Broadway, near Grace Church. Later a Pinkerton operative interviewed every studio in the city with a wanted poster and found the negatives.

There isn't anything unusual about the photograph. The Sundance Kid could have been any mild, harmless drummer of his day, visiting a Broadway studio with his wife to take home a memento of an unforgettable holiday.

While they were in New York, Longbaugh, according to the confidential New York criminal file of the agency, "was treated for an unknown disease by a physician on Second Avenue. He also made a trip to the Pierce Medical Institute at Buffalo, N. Y." However, the Medical Guide of the Western Hemisphere, the New York Medical Guide, the Medical Department of the New York Public Library, and the New York Academy of Medicine, have no record of a Pierce Medical Institute in Buffalo.

On February 20, 1901, Cassidy, Longbaugh, and Etta Place sailed for Buenos Aires, Argentina, on the freighter *S.S. Soldier Prince,* under the names of James Ryan and Mr. and Mrs. Harry D. Place.

A few months later Pinkerton operatives picked up the outlaws' trail and discovered the East Twelfth Street hideout. Robert Pinkerton wrote to his brother, William:

"Longbaugh and his party have been in New York City. It shows how daring these people are; while we're looking for them in the mountains and in the wilderness they are in the midst of society." Pinkerton then went on to suggest: "I think it would be a good thing, if possible, to learn at Buffalo what disease Longbaugh was being treated for as we may in that way get further information from physicians in other parts of the country." The operatives apparently failed to find such an institution, for there is no record of the nature of Longbaugh's illness.

Cassidy, Longbaugh, and Etta Place arrived in Buenos Aires sometime in March, 1901. They checked in at the Hotel Europa, an expensive hostelry, and visited the London and Platte River Bank where Longbaugh opened an account with twelve thousand dollars in gold notes. He gave the Hotel Europa as his address. They went to the government land office in Buenos Aires where they filed an application. They received "four square leagues" in Cholilo, Province of Chubut, District 16 de Octubre.

From Buenos Aires, the trio embarked on a coastwise steamer to Bahia Blanca, further south, and from there traveled by a semimonthly steamer to Rawson. At this point they hired mules and Indian bearers. They reached the District 16 de Octubre sometime in May. Their trip had taken them three and a half months and they had covered more than twelve thousand miles.

The first few months the two western outlaws roamed the countryside, visiting their neighbors, some of them from the western section of the United States, and buying stock. Before the year was out they had purchased 1,300 sheep, 500 head of cattle, and 35 horses.

It appeared that the last of the Wild Bunch were settling down. They became friendly with Dr. Newberry, a dentist of Buenos Aires, who had the adjacent ranch, and were regarded as "highly respected citizens of Buenos Aires."

But the quiet, peaceful life of a cattle rancher was not for Cassidy or Longbaugh. They became restless and, with Etta Place riding with them, began making mysterious trips up and down the coast and into the interior. The ranch was left in charge of a native foreman.

Whenever they stopped at the village Butch distributed candy to the children and a few coppers to the peons. If there were soldiers in the vicinity, the trio would visit the garrison and discuss the country with the officers over bottles of native beer. But Cassidy always made sure that several bottles were sent to the barracks.

Word passed along the jungle trails, and soon the two riders from the west and the beautiful brown-haired woman who was a "clever" horsewoman, were well-known figures to the brown children who ran after their horses; the peons who twisted their broad-brimmed straw hats in their hands as they waited for the coppers; the bored, barefooted soldiers and their strutting officers.

Back at the ranchhouse in the District 16 de Octubre, maps were spread out on the table in the lamplight and plans made. The storm was gathering over the Andes. Soon it would break.

29

"LET 'ER GO."

N late April, 1901, while Butch Cassidy, Harry Longbaugh, and Etta Place were settling in Argentina, Governor M. A. Otero, of New Mexico, was denouncing a "reprieve" he had received supposedly from President McKinley, postponing the hanging of Black Jack Ketchum, the Train Robber's Syndicate member who had lost his right arm in the solo train holdup.

"This reprieve is nothing but a forgery by Ketchum's friends," Governor Otero declared at the state capital, "and may be an attempt to remove him from jail."

To prevent a jail delivery, Governor Otero ordered the outlaw to be removed to the Clayton, New Mexico, penitentiary. On April 25, 1901, the New York *Times* described Black Jack's transfer.

> Since last September, Ketchum has been in jail in Union County, New Mexico. It has been rumored that a band of outlaws of the southwest had taken steps to rescue their comrade. Measures have been taken to prevent this. Ketchum today was removed to the Clayton, New Mexico jail. The sheriff of Union County ordered several deputies to maintain a strong guard and the prisoner was manacled with a heavy steel belt about his waist and his left arm was chained to his lower limbs which were also bound with steel bands. He was placed in a steel lined mail car with grated windows with armed guards inside the car and riding the roof.

Black Jack's friends had tried to force Governor Otero to reprieve the bandit but had failed. April 28 was set as the execution date.

When he arrived at Clayton, Black Jack asked to see the gallows and permission was granted by the warden. Guards armed with rifles and shotguns crowded the jailyard and patrolled the walls as the one-armed train robber, his chains clanking, hobbled into the bright sunshine and was taken behind the high stockade which hid the scaffold.

After inspecting it for several minutes he nodded approval. "Damn good job, boys," he said. "But why don't you take the stockade down so that the folks can see a man swing who never killed anybody?"

Later that day a priest came to see him and the handsome, black-haired Ketchum told him cheerfully, "Go get a fiddle, padre, and we'll all dance. I'll die as I lived."

Later he told his jailers he hoped the hanging would be early so "I can get to hell in time for dinner."

At 1 P.M., on April 28, 1901, Black Jack, calm and smiling, mounted the thirteen steps of the scaffold in the courtyard of the Clayton jail. He joked with the executioners and by moving his head helped adjust the noose.

"All ready Black Jack?" the sheriff called.

"Let 'er go," came through the black hood.

The sheriff let his hand fall and the trap was sprung. The eight-and-a-half-foot drop jerked off the outlaw's head but it was sewed back on. Two hours later, the only Wild Bunch rider to die on the gallows was placed in a pine coffin and lowered into a grave on a rocky knoll in the old Clayton cemetery.

30.

MANHUNT

THROUGH the chilly gray dawn, the column of prisoners in striped uniforms lockstepped their way across the yard of the Salem, Oregon, penitentiary. It was June 9, 1902. At the entrance to the prison foundry building, the men were lined up against the wall and counted by Guards Ferrell and Girard.

"All accounted for," Girard called out. Ferrell nodded and began to walk to the head of the column. Suddenly one of the prisoners jumped out of line and yanked a sawed-off Winchester rifle from beneath his jacket. Girard shouted a warning and Ferrell whirled around. The rifle barked and Ferrell fell, a bullet through his brain.

Harry Tracy, the Hole in the Wall rider who defied the posse in the windy pass nearly five years before, fired a second shot at Girard, but missed. David Merrill, who teamed up with Tracy after David Lant left for Wyoming, jumped to his side, also armed with a sawed-off Winchester. A lifer grabbed Tracy's weapon but was shot down by Merrill.

The prisoners began shouting and milling about the yard and in the confusion both convicts scaled the wall by means of a convenient ladder. Once over they engaged the guards on the top of the wooden stockade. Tracy selected one in the northeast corner. The man was dead before he reached the ground. Another fell, wounded in the right lung and stomach. He died a few minutes later. A third began firing but was shot in the shoulder and toppled from the wall. Tracy dragged him to his feet, and using him as a human shield broke through the outer gate. At the edge of the nearby forest Merrill pointed to the wounded guard.

"What about him?"

"This," Tracy replied and killed the helpless man. A few minutes later the fugitives vanished in the thick underbrush.

Back at the Salem penitentiary the prison population was in an uproar with armed guards herding the convicts back into their cells.

The sirens were wailing and telegraph and telephone lines humming with news of the break. America's greatest manhunt had begun.

The first day of their escape, Tracy and Merrill lay in the woods not far from the penitentiary. At dawn the following day, June 10, they entered the outskirts of Salem, robbed two men of their clothes, horses, and six-shooters, and headed for Portland. Bloodhounds sent from Washington State Penitentiary picked up their trail and a posse started in pursuit. Two law officers in a buggy who were far ahead of the baying hounds were waylaid on a lonely road by the convicts "who relieved them of their buggy and bade them a cheery good morning."

A few hours later they drove down the main street of the little town of Gervais in the stolen carriage with Tracy nodding and bowing to the flustered ladies who wondered who the stranger in the baggy blue suit might be.

On June 11, Tracy and Merrill abandoned the buggy a few miles from Gervais and disappeared in the forest. They were surrounded by a fifty-man posse but blasted their way free. A cordon was thrown about the countryside and "every man within a radius of ten miles who owns a gun" was ordered to join the posse.

But during the night Tracy and Merrill escaped after first holding up two more deputies and stealing their revolvers. The governor of Oregon ordered the state militia to join the manhunt, and two hundred and fifty soldiers arrived on the scene to reinforce the lines.

Pulitzer's *New York Morning World* in a special dispatch declared:

"A spokesman for the man hunters predicted tonight that Tracy is so hemmed in he will be caught within a few hours."

The announcement was premature.

By the morning it was discovered that Tracy and Merrill had broken through the cordon.

On June 14, they reached the outskirts of Portland, stole two horses, and forced a farmer's wife to cook them breakfast. Then they galloped along the countryside to the Columbia River. There they found a man painting a boat and forced him to drop his paintbrush and row them across the river to Washington. They dined at another farmhouse and bound and gagged their host. The bloodhounds were soon baying in the distance and Tracy ordered a stand made, the two men fighting off a force of nearly a hundred men and again escaping uninjured.

After the fight the pair swam the river and worked through the fields to Ridgefield where they stole horses and forced other farmers and their wives to feed them.

On the evening of June 29, Tracy and Merrill again shot their way past a roadblock near Chehalis, Oregon. The next day they were seen on the Northern Pacific Railroad at Tenino, about forty miles from Tacoma. That was the last sight of David Merrill alive.

The entire Northwest was now in a state of alarm. Oregon's

governor ordered the reward raised to eight thousand dollars, and the posses were told, "Shoot to kill on sight."

On July 2, Tracy swaggered onto the stage alone. The sun was breaking through the mist which hung over South Bay near Olympia, the state capital, when a haggard-looking man in a stained blue suit, unshaven and red eyed, walked into the headquarters of an oyster fishing company. He forced the eight men in the building to line up against the wall and selected two to fix him some breakfast.

"I'm Tracy," he said. "Be quiet and you won't be harmed."

After a leisurely breakfast he tied the two impromptu cooks to chairs and gagged them. He herded the six others down the dock and pointed to a large gasoline launch.

"Who is the captain?" he asked.

"Captain Clark," he was told.

"Get him here and no monkey business."

In a few minutes Captain Clark and his son appeared. Tracy nodded to the launch.

"Get in."

One look into the granite-hard eyes was enough to convince Captain Clark. He climbed into the cabin, followed by his son and the six other men.

"Where to?" Clark asked.

Tracy grinned. "Seattle."

The outlaw took a seat in the corner of the tiny cabin, the rifle across his knees and the butts of two revolvers sticking out of his belt. During the twelve-hour journey he joked with the frightened men sitting in a semicircle before him and commented on the weather. Once someone inquired, "Where is Merrill, Tracy?"

Tracy's face set. "I killed him."

After a brief interval of silence the outlaw added: "He had no nerve. During my trial he testified against me. He was scared to death most of the time. When I called him a coward he became huffy so we decided on a duel. We were to start back to back and walk ten paces. I knew he was going to cheat, so after eight paces I turned and fired. The first shot didn't do the job so I shot him again."

There were no more questions.

Once when the launch was in sight of McNeil's Island, Tracy

gestured with the rifle in the direction of the military prison. "Run the boat over there."

"For God's sake why?" Captain Clark asked.

"I want to pick off a few guards from the walls," Tracy replied calmly.

Captain Clark quickly pointed out that they would surely be fired upon, and the outlaw reluctantly changed his mind.

At Meadow Point, near Seattle, Tracy ordered the launch docked. He tied and gagged Captain Clark and the crew but forced one of the men to act as his guide. Later that night he released him. The fugitive made his way to the outskirts of Bothell and lay hidden under some logs in a driving downpour until morning. Later that day he encountered a twenty-two man posse and fought them to a standstill, killing one, a deputy sheriff, and wounding three others. He narrowly missed killing a newspaperman, Louie B. Sefrit of the *Seattle Times*.

The gun battle took place in a weed-choked yard before two small cabins. Three deputies scaled the rusty barbed-wire fence and began beating their way through the high grass and tree stumps. Tracy suddenly rose from behind a stump. He fired twice and two deputies fell. Reporter Sefrit pegged a shot with his Colt and Tracy turned to him. Bullets whistled overhead and the newsman wisely fell, feigning a mortal wound. From where he lay he could see Tracy peering at him through the rain. After a few minutes the fugitive began to back away. Another posseman, scaling the fence, saw him and yelled. The Winchester roared again and the man fell dead in the grass. Still firing, the outlaw scurried through the thick underbrush and vanished.

A mile outside of Bothell, Tracy relieved a rancher of his horse, telling him that he "needed it in a hurry." The owner tried to stop him and Tracy, probably to save ammunition, bashed out his brains with a gun butt. On the way to Seattle he stopped another farmer, Louis Johnson, in a wagon, and made him drive to Woodland Park, a suburb of Seattle. By this time Tracy was hungry and ordered the team tied outside the farmhouse of Mrs. R. H. Van Horn.

The farm woman answered his knock.

"I'm Tracy," the outlaw said, introducing himself. "I would like some food. Be quiet and no harm will come to you."

The frightened woman ushered him and Johnson into the

kitchen. "This is hard work, dodging those posses," Tracy said calmly. He took off his coat and slumped in a chair. "You know," he added as Mrs. Van Horn began preparing the meal, "this is the first time I ever held up a woman. I don't like to tie or gag you so will you please promise not to say anything about my being here?"

"For tonight I will—but not tomorrow," the plucky woman replied.

The outlaw nodded. "Agreed. By tomorrow I will be so far away it won't make any difference."

As he ate, Tracy described his "yachting trip" as "very nice," but said that he was "disappointed" that he didn't have an opportunity of "knocking a few of the guards from the walls" at McNeil's Island.

A neighbor dropped by with a pail of milk and Tracy took his dry clothing. At about eight o'clock that evening there was a knock on the door. Tracy jumped to his feet. With a revolver he motioned to Johnson and the neighbor.

"Say anything and I will kill you."

Mrs. Van Horn nodded and went to the door. It was the butcher boy. As she paid her bill she managed to mouth the word "Tracy." The startled boy understood and ran down the road. The farm woman returned to the kitchen, sat at a table, and nonchalantly added her bill. Tracy watched her through narrowed eyes. Satisfied, he returned to his chair to joke with his two prisoners.

The butcher boy, meanwhile, had sounded the alarm and a posse surrounded the house. Three men wormed their way through the bushes and lay in wait less than six feet from Johnson's wagon.

At about ten o'clock Tracy yawned and, thanking Mrs. Van Horn "most courteously" for the meal, stepped down the path using the two men as a shield. The rifles of the posse covered him every inch of the way, but at an order from the sheriff held their fire to wait until Tracy climbed into the wagon alone.

Three members of the posse sprang to their feet and ran toward Tracy. Suddenly one shouted, "Throw down your arms, Tracy."

The outlaw spun around and fired several shots in rapid succession at the moving shadows. His incredible marksmanship was effective.

In its account of the shooting, the *New York Morning World* correspondent wrote:

One of the dead men was shot in the face, in the shoulder, and in the breast. His left arm was also shattered. His body bore eloquent evidence of Tracy's magnificent marksmanship. After he had killed Policeman Breece he dropped on one knee and taking deliberate aim in the darkness put a bullet through the heart of Game Warden Rawley. Deputy Sheriff John Williams was Tracy's next victim. The bullet struck his rifle and passing through his breast, killed him.

The posse fired several rounds at Tracy but the outlaw scaled a fence and disappeared into the night.

For days Tracy roamed the countryside. He held up another farmhouse and forced a hired hand by the name of Anderson to become his pack horse. He next appeared at a logging camp "more dead than alive," as the *World* reporter declared, and ordered the men in the camp "to cook him a meal and supply him with provisions." Later that night he vanished in the darkness with Anderson carrying the supplies—after warning the loggers not to sound an alarm "for an hour or two."

The next heard of Tracy was at Renton where he compelled a family to shelter him and his human pack horse for the evening and to cook him a meal.

"I'm Tracy," he told the farm woman. "I suppose you heard of me. But don't be afraid. I never harmed a woman in my life."

That evening, rifle in hand, he went down to the spring and filled a bucket. He came back grinning. He told the family he had spotted the special train coming down the tracks loaded with possemen.

"I reckon there were some men on that train looking for me," he said in mock surprise.

While the small army of law officers crawled cautiously through the brush surrounding the farmhouse, Tracy insisted that the afternoon meal be served. He was completely at ease, telling jokes and describing the highlights of his escape. Once he rose and looked out the window.

"It's a shame that my trousers are unironed with so many ladies here," he said when he returned to the dinner table. "Perhaps I had better go out and capture a deputy."

When one of the ladies in the house said that she was frightened to go home alone, Tracy chivalrously volunteered to accompany her, pointing out that any man could call himself lucky if he had a chance to escort a charming lady home in the moonlight.

It was late afternoon when Tracy decided that he must leave. Again and again he thanked his unwilling hostess, wished everyone happiness and luck, and then opened the front door. At that moment the unfortunate Anderson was discovered tied like a mule to a tree and the posse broke their lines and began running toward the spot. Tracy walked through the woods and, when he was grabbed by two deputies in the gathering gloom, escaped by informing them, "I'm a newspaper reporter." He was released with a warning to "be on the lookout."

Bloodhounds were again put on his trail, as the *World* correspondent reports, but he threw them off by scattering red pepper behind him and made his way into Seattle where he spent a night of revelry with two crooks who were also fugitives from the law.

The following week he entered a country store and called a nearby sheriff on the telephone.

"This is Tracy," he said. "I just wanted you to know I'm still around." When the law officer began sputtering, the outlaw told him: "Don't feel too bad. You've done much better than the other sheriffs. At least you spoke to the man you were after. Good-by."

Weeks later he showed up in eastern Washington headed for Hole in the Wall. He came upon A. B. Shruer, who was hunting deer, and ordered him to throw up his hands. Shruer, believing it was a joke, refused and Tracy, not in a joking mood, fired a warning shot. The powder blast burned the hunter's hands.

"I'm sorry I hurt you," he said, "but when I say throw up your hands, I mean it."

The desperado walked over to the fire and examined the food cooking in a small pot. "I'm hungry," he said, and squatting down began picking out bits of meat. "Come on," he invited Shruer, "have some supper."

After he had finished eating the fugitive scanned the sky. "I guess it's going to rain." After he had disarmed Shruer he said "goodnight and disappeared into the woods."

The *New York World*, which told the story, explained unnecessarily: "Mr. Shruer did not attempt to detain him."

For days there was no news of Tracy. Then he was sighted in a small sloop riding the treacherous waters off Deception Pass in Puget Sound. Again the manhunt was in full swing. Instead of horses, bloodhounds, and carriages, the posse took to revenue cutters, gasoline launches, and steamers.

"The war against Tracy, the outlaw, is now a naval war," the *New York World* correspondent declared. "Two steamers, the revenue cutter *Grant* and the *Scout,* are on the sound with three posses embracing some of the most noted man hunters in the entire west. All the towns are ready for him with posses trying to head him from the Olympia mountain country. 'If he gets there,' one deputy said, 'his leave on liberty will be a long one.' The mountainous country in that section is densely wooded and terribly precipitous."

After a twenty-four hour search covering one hundred and twenty-five miles of the sound and its adjacent area, the weary posse returned to Seattle. Tracy had again made good his escape.

The cutters patrolled the sound and the bloodhounds bayed helplessly. Tracy vanished. It was thought that he had made his way to Hole in the Wall, but he suddenly appeared in a running gun battle with a farmer and his son. He was wounded in the right hip and took refuge in a dense swamp. How long this incredible man stayed there is not known. It must have been a terrifying ordeal splashing through the scummy water, eaten alive by the clouds of mosquitoes, hungry and thirsty and the wound in his hip like a white-hot coal.

He emerged at last to find food and slept one night in a barn. He was discovered and had to shoot his way through a sheriff's posse. That same afternoon he "exchanged shots" with another band of manhunters and escaped by jumping aboard a passing freight train.

A few days later, according to the *New York World,* "he met a man on a road and told him that his wound was bothering him a great deal."

In August Tracy reached the country south of the Colville Indian Reservation. He was exhausted and vicious as a wounded wolf. He was spotted on a ranch a few miles from Creston, Oregon, and the telephone summoned a posse of Lincoln County citizens.

He broke out of a trap and began to move down a broad valley, pausing now and then to exchange shots with his pursuers. The duel lasted most of the afternoon and, as the purple twilight closed in, the exhausted fugitive made a stand behind a large boulder.

74. Clement Rolla Glass, manager of the Concordia Tin Mine, who employed and befriended Butch Cassidy and the "Sundance Kid." *(Courtesy Percy Siebert)*

75. The Concordia Tin Mine in Bolivia. Cassidy and Longbaugh bunked in the first white house on the mountainside. *(Courtesy Percy Siebert)*

76. Cassidy and Longbaugh's bunkmates at the Concordia Tin Mine. James Patrick Ahern, fourth man from the left, as night watchman, prodded the strange blanketed figure of Longbaugh to ask who he was and narrowly missed being shot by Cassidy. *(Courtesy Percy Siebert)*

77. Percy Siebert, engineer at the Concordia Tin Mine, was the closest thing to an honest friend that Butch Cassidy ever had. *(Courtesy Percy Siebert)*

78. The La Paz stage. Cassidy and the "Sundance Kid" were friends of Harry Hutcheon who owned the stage, and so, though tempted, would not rob it. *(Courtesy Percy Siebert)*

79. San Vicente where Cassidy and the Sundance Kid died, as it must have looked to them. *(Courtesy Victor Hampton)*

80. The bario where Cassidy and Longbaugh were killed. The outlaws' rifles were stacked where the man sits on the far right. Both died inside the hut. *(Courtesy Victor Hampton)*

• 81. Sketch depicting how Cassidy and Longbaugh died in San Vicente, Bolivia. This sketch is based on sketches supplied for this book by Victor Hampton and Sue Butler.

He fired several times at the deputies who dodged from rock to rock but, owing to the gathering darkness and his exhausted condition, missed each time. The posse began a flanking movement and Tracy made a dash for a nearby wheat field. Several rifles barked almost in unison. The outlaw stumbled and fell but dragged himself foot by foot into the field as the bullets thudded in the ground on all sides.

A second posse arrived and the field was completely surrounded. In the silence a shot suddenly rang out. The manhunters waited all that night, peering anxiously through the tense blackness. When the sun came up the wave of men moved across the field foot by foot. Tracy was found with a bullet hole in his right temple, the revolver still clutched in his hand. The most famous manhunt in America's criminal history had ended.

31.

KID CURRY ESCAPES

WHEN the jury in November, 1902, convicted Harvey Logan, the Kid Curry of the Wild Bunch, it soon became clear that there was no jail strong enough in Tennessee to hold him. Logan had always boasted he would never stay behind bars, and the Pinkertons wired the Knoxville County authorities to be on the alert.

"There is not one good point about Logan," William Pinkerton warned the Tennessee authorities. "He has not one single redeeming feature. He is the only criminal I know of who actually does not have one single good point. He is desperate and will use any means to escape."

The federal authorities agreed with Pinkerton and Logan was sentenced to twenty years at hard labor in the Columbus, Ohio, penitentiary. Kid Curry ordered his attorneys to appeal his conviction and the case went into the slow-moving legal machinery.

It was heard by the United States Circuit Court of Appeals, Sixth District, in the spring of 1903. It must have startled the dignified robed justices to hear the court clerk call out the case of:

"Harvey Logan, alias Kid Curry, alias Harvey Curry, alias Bob Jones, alias Tom Jones, alias Bob Nevilles, alias Robert Nelson, alias R. J. Whelan, alias Charles Johnson—Plaintiff in error versus the United States, defendant in error."

After a lengthy argument the high court confirmed the conviction. Logan was removed to the Knoxville County jail while federal authorities began preparations to remove him under heavy guard in a steel mail car to Columbus.

The Knoxville County jail was a two-story white brick building overlooking one of the town's principal streets. One side of the wall was covered with ivy and at the front entrance there was a hitchup post. In the back of the jail was a small yard open on all sides, where Sheriff Fox, who had temporary charge of the prisoner, kept his two-year-old mare. Prisoners and the sheriff's men usually entered the jail from the yard through a basement door which led up into the sheriff's office. Overhead was a small porch where the sheriff smoked his after-dinner cigars.

Logan was on the second tier and had the freedom of the cell block. Running parallel was a small corridor where the guards sat. At the far end was a barred window through which the Tennessee River could be seen. The outlaw was guarded day and night in twelve-hour shifts by guards Bell and Irwin.

At 4:15 P.M., Saturday, June 27, 1903, Logan rose from his bunk and stretched. He smiled at Irwin and walked to the end of the cage and looked out at the river. The guard joined him, on the other side of the bars. The sun was setting and its rays cast a fiery sheen on the water.

"A beautiful sight, eh, Logan?" Irwin asked.

Logan nodded. "It sure is, Charley," he said feelingly, "but I think the river is rising slowly from so much rain."

As they stared at the glittering river, Logan suddenly pointed to some object in the river. They discussed it for a few minutes and then Irwin turned to take his position in front of the cell block.

Logan suddenly threw his hand out and a thin wire lasso hissed through the air. The outlaw jerked hard on the noose and pulled the guard against the bars. Irwin struggled, but the noose turned into a strangler's cord. In a moment Logan had tied the guard's hands between the bars with strips of tough canvas torn from an old cot.

"Now to make Bell let me out," Logan growled.

"Bell has nothing against you, Logan, don't harm him," Irwin pleaded.

"This is a life or death question with me. I'd rather be dead than behind bars. I'll kill anyone that gets in my way," the desperado replied.

Logan then ran into the small bathroom at the end of the block and came out with several pieces of window molding. He bound the sections together with canvas strips and then from beneath his mattress produced a large rusty hook. Lying flat on the floor he carefully raked the floor of the guard corridor, trying to reach a cardboard box containing a .45 caliber Colt and a .38 caliber Smith and Wesson. It was a breathtaking few minutes. The hook was just an inch too short. Logan strained against the bars. Then at last he hooked the box and dragged it to him.

He spun the cylinders of the revolver and stuck both guns into his belt. Reaching into Irwin's pocket he drew out a watch, gave it a quick glance, and returned it.

"I only want to see what time it is, Charley," he said almost apologetically. "I don't want anything that you got."

It was then 4:30 P.M. Logan had obviously planned his break to the split second.

He began rapping the cell bars with a bottle and calling out Bell's name.

The guard appeared only to stare down at two barrels poking out through the bars.

"Open up, Tom," Logan ordered, each word an icicle. "I don't want to hurt you, but I'll kill you if you don't open this door. I have nothing against you, but Fox had better stay out of my way. I'm getting out of here. Open this door."

Covered by the guns Bell fumbled at the combination lock. It didn't open at first, and the sound of the revolvers being cocked was loud in the stillness.

"Don't fool me, Tom," Logan warned.

A moment later the door swung open and the train robber spun Bell around. Jabbing the revolvers in the guard's back he marched him to the main office and down the basement steps into the rear yard.

Curiously, Sheriff Fox's mare was there and Logan ordered Bell to "saddle her up." R. P. Swanee, an Italian helper and an ex-prisoner, walked into the yard and was ordered to help the guard. In a few minutes the horse was saddled. Suddenly the sheriff appeared on the porch overhead and shouted down: "What's going on down there."

Bell replied, "You'll soon find out what's the matter if you don't get inside."

Pushing aside the guard and the ex-prisoner, Logan vaulted to the saddle and, with a pistol in one hand, booted the mount out of the yard.

Directly across from the jail he saw a little girl playing with her dolls in the grass. About this time every evening it was the outlaw's custom to wave to the child and call out hello from the jail window. As he saw the child jump up and wave to him, Logan shook his head and pressed a finger to his lips.

A man who lived a few doors from the jail saw the outlaw pounding past but thought "it was a liveryman taking a horse to a customer." He did, however, look at his watch and saw that it was 5:05 P.M.

The Wild Bunch rider galloped down Prince Street, then into Hill Avenue and Gay Avenue. He rattled across the wooden Tennessee River Bridge to disappear in a cloud of dust along the Martin Mill Pike.

At 6:30 P.M., Logan, who was now "riding leisurely," according to eye witnesses, approached a country store about five miles outside of Knoxville where he stayed long enough to smoke a cigar. A crowd gathered, and several persons who recognized the outlaw struck up a conversation. Logan readily answered all questions and it was only after several men "got into a huddle" that he decided not to stretch his luck too far and rode off.

At least ten other farmers and passing travelers saw him riding down the road, apparently without a care in the world.

Back at the jail Sheriff Fox, Bell, and the Italian ex-prisoner found Irwin and untied him. The *Knoxville Sentinel* declared that Fox had armed himself with a revolver after Logan had leaped into the saddle but couldn't find a rifle "because there wasn't any on the place."

Due Dec ~~2~~
~~2~~ 16

Irwin told his story of how he had been lassoed by the outlaw, adding: "I simply knew he had me and that if I created any trouble he would cut my throat and kill me. He could have done that and accomplished his purpose in getting away as easy as not."

Bell said:

"I was so taken by surprise when he shoved the pistol at me through the bars that I hardly realized what had happened. He could have killed me, had I not complied with his requests.

"I opened the cell door to save my life. I do not regret my actions as I knew Logan would have shot me if I did not do so. He would have covered every man who came up until that door was unlocked. With those pistols he had control of the situation."

It was at this point that the escape became incredibly bizarre and ludicrous.

R. W. Austin, United States marshal, and W. D. Wright, United States district attorney who had prosecuted Logan, strolled down the street, passing the jail at 5:15 P.M., exactly one hour after the outlaw had lassoed Guard Irwin.

"I saw Sheriff Fox passing in a leisurely manner," Austin said later in a public statement and I said, "Hello, sheriff, how is Logan?" He replied "He is gone." I replied, "Why, you must be joking." He answered, "No, it is a fact."

Incredulous, Wright and Austin accompanied Fox to his office, where, as Austin declared, "we obtained the story of Logan's escape. Mr. Fox also told us at that time," the marshal reported, "that he had found out two weeks before that Logan had a map of the country south of the river. We also learned that Logan had use of the corridor. Mr. Wright stated that he had ordered the sheriff not to let Logan out of his cell and I had given the same order. I asked Mr. Fox if he had done anything about hunting Logan and he said he would have a posse go after him. This was an hour after Logan had escaped.

"I then began to phone all over the country, calling to my aid all the deputy United States marshals and sheriffs. Both the sheriffs of Blount and Sevier Counties stated they would start at once and did with posses. I was in frequent communication with all parts of the country, sending out descriptions of him and using the telegraph to contact many points."

Before they had hurried from Fox's office, Austin and Wright ordered the sheriff to meet them at Wright's office at 8:30 P.M. At that hour Fox had not showed up and both men began searching for him. It is indeed a weird scene to imagine the two federal law-enforcement officers hurrying down the streets of Knoxville looking for the county's sheriff, while the most desperate outlaw in the country trots leisurely along the dark roads mounted on the sheriff's mare. But each passing hour was to be more weird than the last.

About ten o'clock, Wright and Austin found Fox sitting in conference with one of Logan's attorneys.

"Fox acted as the spokesman and told the story of Logan's escape," Austin said. "He made the statement that Irwin's neck showed where the wire noose had caught him. I then turned to Mr. Wright and said, "Did you not tell me you examined Irwin's neck and found no marks?" Mr. Wright then said that was true. We then left the office, saying that we did not intend to discuss the matter in the presence of Logan's attorney. Federal Judge Clark was also notified of the escape and ordered me on Sunday morning to make a full and detailed investigation of Logan's escape. I also notified the Department of Justice in Washington, D. C., the Pinkerton National Detective Agency, and the Union Pacific Railroad."

Mr. Wright was more succinct in his statement to the *Knoxville Sentinel*. "I looked carefully at the neck of Irwin, the guard. I found no marks to show that he had been roughly treated."

The following Monday, Austin exploded another sensation. "I was told two weeks ago by Sheriff Fox that Logan's friends would pay as high as ten thousand dollars for his escape. I also learned that attempts had been made to bribe the watchman. Upon receipt of this information I immediately applied to the United States Circuit Court of Appeals to issue an order to have Logan transferred at once to the jail at Cincinnati but had not received the order up to this time."

That same day the *Knoxville Sentinel* reporter, who had scooped the country on the outlaw's escape, wrote:

It was only in February that Sheriff Fox stated to a *Sentinel* reporter that he wished Logan would be taken away, as he was afraid he would cause a great deal of trouble before his case was finished. He also said he did not know in what way the trouble would come but was very apprehensive that he was a very dangerous man to have in his jail and would by some means make trouble for him and his deputies. He said he wished he would be soon taken to Columbus.

The country, meanwhile, was in a state of alarm. Posses scoured Tennessee and the neighboring states. The wires hummed with orders from William Pinkerton to Denver and Kansas City. Crack operatives saddled their horses and began their lonely and dangerous trips. The sheriffs of Utah, Wyoming, and Colorado, no longer cowed by the Wild Bunch riders, searched Hole in the Wall, Robber's Roost, Brown's Hole, and Powder Springs. There were still watchers on the hills. The stolen horses and the fugitives slipped into the small hidden canyons and the posse found nothing but the dead fires and the scraps of dried hides.

A small army of homeless drifters and tramps were arrested as Logan, only to be released after weary Pinkerton operatives peered into countless cells and shook their heads.

Back at Knoxville a full-scale investigation of the escape was begun at the insistence of the federal judge. The Pinkertons, together with the marshal and the United States district attorney, held several sessions behind closed doors of the jailhouse, questioning witnesses and watching guards Irwin and Bell re-enact the break.

The evidence showed how cleverly Logan had planned his escape. After his conviction he shammed several wild outbreaks, smashing the furniture, battering the sink with a small broom, and punching the wooden molding about the windows in his berserk rage. He finally was able to unwind the fine wire from around the sweep portion of the broom and loosen some of the longer sections of the molding. The rusty hook was from an old wooden bucket he had kicked to pieces. The findings of the investigators were rushed to Washington.

"While the manner of Logan's ultimate escape was rather ingenious," George S. Dougherty of the Pinkerton New York office announced a short time later, "it is apparent that he had some help, for today the United States government has brought a civil suit against the officials of Knox County for $10,000 damages for permitting this criminal to get away."

Two weeks after his escape, Logan was reported to have been seen passing through several small towns in the Great Smokies of

North Carolina. A large posse, headed by Lowell Spence, the Pinkerton operative, spent two weeks searching the rugged country but without success.

For Logan there remained nothing but Butch Cassidy and the Argentine pampas. Passage money was needed and, like his leader, Kid Curry decided he had to hold up a bank or a train. With a weak facsimile of the Wild Bunch he stopped a train near Parachute, Colorado, on the afternoon of July 7, 1903. The safe was blown open with dynamite but it was empty. Logan and his gang fled closely pursued. The chase lasted for two days. On the second evening the train robbers were cornered in a mountain gully and there made a stand. A furious gun battle followed. In a brief silence the posse heard a man behind a boulder call out: "Are you hit?"

The answer was, "Yes, and I will end it here." There was a single shot. The battle in the gully was resumed but the other train robbers escaped. Returning to the gully the posse found the body of the dead outlaw, who had shot himself through the right temple. At Glenwood Spring, some townspeople identified him as Tap Duncan, a puncher who had worked in the vicinity.

The Pinkerton agency in Denver heard of the robbery and shooting and requested a photograph of the dead man. A copy was sent and Superintendent James McPharland declared that the dead man was Harvey Logan.

The announcement created a furor. Sheriffs, marshals, and railroad officials openly doubted it. The bank in Cody, Wyoming, was robbed and the headlines cried that Harvey Logan and the Wild Bunch were again on the loose. Buffalo Bill, a whisky-soaked ghost out of America's past, after whom the town was named, gathered a posse together to chase Kid Curry, but "decided to go hunting instead," as the Cody paper declared.

"To answer the endless questions," William A. Pinkerton ordered Lowell Spence to go to Glenwood Springs, Colorado, and have the body exhumed. Operative Spence, who is living in quiet retirement in Chicago at the age of eighty-seven, told this writer:

> The body was exhumed and I identified it as Harvey Logan. There was no doubt about it. He had shot himself in the left temple. Chief Special Agent Canada of the Union Pacific Railway, who made the trip with me, said it was not. I was laughed

at a number of times for making this identification, but I knew it was Logan's body.

Mr. Canada had seen Logan only once and then behind the bars of the Knoxville County jail. I had seen him awake and asleep in the jail and on the streets of Knoxville going to and from the courthouse and sitting in the court rooms for hours at a time. The body that was exhumed that day was that of Harvey Logan, the Kid Curry of the Wild Bunch."

The controversy lasted for a year. On July 7, 1904, Robert Pinkerton in New York, telegraphed his brother William in Chicago:

Suggest Spence go at once to Knoxville with photograph. Have him show it thoroughly. If identified please advise us. Notify all western offices to publish on instructions from you. Annual report 1902 has very full story. If Spence succeeds in getting photograph identified then he is to telegraph Chicago. We will notify all eastern offices to arrange for publication of an article showing that identification has been made of the dead outlaw as Harvey Logan, alias, Kid Curry.

Spence made the trip to Knoxville and the photograph was identified by state and federal officials. There could no longer be a doubt that the cowpuncher, Tap Duncan, resting in the tiny graveyard in Glenwood Springs, Colorado, was the notorious bad-man, Harvey Logan. Like Harry Tracy, Kid Curry, the tiger of the Wild Bunch, had chosen death rather than life behind prison bars.

OPERATIVE DIMAIO

FRANCIS P. DIMAIO found out long before 1903 that his life as a Pinkerton operative was filled with the unexpected. Strange and dangerous situations were commonplace. Like the day in 1890 when he was summoned by William Pinkerton to be informed he was to be arrested within a few days by the United States Secret Service as one of the country's biggest counterfeiters.

Dimaio, who looked more like a quiet, peace-loving business-man than one of the agency's crack detectives, was not surprised. It was all in a day's work. Within a few hours he knew the plan. Several powerful Black Hand killers and extortioners were lodged in the county jail in New Orleans. Someone had to break them. That was to be his job. He was to be arrested as an important counterfeiter and, after a fanfare of publicity, thrown into the cell with the killers. He was told very bluntly what to expect if the Mafia saw through his disguise.

The play went off without a hitch. In New .Orleans he was arrested and described by the Secret Service as the country's biggest counterfeiter. Every paper in the country played the story big. He was arraigned and thrown into the old Parish Prison. He stayed there for weeks. He cursed the jailers, threw money about like water for special privileges, and boasted about the powerful interests working in his behalf. The gang was impressed.

He cleverly split the Sicilian killers into two factions, whispering in one ear, then another. Soon they were at each other's throats. He kept goading one of the leaders. Finally in a rage the killer spilled the story, disclosing the names of the other members of the gang, some of whom were powerful New Orleans leaders. So he could tell his story to the grand jury, Dimaio was safely removed from the cell "on a writ."

There were many other exciting episodes. No two days of his

life were alike. So on March 8, 1903, while successfully concluding
an investigation in Sao Paolo, Brazil, he was not surprised to
receive a cable from Robert A. Pinkerton in New York, which
read: "Proceed at once to Buenos Aires. Await letter of instructions."

Dimaio packed his bags and that night boarded the French
liner, *Chile*. He arrived in Buenos Aires on March 10 and registered at the Hotel Metropole. The next day he received the letter
of instructions from New York. It was an order to find Butch
Cassidy and his two riders. The agency had trailed the outlaw
leader, the Sundance Kid, and Etta Place across the country to
the steamship line in New York City. The famed portrait taken in
Texas, along with the pictures the Sundance Kid had taken of himself and Etta in New York, were included.

The next morning Dimaio began his investigation. He went to
the American Legation and interviewed Secretary Eames who was
taking the place of the minister, who was ill.

"Mr. Eames was very helpful," Dimaio wrote in his report. "He
gave me an introduction to Dr. Newberry, an American and leading dentist of Argentina, and also a letter to Dr. Francisco Beasley,
chief of police of Buenos Aires.

"I contacted Dr. Newberry, a man about 45, light complexion,
light brown hair and mustache. He is very neat in appearance. I
showed him the pictures of Cassidy, Longbaugh and Etta Place
and he informed me that as Mr. and Mrs. Place and James Ryan
they were located on a ranch at Cholilo, Province of Chubut,
District 16 de Octubre. Dr. Newberry, who had the adjoining
ranch, describes Ryan and Place as very fine gentlemen and well
liked by all those they came in contact with. They posed as cattlemen. Dr. Newberry said that it would be impossible to bring them
out through the jungle as it was the rainy season." To reach the
outlaw's ranch Dimaio discovered that he would have to travel
two hundred and fifty miles south of Buenos Aires to Puerto
Madryn and from there travel on muleback through the trackless
pampas. He cabled this information to the New York office and
was ordered "to block all avenues of escape and arrange for the
local police to cable us at once should the outlaws start traveling
in the direction of the United States or any port." Dimaio saw
Chief Beasley and arrangements were made to keep a lookout
for the outlaws.

Dimaio stayed in Buenos Aires for several weeks, scrutinizing every passenger that came down the gangplanks and interviewing every American who had come from the interior to escape the rainy season.

He became acquainted with a salesman by the name of Steele and showed him the picture of the Wild Bunch.

"Sometimes I'm out on the road for as long as six months," Steele told him. "I see a lot of people and visit a lot of places. I'll keep my eyes open for these people."

On the theory that the outlaws had banked their money to keep it safe from thieves in a strange country, Dimaio toured the banks. At the London and River Platte bank in Buenos Aires the manager gasped when the Pinkerton operative showed him the pictures of Cassidy, Longbaugh, and Etta Place.

"My God," he said, "that's Mr. and Mrs. Harry Place and Jim Ryan."

"Have you seen them in this bank?" Dimaio asked.

The bank official stared at him. "Seen them? Why, they opened an account here."

The books were produced and they showed that Longbaugh, as Harry D. Place, had opened an account on March 23, 1901, with $12,000 in United States gold notes. The Sundance Kid had given the Hotel Europa, an expensive Buenos Aires hostelry, as his address. On May 16, 1902, he cashed a check for $3,546. On August 14, the same year, he withdrew $1,105.50. The banker, wiping his forehead after Dimaio sketched the career of the Wild Bunch, promised "to be on the alert for them."

When the detective searched the files of the Argentine Government Land Office in Buenos Aires, he discovered that the outlaws had filed a second application "for the right to buy the land and improve it."

Dimaio also wrote out a long wanted poster with detailed descriptions and pictures of Cassidy, Longbaugh, and Etta Place. They were printed both in Spanish and English. To make sure they gained wide circulation, he tramped about the city distributing them to post offices, banks, railroad depots, hotels, steamship lines, ticket agencies, livery stables, and mining offices.

After a last conference with Beasley he returned to the United States, arriving in New York City in June, 1903, where he conferred with Robert Pinkerton. A few days later the agency head wrote to Chief Beasley, enclosing twelve more pictures of Cassidy, Longbaugh, and Etta Place. The agency head also disclosed that arrangements were under way to arrest the Wild Bunch riders under an extradition treaty between the United States and the Argentine Republic. The letter has the wonderful laconic precision of police communications.

"All these men are desperate," Pinkerton warned Beasley, "and if an attempt is made to apprehend them, they are sure to resort to firearms. Longbaugh (or Place) is the most desperate of the two. Cassidy (or Ryan) is the next. Either of these men would not hesitate to take a life to escape arrest, and whoever attempts their arrest should be fully advised and prepared for any emergency. They are all good shots with rifle and pistol. In this country, before commencing as bank and train robbers, they were cattle thieves, or what are known in this country as cattle 'rustlers' and will undoubtedly engage in the same business in South America.

"We write you thus fully that you may be informed of the nature and character of these men, and being fully advised, in case you should be called to act against them, you can have your officers fully prepared. It is our firm belief that it is only a question of time before these men commit some desperate robbery in Argentina. They are all thorough plainsmen and horsemen, riding from six hundred to a thousand miles after committing a robbery. If there are reported to you any train or bank robberies or any other crimes, you will find that they were undoubtedly committed by these men, who sooner or later will engage in the commission of some desperate crime in your country."

The letter and the pictures of those "desperate men" were sent to Chief Beasley. Dimaio was given another assignment. He will appear again.

BANDIDOS YANQUI

ON a bright March morning in 1906, as Pinkerton had fore-seen, Butch led his three raiders into the town of Mercedes, Province San Luis, in Central Argentina, five hundred miles west of Buenos Aires. There was only Longbaugh, Etta Place in rough jeans with her long brown hair rolled up beneath a broad sombrero, and a young American outlaw fugitive named Dey.

The town was quiet with few people on the streets as they rode up and dismounted in front of the Bank of the Naçion, facing the Villa Mercedes. Cassidy, Longbaugh, and Dey entered while Etta held the horses. The clerk smiled a welcome. Rancheros Yanqui. It meant good business. His smile froze when he saw the revolvers. Butch tersely warned him in Spanish not to make any outcry. Dey and Longbaugh vaulted the counter and began sweeping the gold and securities into a sack. At this point the manager of the bank returned from a rear room and shouted when he saw what was happening. A gun barked. Who pulled the trigger nobody knows, but the banker was killed instantly.

The robbers slowly backed out of the door, one throwing the heavy sack across his saddle. In a moment they were galloping out of town. A small band of citizens chased them for several miles but lost their enthusiasm for the manhunt when one of the bandits wheeled about and charged them, firing rapidly. With the bullets whistling over their heads, the possemen turned and fled.

It was fifteen days of hard riding back to 16 de Octubre. The twenty-thousand-dollar loot was divided and Dey said good-by. He traveled to Bolivia and, according to the *New York Herald* of September 23, 1906, checked in a hotel where he met a Dr. Lovelace from Texas. One night Lovelace saw the bag filled with sovereigns. When he commented, Dey replied solemnly: "The Lord has treated me very generously lately."

Meanwhile Dimaio's legwork had produced results. The San Luis police contacted Dr. Beasley in Buenos Aires with descriptions of the bank robbers and killers. There was no doubt in Beasley's mind who the outlaws were. He sent a patrol to the ranch, but the Bandidos Yanqui had fled—first selling the ranch to a Chilean beef syndicate. Butch had ordered the gang split up until the hunt died down. He drifted south, and Longbaugh and Etta crossed the border into Chile by the highway to Santiago.

A few months later Cassidy summoned them for their second South American strike. It was at the seaport town of Bahia Blanca, five hundred miles from Mercedes and that much south of Buenos Aires on the Atlantic Ocean. The victim again was the Bank of the Naçion. Ironically, the loot was twenty thousand dollars, the same as the first holdup. Etta, "that slim young man," as the police later described her, played her role as the gang's horse holder.

Cassidy shot the horses of the pursuers but evidently took good care not to shoot the men themselves.

The same month that strange triangle rode into Bolivia from Bahia Blanca. They had to go almost one hundred and fifty miles to reach the Bolivian frontier and Eucalyptus, where they struck again, is more than a hundred miles from the frontier. Assuming that they made the major portion of the journey by rail and not horse, consider the competent bravado necessary to buy tickets at the station unquestionably watched by the police.

They held up the Bolivian pay train at the Eucalyptus station. With them was a new rider, McVey, of whom nothing is known.

In this robbery Cassidy used the well-tried methods that had served him so well in the states: hold up the engineer of the train, force him to run the express car some distance from the rest of the train, force the express messenger to open the safe and turn over its contents. There were several packages addressed to various railroad employees in the safe, and when the bandits learned this, they returned them to the express messenger. It is said that this was the reason the railroad employees refused to join the posse who set out after the gang a few hours later. There is also another tale about the holdup which has a Bolivian cavalry colonel in a nearby garrison refusing to permit his men to join in the manhunt because he had become acquainted with Cassidy and "liked the Americano."

At the risk of seeming trite we believe that to every criminal the day of reckoning must eventually come. None the less it might be well at this point to consider Cassidy's striking but evil competence; the intelligence that went into his planning and his careful arrangements. There were the timing, the rendezvous, the horses and the undependable railroad schedules; the soldiers and the police; the bribe and the waiting for the answer and the scaling of that great barrier of strangers in a strange land.

After the robbery, the wild triangle traveled to the eastern slope of the Andes and the head of one of the Amazon tributaries. It is believed they made their camp in the abandoned Jesuit Mission of Sacambaya.

The following summer Cassidy decided to hold up the Huamuni Mines in Bolivia, operated by a Scottish firm, Penny and Duncan. To plan the robbery he obtained a job as head of the mine watchmen, guarding the pay roll.

The story of his gratitude for the treatment he received from his Scottish employers seems naïve, yet with his good cheer and camaraderie it is possible that he did let go his plan and certainly he did learn of the plot by some local bandits to kidnap Penny, the owner, and did furnish him with a bodyguard.

After a few months he collected his pay and left. Before the fall of 1907 he joined the Sundance Kid and his lady love to plan the next robbery.

In the late fall of 1907, back they rode into the town of Rio Galleos, Argentina, and checked into the Hotel Uglesich. They were well dressed in English riding clothes and rode small, rough-haired Patagonian ponies. Longbaugh and Etta Place registered as Mr. and Mrs. Lewis Nelson and Butch as Henry Thompson, Mrs. Nelson's brother. They stayed in town a month mingling with the local society and spending freely. They posed as wealthy cattlemen who were on their way back to the states. One of the first visits they made was at the local bank, where they introduced themselves to the manager, Mr. Bishop. They were soon daily visitors.

On December 7, 1907, at 2 P.M., Cassidy entered the bank. It was a nasty day with high winds and a driving rain. The teller smiled and nodded. But this was not the cheery affable Mr. Thompson he knew. It was a hard-faced man armed with two revolvers who stood before his window. Behind him was Nelson, no longer grave and courteous but waving a gun and a straight razor.

"Make an outcry and I'll cut your throat," Longbaugh warned. He unrolled a sack and motioned to the money drawer. With one eye on the razor the clerk flung open the drawer. Bishop, the manager, came upon the scene and was pushed against the wall. The sack was filled with ten thousand dollars.

There can be no question that they apologized to banker Bishop for the inconvenience caused him, sent apologies to his wife, and all the time superbly played to the hilt the role of the Gay Desperadoes. On this note, they vaulted into their saddles and headed through the rain for the hills.

They met Etta several miles outside of Rio Galleos and struck out for their hideout. A chase started, but Butch shot the horses of the leading pursuers and they got away.

Two years passed. Nothing is known about what they did during that time, but it must be remembered that they were desperate and bloody men whose lives had been filled with only crime and violence. What few fleeting pleasures they had experienced were evil and sordid.

They appeared again on the evening of December 27, 1910, entering the store of the Compania Mercantil Chubut in Arroyo Pescado, of the District 16 de Octubre, breaking open the safe, killing the manager, and forcing several employees at gun point to load their pack mules with supplies.

On January 29, the police chief of the Territorio Del Chubut wrote to Robert A. Pinkerton in New York, giving details of the robbery and requesting photographs of Cassidy and Longbaugh. He also revealed several Montana train and bank robbers to be in Argentina. He wrote:

> One of these men, I know for certain has been a spy for Ryan [Cassidy] and Place [Longbaugh] and let this out when under the influence of liquor. Ryan has been in Bolivia under the name of Gibbon and I believe he is actually in Santa Cruz, about 400 miles to the south of this place. I would be very pleased if you would send me all the data that you have about the Wild Bunch which had its hiding place in Hole in the Wall in the west some years back. We believe they have gotten together here again and intend to operate in this part of the Republic as they know we have no police and that they have so many good hiding places in the mountains.

In a report filed that year Robert A. Pinkerton wrote:

> Our persistent search for Cassidy and Longbaugh resulted in their fleeing from the United States to the Argentine Republic in February, 1901. They have proceeded to the interior, settling and taking up government lands at 16 de Octubre. They have been parties to committing bank and train robberies in Southeastern Argentine Republic, i.e., riding to the scene of the robbery on horseback, dismounting, leaving the horses in charge of Etta Place, the common law wife of Harry Longbaugh, attired in men's clothing, and during business hours, at point of fire arms, forcing bank employees to hold up their hands and to remain passive while they committed their robberies. The latest report on these outlaws places them in Southwestern Argentina near Norquin, province of Nequien, close to the Chilean border. Warnings have been sent to the South American authorities to watch for further criminal attempts.

An informant reported to the agency that an American bandit who answered the description of Cassidy was in the penitentiary at Antefagasta, Chile. But as he himself said in conclusion, he was unable to verify his information. The report said in part:

> This man was seen by the informant and talked to; that he, with two other North Americans and a woman, had been in Chile robbing banks and like; that one night the three Americans after drinking a lot of native liquor, started fighting among themselves and two of them were killed after which it is stated, Cassidy went to work for the Nitrate Mining Company as a pack master, conveyed the mineral and guarded the money on the way back to the mine. He did considerable business with the Bank of Antefagasta, and in this way got acquainted with the bank officials. One day he appeared at the bank with an American woman. She is supposed to have gotten the cashier or a bank official in a separate room and then Cassidy robbed the bank. In attempting to escape, Cassidy killed the Mayor of the town; his horse stumbled and in the fall Cassidy broke his leg and was captured. However we cannot verify this story.

> We secured additional advices to the effect that in the hold-up two North American bandits were killed. We communi-

cated with the authorities after learning of this with the object of securing photos and other means of identification but were advised that no photos were taken.

The unverified reports and the rumors were coming to the agency from all over South America. Like Jesse James in those last years, Butch Cassidy and his gang were everywhere. In Los Angeles, "Informant Number 85" told a Pinkerton operative that he saw the Wild Bunch in June of 1907 when Cassidy was returning to Wyoming. "I have heard since," he declared, "from a good source, that he was killed on the Green River in the winter of 1905-1906. I can tell you that Butch Cassidy is dead, that he was filled full of holes on the bridge at Green River, Wyoming."

But Cassidy was far from being riddled with bullets. According to Arthur Chapman, who wrote the famous poem "Out Where the West Begins," Cassidy the outlaw, the son of a Mormon bishop, the rustler and the horsethief, the laughing cowboy—and who can deny it—was rapidly becoming the Robin Hood of South America. Chapman repeats the story told to him by a Mr. Siebert, who was in the country at the time and knew Cassidy.

"All over the pampas of Bolivia, Cassidy seemed to have the friendship of the Indians and the half-breeds. As soon as he entered an Indian village he would be playing with the children, and he usually had candies and sweets in his pockets to give them. Because of this friendship, when he was hard pressed by the authorities he would always find a hideout among the native population."

There are two versions of the death of Cassidy and how the triangle fell into its last segments. One story is that Butch and the Sundance Kid—the woman had been left somewhere—stopped at the police station in the tiny village of San Vicente, near the Grande River, Bolivia, and asked for food. The police station, as was the custom in Bolivia, was also the inn where travelers could find food and shelter. The outlaws removed their rifles, saddles, and equipment and piled them in a corner of a small courtyard. Outside, one of their mules, suffering from a saddle gall, began rolling in the dust and attracted the attention of the constable in charge of the San Vicente station.

As he languidly eyed the animal, something clicked in his mind.

He had seen that brand. He searched his memory and at last it came to him. There had been a robbery at the Bolivian Aramyo mine. A muleteer who had been there at the time of the holdup was a friend of his. A mule so branded . . . how did the Yanqui . . .

The constable sent a messenger to the captain of a nearby company of Bolivian cavalry. The station was surrounded. The army officer walked into the courtyard, pistol drawn.

"Surrender, Senores," he began. They were his last words. Cassidy shot from the hip and killed him. The sergeant of the troop rushed forward with some men and joined his captain. Revolvers blazed from behind the barricade of tables and chairs. Soldiers gained the wall to pour in a cross fire. Longbaugh made a dash for their rifles and was wounded. Butch ran across the yard, was also wounded but managed to bring in the Sundance Kid.

The battle lasted all afternoon and into the night, the blackness lurid with gun flashes. Cassidy was wounded again when he made another desperate attempt to cross the courtyard and get their rifles. The battle settled down to a siege. Then, at about ten o'clock, the soldiers on the walls heard two shots. They waited all that night, fearing a trap. In the morning they found Cassidy dead, a revolver clutched in one hand. He had killed the dying Sundance Kid, then turned the gun on himself. In their packs the soldiers found the loot from the mine and the gold watch the outlaws had bought for Etta Place at Tiffany's eight years before. The dead were counted. There were twenty bodies sprawled about the courtyard and on the walls and almost twice as many wounded.

If this is the ending, the woman who seemed to have held the triangle together, either by love or sex, is not accounted for.

What happened to Etta Place? It is natural to recall the legends of the death and re-birth of the hero and the villain: Morgan the Rebel Raider, who never died in the peaceful garden that twilight; Jesse James, who still rides—and then there are Ney, the Dauphin, and a score of others.

So now we come to the second version from a living witness. He is Francis Dimaio, to whom Robert Pinkerton sent that curt order in 1903. Dimaio, at eighty-four, is now living in Dover, Delaware, in retirement. He had an experience in 1912, which is in contrast to the end we have just described and drops the final curtain on not only the two men but the woman, who belonged to either one or both of them.

Dimaio, a cheery, white-haired gentleman, told this writer that he took a seat in his favorite restaurant in Cincinnati late one day in December, 1912. It was dusk, and when the lights were turned up a voice called: "Why, Dimaio!"

He looked up from the menu and saw a man getting up from a nearby table. It was Steele, the salesman he had met in Buenos Aires and who had promised to keep a lookout for the Wild Bunch riders in 1903. The men had dinner together and, as they lighted their cigars, Steele said:

"I have been wanting to tell you, Frank, about those outlaws you were looking for in Argentina."

Dimaio looked up. "Yes, what about them?"

Steele took a deep puff on his cigar. "I saw them."

"Where?" the operative asked quickly.

Steele told his story. In the early part of December, 1911, he had made a trip to Mercedes, Uruguay. He had checked into the hotel and walked up to his room when a friend called, "Come on down and see the Bandidos Yanqui we have killed." Steele hurried to the small public square. Six boots stuck out from beneath a canvas shroud. The policeman drew it back.

"It was Mr. and Mrs. Place [Longbaugh and Etta] and that man Jim Ryan [or Cassidy]," he told Dimaio. "They had been riddled by the soldiers while trying to rob the bank. The woman was outside with the horses and was shot down first. The two men rushed out and were killed in the street."

"Are you sure?" Dimaio asked.

Steele nodded. "I compared them with the poster you gave me and there was no doubt about it. The police also said they were the same three."

That that was the final act, Dimaio has no doubts. "I am sure Mr. Steele was not mistaken," he said. "He was an intelligent, level-headed man and not one for making rash statements. Cassidy, Longbaugh, and the woman were never heard from again after that date, and that seems to confirm his identification.

"At first we thought Mercedes, where they were shot down and where Steele saw the bodies, was the small town in Argentina where they had robbed their first bank. But Mr. Steele undoubtedly meant Mercedes, Uruguay, where an important hotel for salesmen was located at the time. The Mercedes in Argentina at the time did not have a hotel."

And so it ends. Far to the north, Hole in the Wall, Robber's Roost, and Brown's Hole had gone back to the empty quiet of geologic time and the fire Butch Cassidy had brought to the Andes was out.

POSTSCRIPT

Looking back at other robber eras, one is struck by the fact that although the specific crimes or acts of violence are frequently forgotten, the romantic pageantry always remains. Thus will it be with the life and times of Jesse James and his Missouri bravos and Butch Cassidy and his Wild Bunch riders. One may not be able to name the place or the time of a certain robbery. But who can forget the thrilling rides across the plains with the posses far behind; the thunder of horses as the army of desperadoes rides through the narrow gorge out of Hole in the Wall to repulse the stockmen's army of mercenaries; the lonely outlaw watchers on the rims silhouetted against the clear, Western sky; the blue-eyed boy whose name in the family Bible was Jesse Woodson James, leading his howling ex-guerrillas across the public squares of the small towns, their revolvers blazing at the street lamps, the painted signs, and the store windows; Frank James, coming out of the unknown to unbuckle his gun belt and dramatically surrender to the governor of Missouri.

However, making all allowances for the grand pageantry and melodrama, we must, after an examination of their lives, come to the rather commonplace conclusion that crime does not pay. It is difficult to find any nobility or splendor in their lives. Nonetheless, to give the devil his due and perhaps hustle the angels in the process, we do come to admire, however grudgingly, the vitality, self-confidence, recklessness, and gusto of these men, particularly Butch Cassidy. In connection with the leader of the Wild Bunch, we might possibly say that which is said about better men: nobody else could have done it.

It was different in the case of Jesse James. There was an unrevealed evil about him that fascinated the scores of people who made it impossible for him to be taken. Countless books and newspaper and magazine articles are yet to be written about him, but of necessity they must all skim the surface of his life. Although many claimed it, Jesse James bared his soul to no man. When Bob Ford pulled the trigger in 1882, the dark secrets of this strange man's mind were lost forever.

Outlaws, train robbers, cold-blooded murderers,. they are in Bunyan's class: out of size, out of drawing. One can conceive the thief or the gunman made harmless or returning to his place in society through modern psychiatry, but it is impossible to visualize these gigantic figures undergoing "rehabilitation."

Jesse James or Butch Cassidy on a psychiatrist's couch telling all . . .

It is probably safe to say that most psychologists have concluded that a sense of guilt or sin is the basis for all neuroses. If this is true, certainly there was nothing neurotic about these desperate men. What then was the cause? The records are too inconclusive to judge more than eighty years later, but as one ponders the question and the answer, which is never the right one, a line comes to mind. It is from *The Mikado,* and it ends "everything is the source of fun." In a way it could apply to nearly all of them. When Todd, that bloody guerrilla leader, invited Cole Younger to come to town and kill some Kansas Red-Legs, he called it "fun." When the Wild Bunch swung into a town to spray it with bullets and to drink themselves insensible or to engage in a gun duel, they called it going to town and having some "fun."

Ironically, these same men did produce some good. Although such a statement might be compared to saying that a better race of deer was bred because of a vicious cougar who lived in their forest, the outlaws of the Middle Border and the Far West helped to develop the same forces that finally destroyed them. Certainly the outlawry and violence did point up the corruptness of some law-enforcement officers and the cowardice of others, and finally awakened the communities to appoint better men to protect them.

INDEX